To Dance with God

To Dance with God

FAMILY RITUAL AND COMMUNITY CELEBRATION

Gertrud Mueller Nelson
with illustrations by the author

PAULIST PRESS
New York/Mahwah

Acknowledgments

The Publisher gratefully acknowledges use of the following materials:

The English translation of the Good Friday Reproaches and the Exsultet (Easter Proclamation) from *The Roman Missal* © 1973, International Committee on English in the Liturgy, Inc. All rights reserved.

The poetic English translation of the Pentecost Sequence from *The Roman Missal* © 1964 by the National Catholic Welfare Conference, Inc.

Excerpts from "Little Gidding" in FOUR QUARTETS by T.S. Eliot, copyright 1943 by T.S. Eliot; renewed 1971 by Esme Valerie Eliot. Reprinted by permission of Harcourt Brace Jovanovich, Inc.

Library of Congress Cataloging-in-Publication Data

Nelson, Gertrud Mueller.
    To dance with God.

    Bibliography: p.
    1. Fasts and feasts.   2. Rites and ceremonies.
I. Title.
BV43.N44   1986   263'.9   86-9459
ISBN 0-8091-2812-8 (pbk.)

Published by Paulist Press
997 Macarthur Boulevard
Mahwah, New Jersey 07430

Printed and bound in the
United States of America

Contents

Part Two

In Appreciation

This book came into being because of the sustained good will and the cheers of encouragement from many people who believed in the effort. Without their confidence, the effort would have remained a pile of disjointed ideas and experiences.

I am grateful to my parents, Therese and Franz Mueller, who raised me in a household with an unusual awareness of the richness of the life of the Church. Their gift that could connect the sacramental life of the greater Church with the sacramentality of the "little church" has stood me, my own family, and many other families who were touched by their gift, in good stead. I am grateful also that they wisely extended to us the folk stories and customs out of their national heritage. These lent me a richness and a grounding that added meaning to the important issues of growing up.

I am indebted to many whose writings clarified, ratified and expanded the insights and experiences that are mine by inheritance and good fortune. Readers will recognize my great indebtedness to the psychological work of C. G. Jung and the liturgical inspiration of Romano Guardini. The works of Mercia Eliade, Josef Pieper, Gerald Vann, Aidan Kavanagh, Rosemary Haughton, Eugene Kennedy and others have lent insight and inspiration over many years.

I want to acknowledge with appreciation those families, the religious communities, and my own worshiping community who required of me the discipline to organize and formulate many of these ideas. They have also been trusting, graceful and adventuresome in their expression of the mysteries of life and have endorsed these ideas with creative ingenuity and delightful results. In my own community, members have made contributions to this effort in ways that they may not even guess. To them, I am especially grateful, because through the warmth of friendship and community, through our worship together, we are sustained and carried through the experiences that are a part of every life.

Bernard Campbell, our former pastor, and now an editor with Paulist Press, has helped at both ends of this project. As a pastor he had an unusual respect for the ministry of lay people and a great good humor as we created our celebrations. In his editorial role, he addressed these efforts again and suggested they be put into book form. Without that suggestion and his confidence that it would come to be, it would not, indeed, have been conceived.

There are also some friends on whose good nature and talent I particularly drew. Dennis Clark has been a great help with his steady motivation and his orderly insights. Lowell Storms read the manuscript as it evolved and must consider himself one of the primary midwives for his support and faith in me. Nancy Hatch made countless "house calls" to check the well-being of the book's process and has helped immeasurably, poring over the manuscript with careful attention to detail as it progressed to its final completion. Her wisdom and experiences lent a fine sounding board for ideas. Arline Paa and my sister, Hildegard Kerney, spurred me on, checked the recipes and were my test kitchen—on many levels. Patty Mittendorff has been a "test kitchen" for everything from the paradigms of ritual making to a willingness to listen and to read. Her response has been generous and her stories and insights of special value.

My family, who knows the content of this book through experience, is an important ingredient in its makeup. My son Peter has been unflagging in his encouragement that I write what needed saying even if he thought I left out too many stories. My daughter Sara has lent me her special variety of confidence and wisdom as well as her considerable writing skills as "in house" editor when I needed her. Many thanks to Annika, my youngest daughter, who was courier to the post office and my cook when I needed rescue. And to my husband, Jerry Nelson, my thanks for his years of creative participation, insight and support as we built the ceremonies that mark our family life. His loving support and good humor through the process of bringing this book to birth have been invaluable.

Part One

CHAPTER ONE

To Dance with God

Some years ago, I spent an afternoon caught up in a piece of sewing I was doing. The waste basket near my sewing machine was filled with scraps of fabric cut away from my project. This basket of discards was a fascination to my daughter Annika, who, at the time, was not yet four years old. She rooted through the scraps searching out the long bright strips, collected them to herself, and went off. When I took a moment to check on her, I tracked her whereabouts to the back garden where I found her sitting in the grass with a long pole. She was affixing the scraps to the top of the pole with great sticky wads of tape. "I'm making a banner for a procession," she said. "I need a procession so that God will come down and dance with us." With that she solemnly lifted her banner to flutter in the wind and slowly she began to dance.

My three year old was not a particularly precocious toddler. I think, rather, that she was doing what three year olds do when left to their natural and intuitive religious sense and I was simply fortunate to hear and see what she was about. Mothers are often anthropologists of sorts and their children the exotic primitives that also happen to be under foot. This little primitive allowed me to witness a holy moment and I learned all over again how strong and real is that sense of wonder that children have—how innate and easy their way with the sacred. Here, religion was child's play. And of course I had to wonder what happens in our development that as adults we became a serious folk, uneasy in our relationship with God, out of touch with the mysteries we knew in childhood, restless, empty, searching to regain a sense of awe and a way to "dance with God."

While it was natural for us at one time in our lives to be at ease with God, it is also natural to the human condition that our connection with the transcendent become complicated and precarious. Life's tasks of learning to think and compare, to sort and choose began with our taste of "knowledge of good and evil" and for that fruit we have developed a great appetite. That knowledge changes our innocent relationship with God. And we spend the rest of our days circling the garden of our original innocence, yearning to find our way back in. The route we choose is marked with the mysteries of the human condition: peak experiences and pitfalls, births and deaths, joys and sufferings.

Our "fall" from innocence is double edged; it is both our sickness and our salvation. It is our painful, guilt-ridden split and separation of what is human from the divine. But it also sets us forth on the natural and saving journey of the human process to ultimate wholeness. Our way back to a connection with God is through the profound experience of our humanity and the discovery of meaning. When we are struck with the meaning of our most human experiences, we are most closely connected with the divine.

Knowledge and Belief

We are the children of the Enlightenment. The fruit of knowledge continues to be our value. We have come to prize it as never before. We have become the most intellectual and scientific society, profoundly proud of our thinking skills. We have developed these skills to such a degree that we can penetrate life's mysteries from its most basic molecules to all of outer space—and we proceed to demystify them. We can manipulate molecules and probe and even people that mysterious moon.

Science changed our views, improved our condition and redirected our hopes to such a degree that every problem and even every mystery became an issue which science would solve. Even while the great scientists themselves, with a growing humility, see that every question answered only reveals more and terribly complex ones, we develop a view that a continually advancing science will provide all the answers. It will bail us out of one crisis after the other, and it will produce thinkers to answer all questions even in terms of meaning and the quality and condition of our lives. So seductive is this hope and this fantasy that the general population still clings to this new faith and chooses not to question its validity or truth even as they proceed to search for meaning.

While science pulls us out of our original religion, the churches have done their share to push us out. We became particularly vulnerable to the lure of scientism because the churches, resisting the same intellectualizations, entangled themselves in self-preserving apologetics, dogmatics, and morality. They created a heavy overlay, crusting over religious mystery, losing touch with their own meaning. In the Catholic Church, the profound mystery of dogmas was distorted by rules and the mandate to believe them on a literal level, because the understanding of the truth of myth was lost. In some churches, religious rituals were abandoned because they reeked of popery, and they were left with an anemic expression. In many Catholic churches, the rich heritage of symbol, of ritual and ceremony, degenerated into dry, mechanical rubrics which were followed by the book and returned little or no meaning to the people.

While some closed their eyes and tried to believe the dogmas of the Church literally and avoided the use of their intelligence, others were able, with some grace and wisdom, to translate the truth of dogma into a living language and integrate it into their understanding and experience. But many people, armed with a desire to be reasonable, learned to protest any belief or any mystery that could not be scientifically proven. Science and the value of knowledge became the enemy of religion. Because churches, for all their apologetics and application of reason, celebrate mysteries and espouse dogmas that a purely intellectual approach will seek to refute or dismiss, many people were left without a faith, and without the resources that help one find meaning. But this did not eliminate the continued search for meaning. We found we could not intellectualize our way into faith. Rather, many found that they had "thought" their way out of faith and out of a religious system, a system of being which nourished them in ways that they never knew, until they left it.

Years ago, Carl Jung warned against our heady application of the intellect to mystery. He said that we make a big mistake if we try to rationalize dogmas and if we tamper too much with our ancient traditions. Our intellect, he said, does not understand the secrets of religious mystery. "We are not far enough advanced psychologically to understand the truth, the extraordinary truth, of such ritual and such dogma."

Jung said these things in the 1930's. And, of course, we went ahead and applied massive intellectual arguments to our beliefs to shore them up or to talk ourselves right out of a system of meaning.

Today there is evidence of a new search for faith and meaning. I meet many people whom I would see as intellectually honest, in search of meaning, seeking ways to make sense of, engage and celebrate their human experience. Often they are young couples, their first child is just born, and both mother and father have been fully engaged in the wonder of every stage of this child's coming into being. I have seen these people seek out and even renew their commitment to the Christian heritage and to a Church community after years of non-commitment to any formal religious expression. Their faith, with regard to certain primary articles of doctrine, may still be "lost" because they could not give you a rational argument about what is "really true" and how that might be. But can anyone ever pick up an old faith of years ago like some slipped stitch and continue in the same old pattern as before? Can we read Jung's warning and turn the clock back to the good old days and simply reconstruct "that old time religion"?

Most of us would agree that we cannot go back to where we once were. Individually and collectively, new experiences change the way we understand the world. Perhaps these experiences have even made the search for lost faith and meaning more poignant. We do not grow without increasing our convictions and beliefs, but neither the blind, unthinking faith nor the faith which was shored up with intellectual arguments seems to speak to this new, accumulated awareness. Indeed, our new consciousness has a feeling and a knowledge which is emotional and intuitive.

It may well be that we are entering an age where we are willing and ready to allow our scientific knowledge and understanding to exist in concert with our need for a symbolic life. New and fresh approaches to what is old and primal in human religious expression will emerge from our increased understanding of human nature. The sciences of psychology or anthropology can illuminate and breathe new life into fundamental Christian concepts. Mythology and liturgics are enhanced and revitalized by our increased understanding of the human condition. This new development will help us to heal the rift we have suffered for so long between knowledge and belief.

The Poetic Church

Perhaps the Church which Jung and others recognized as vital to the life and richness of our humanness and our wholeness is about to be rediscovered. What we have lost touch with lies in the poetic aspect of the Church which has always been there for us, which has always been centered in the cycles of our human development and which has nourished us through rite and symbol, through rhythmic repetition. This Church celebrates our cycles and seasons, inviting us to see and engage and feel and touch and be aware and grow and be transformed. Through myth and symbol the experiences which make up our daily lives are affirmed and made sacred.

This creative and poetic Church helps us to pay full attention to what we might otherwise deem ordinary and commonplace. Rites and symbols use the ordinary and earthy elements of our existence and, by encircling them, ratify, sanctify, complete. The ordinary becomes the container for the divine and safely holds what was uncontainable. The transcendent is disclosed in what is wonderfully familiar: bread, wine, fire, ash, earth, water, oil, tears, seeds, songs, feastings and fastings, pains and joys, bodies and thoughts, regressions and transformations. It draws its action more from what is most human in us than from theology. In its creative function, the Church speaks directly to the heart, a heart which hears symbols, not rational vocabulary.

The dawning of a renewed faith to which I see people striving to go forward is one which connects us to our forebears, to our ancient roots, to all those who went before us and to all who will come after us in the development of our human existence. Celebrating together binds us together with a common symbolic form, a unique identity and a tradition in which to be founded. To celebrate as a Church community, to commit ourselves to the realities in its history, to its traditions, to its forms, to its leadership, is also to commit ourselves to its reformation and growth. We are this Church. As its people we know that the mysteries of the human condition never change, but our understanding, our growing awareness, our expressions, need our expanding and changing insight and creative efforts. Our renewed faith will intersect the theological issues and the historical facts of the Church and speak to what is our common human experience.

Through this book I hope to underscore the forgotten values of myth, ritual and ceremony as a vital expression of our experience. I hope to return to individuals, to families and to worshiping communities the resources that help us find meaning. In the first part of the book I explore that yearning for transformation that we know as part of the human condition and the ways in which we look for the touch of the transcendent. In the second part of the book I review the seasons and feasts of the Church year. I have included family and folk traditions to jog imaginations. Given the paradigms that create ritual, translate myth and celebrate our daily lives, readers will discover the tools that can return meaning to simple life issues as well as to the major issues that make up our experience. The creative function of the Church's heritage is reconsidered as a rich fund for family and community expression. I hope to encourage an openness and another way to see the mythic truth of dogmas—a way to honor the wisdom that lies at the heart of religious mystery. For the ritual expression of mystery is an expression of our most fundamental human condition.

CHAPTER TWO

The Hints of Transcendence

A Religious People

Since the beginning of time, humankind has centered and located itself in the sacred. Now, in very recent history, we have created as wholly a secular or desacralized world as there has ever been. We have evolved a new, non-religious society, where we think ourselves to be free and unencumbered by taboo and by the irrational, a world where we think that we can create ourselves.

To see some evidence of this progression, one need only to look at the medieval cathedral in the center of the square, with the rest of the city oriented around it. Move over sea and time, and see the little white churches at the heart of the New England village. And then go west, to California, where the restless freeways are strung along the coast, punctuated periodically with food-shop-and-rest stops. Along the old road, the early missions are engulfed by urban sprawl.

The completely secular world of modern society is a recent phenomenon. It arises out of our historic surge of thinking and intellectualization. And it is as much a result of humankind's search for the truth as it is a reaction against that aspect of the Church that claimed to have every answer, if you would only close your eyes, ask no questions and obey. Hardly have we created this desacralized world and we are aware of the emergence of a new religious consciousness, a longing, a yearning for what feels to be missing. There must be something more.

Mircea Eliade, of the University of Chicago, points out, "To whatever degree he may have desacralized the world, the man who has made his choice in favor of a profane life never succeeds in completely doing away with religious behavior."

The human inclination to search for the religious experience is primal. Humans are religious beings and our religious nature is at the root of who we have become; we cannot deny or shrug off our long history and our origins. The point is that we are not as free to choose or not choose our rituals and symbolic behavior as we may think. Our only choice is between conscious rituals and unconscious ones, those which enrich, dignify and enliven our lives and interactions and those which enslave us, which deaden life and block us from deep human relationship and meaning.

The Symptomatic Way

Without a way to consciously feed and express our naturally religious nature, we create a vacuum, a void which is quickly filled in with its unconscious counterpart. Our religious hunger is not passing away; rather, our loss of a religious nurturance only makes us more aware of our hunger. We want meaning, fulfillment and wholeness.

Rushing in to fill the void are the low-grade religious experiences which bedevil and taunt. We still search for meaning and the religious experience, but the powerful is more often encountered through the back door. Instead of having ritual ways to meet the awesome, we are overawed by our ritual habits, our fears and symptoms. In place of the periodic, holy fast, we have become slaves to our perennial diets. In exchange for "carrying our cross" in the constructive suffering that every life requires, we complain of low back pain. The old taboos, which we think we are freed of, crop up as new varieties of superstitions, and we take another vitamin. The neurotic is religious material done unconsciously. Compulsive behaviors are the rites and ceremonies of the unconscious which have taken control of our nature. Symptoms and compulsions are the symbolic language of the soul, begging to be translated out into consciousness, asking to be heard and enacted on the correct level. Neurosis is the modern parody of religion and is the consequence of our lost orientation to the sacred.

The Boar in the Bedroom

We have lost faith in the reality of the unconscious—the real, though elusive symbols that people our inner world; and we forget to pay those symbols homage. Again, I learned a lesson from the "primitives" in my care. When my son Peter was around three years old, he had a great fascination for any book with animals in it. But for several weeks, one book in particular was singled out as the most important. There was a painting in this book which I think was by Peter Paul Rubens and it depicted a very dramatic boar hunt. The hunted boar, foaming at the tusks and with fire in his eyes, all but charged out of the page at you. I really didn't much like this picture. Nor could I imagine what a gentle little boy living in the safety of the suburbs could possibly understand was going on here. But this picture, of course, was the one that Peter found the most wonderful, and he could flip through that fat book and find his special page every time. He sat in the corner of the couch and stared at it wordlessly every chance he could. When he had had enough, he closed the book and put it away. When we "misplaced" the book on the highest shelf he could always trace it and get it down. It engaged him fully; he had complete control over that boar as long as it was between the covers of the book. Naturally, it came to pass that this boar became a night-time visitor to our house. Peter knew him well; he told us his boar was the same color as the night—he blended so well into the darkness that getting up to go potty was a real hazard. You could walk right into this boar and not know it until it was too late. At night, Peter had no control over his boar. He would wake and he would call out to us: "The boar is here!" His fear was electric. My husband and I took turns getting up to deal with the animal. The idea of this night-colored boar made the hair stand up on *my* neck. When it was my turn, I hurried down the hall determined to save Peter but half-hoping not to slam into a great bristled body. We didn't doubt the reality of Peter's boar. His fear was so real. And we devised a way of exorcising him.

It is a great temptation for parents, naturally impatient with these night-time interruptions, to flick on all the lights, rustle the curtains, kick under the bed, call into the closet and show the child that there is no boar. "See, no boar! It's *only your imagination!*" we want to say. But that doesn't work. It negates the reality of the inner world. The characters of our inner world are real and are to be taken seriously. For a small child the primordial fear of being abandoned to wild beasts is still an inner reality. Peter needed to know without a doubt that his parents could save him from any old boar and they would.

Jerry and I had a week of dealing with the boar. We went into Peter's room. "What shall we do with him, Peter?" we'd ask. "Frow him out da window!" We crawled under the bed, grabbed the boar by the scruff of the neck, hauled him out and dragged him to the window where we shoved him out and banished him for the rest of the night. Finally, his Papa was extra-brave. The beast had visited once too often, so the next day Peter and his Papa drew a large image of the boar. Peter colored in the tusks and he put the fire in his eyes. They took the boar behind the garage and they burned him. Peter was reassured. Parents can handle anything.

There were other ways to understand this boar and perhaps other ways of dealing with him. We learned as we gained practice in raising our children. Had Peter been a little older and had he wanted to study his boar picture, we might have referred to it as his "angry boar." We might have wondered what made this boar so very mad and sad? And Peter could have had some ideas. Bit by bit it could become clear that this mad boar had any number of reasons to show fire in his eyes. For one thing, "His mama says, 'No cookies for you, boar!'" "Oh, that must make him very mad! Show me how angry that makes the boar." And Peter could risk showing us just how angry were his feelings.

As a boar it is okay to grunt and spit in rage. As a boy, that isn't proper behavior. As a mother I had to learn how to give Peter back his feelings. Anger and frustration are a part of being human. Small boys have reason to feel plenty of it. Now, how could he know his feelings and express them properly? It was hard for me to allow that this small tousled-hair fellow could have black, bristly feelings, and I am sure I was reluctant to acknowledge them. The very real inner boar of night-time can have a proper outer expression.

Because of the power of the night world, many people know intuitively the importance of a planned ritual for their children's bedtime. Without giving the process sufficient attention, parents often compel the child to devise his or her own ritual, and we know these can be lengthy and impractical. Instead the parents take control. Using some of the child's ingredients and devising a short but certain routine which always has some permanent elements and some small changeable ones—which always has a beginning, a middle and a certain, clear ending—the process can be comfort and a proper ending to the day. Surrounded with warmth and strength, perhaps with a parental blessing and some prayers to Him who protects us all, the child can turn from the active and event-filled day and make the transition into what Dylan Thomas called "the close and holy darkness."

Without conscious rites to close the day, even the enlightened adult can come up against some curious compulsions, habits, or superstitious behaviors which are an attempt to close the day and guard against the powerful and unknown elements of the unconscious. Imagine the adult who wants to go to sleep. Have you ever settled into bed and then wondered if you locked the back door? You get up to check again. While in the kitchen you make certain you turned off the oven. As long as you're up, maybe you ought to have a quick cup of hot cocoa—to help you sleep. You make another trip to the bathroom, check in the mirror again—those crow's feet around the eyes—and dab a little cream on a possible new wrinkle. Before you crawl into bed this time, you might check under the bed. Nothing. You settle down. Ah, but you forgot to close the closet door. Unclear about what the fear is and distracted from a more meaningful way to close the day, you are driven through your routines until you finally sleep.

Commercial Offerings

So strong is the longing and need of humankind for meaning and transformation that much of the success of the advertising profession lies in attempting to answer that need. Without the essential mysteries of conceiving and waiting and birthing and creating and yielding up and dying, we want our religious experience and we want it now. We feel we have no time to wait around. And we dread being bored. So the commercial world promises us romantic love, perfect communication between the sexes, gleaming bathrooms, painless diets, adorable children, and riotous weekends if we just shell out for the right toothpaste, rub a magic potion in our arm pit, pop a pill, purchase a toy or serve the right beer. Unclear and distractible, the human condition being what it is, we are quick to believe that the religious experience and transformation can be had for the buying and that without pain or waiting.

Recognizing the Transcendent

The search for the transcendent does not satisfy on this level. Indeed, it is the very problem of levels that brings us to discuss how and where we might search for and be touched by the power of God. We make a mistake when we believe, "Lo, he is in . . . the toothpaste." The transcendent is elusive and nothing we can package, shelve and trade on. Nor is it appropriate to fill in the blanks with substitutes. The prophets in the Old Testament often warned against taking a mistress when you were weary of your wife. They said not to be fooled. The God we seek is already with us. Such is the human condition that in times of quiet desperation we would be tempted to dispose of our tired old toaster and get us a flashy new model, and our relationships in like manner! . . . The God we seek is already with us.

Happily, the Almighty does manifest himself to us in fleeting glimpses, in the flash of a moment, in an instant of recognition. These experiences are real. They punctuate life with meaning and lend us courage to press on in our search for wholeness. The poetic, the symbolic, the sacramental, the mythic, though it is elusive and fleeting, is just as true and real and just as valuable as what is rational, historical, scientific. One is true on an inner level and the other on an outer level. On the creative level, our recognition of the tremendous takes place. What we know in our hearts to be true can be honored with the heart; it can only be caught by the heart.

The religious experience, the "epiphany" we all long for, may be so utterly a part of our daily lives that we may be looking elsewhere, traveling great distances only to discover what was truly close at hand. Sometimes the sacred moments in our lives are deceptively simple. We expect the religious experience to come in a different size or color. We are taken by surprise, or sometimes we are sadly numb and absent, unprepared to be fully present to the mystery of the moment because we did not stand ready and vulnerable to the nature of things, because we were not willing to look beyond appearances, moving from visible reality to invisible reality.

In considering how the sacred can reveal itself to us, the story of Moses is a perfect paradigm. Scripture is full of characters who are crippled in some way: inept social failures who wander about doing the menial tasks that so resemble the sort of tedious duties that sometimes fill our days. We despair of anything so glorious as a religious experience as we drive the kids to music lessons or pay the bills. Furthermore, we dare the Church to cough up a religious experience for us. We feel like the lisping Moses who has been relegated to the desert to herd sheep who couldn't care less if Moses has a speech defect or if he even speaks. Moses roams the landscape with his flocks when, behold, a bush appears on the horizon, and furthermore, even though this bush is on fire, it is yet not consumed. At the moment that he sees the bush, he says to himself, "I must go and look at this strange sight and see why the bush is not burnt."

In looking at the bush, Moses might have recognized it merely as a bush, or merely as a fire, and then he would have trod on, herding his sheep, untouched. But instead, he turns aside for a moment from his outer purpose of herding these sheep. He looks. He allows and accepts the great paradox of opposites in this phenomenon; by superimposing and holding the tension of two opposing factors, his vision pierces through the ordinary world of appearances. The ordinary bush and the Spirit-fire become one. Through his recognition, the impossible is made possible. He allows a third and wondrous thing to happen: God speaks to him and calls him by name.

Moses, attentive to what he sees, names the revelation, makes it conscious and in turn is named by the Transcendent. From that moment, Moses himself is changed. Oh, he still lisps, he is still a misfit of sorts, he is still ordinary, but he allows his vision to affect the very purpose of his existence. His world view is changed and his life takes on new meaning. He becomes a prophet and leader amongst his people.

We know something of the same paradoxical reality—when we have come to the end of our rope. There is no answer on the horizon. So we have listed all the pros to our decision making on one side of the paper and all the cons on the other and they come out fifty-fifty, and for a moment we have no recourse but to hold still and say that both opposing sides hold the truth together and we cannot choose one side over the other without losing something very important. For a fleeting moment we see the delicate harmony of contradictions, and a third, a powerful thing happens beyond mere insight. We are flooded with a strange peace and know that we are in the presence of something much bigger than the decision. In the moment that we accept what reason would hold as impossible, God calls us by name.

Could it be that God speaks to us as he always has, just that we have forgotten his language or gotten distracted in ways that human nature has always gotten distracted and wandered out of earshot? Perhaps his revelation amongst us is not more elusive than it ever was. Rather we are unbelieving, less open to seeing, unwilling, again, to accept the challenge of what is still unknown to us. Most of all, I think that we do not recognize and name as religious experience the revelations that do occur in our lives because we have forgotten the value of what is inner, non-practical, non-rational, elusive. And we have forgotten that the *tremendum* has always revealed itself in the ordinary. That is what the mystery of God's flesh-taking, the incarnation is all about.

When we allow ourselves to believe this truth, we stand in the right attitude toward the transcendent. Heaven and earth become a single reality, and we have experienced the numinous. We are touched in that terribly mundane moment, when we witness the impossibly divine. These glimpses are the ones which a friend of mine calls "the freebies," those that we have done nothing terribly special to deserve, but have only stood in the right place at the right time in the right attitude. Then we are touched when we see that father, ever so lovingly, show his son how to swing that bat. We catch our breath when we slice open the dusty yam and see its orange-gold flesh. We feel a deep and full satisfaction when we have connected with our spouse in a conversation over coffee. These are sometimes experiences so ordinary that, when we try to share them a little later with a friend, we are not at all certain that they will understand what was so special about our moment of revelation. Can we even describe it?

Let me try it; let me try to recount one such homely experience and see if I can let you in on its mystery. The other day I sent my daughter Annika to the market for a bunch of asparagus. Annika is sixteen and has just discovered a creative outlet in printing on fabric. I interrupted her printing to send her on this errand. A guest was coming and I was in the midst of things when I discovered I'd forgotten to pick up asparagus. She put aside the stamps she had carved out of erasers and potatoes to print with, washed off her paint smudges and hurried to the market down the hill. When she came back, she slid the brown bag across the counter to me and said with delight, "Now just look at what *else* I bought." She let me fish in the bag, inviting me to come up with her surprise. I reached in and pulled out the asparagus, and I pulled out a fat yam. "But we don't need this. It doesn't go with the menu. What ever did you think we could do with a single yam?" I carried on about the absurdity of the purchase and its impracticality. "No," she said, "just look at it. Have you ever seen such a fine, fat root? It's beautiful. I bought it for me, to make a large print with. My erasers and those little potatoes are so small. Besides, it's just too lovely." Later she sliced open the yam and then exclaimed about the color inside, urging me to look as it lay split and golden-orange on the cutting board. Then I had to look at Annika, socks all baggy around her ankles, sweatshirt spotted with paints, and face glowing with an utterly new discovery. And she was sharing it with me. We both saw it. A wonderful yam, a perfectly glorious fat, firm root.

There! I tried to share my story, and of course I worry that you won't believe me or haven't caught what I wanted to share. Is it simply too ordinary? Or is it wonderful—to consider a teenager sidetracked in the produce over a "wonderful root"? The artist in myself sees the emerging artist in my daughter. I understand, all over again, that being awake for the religious experience is the realm of the artist in all of us. The ordinary, not having been noticed by anyone else, becomes wonderful. For a moment, my practicality threatened to be the enemy of the numinous. It always is. The vision that we long for lies just the other side of the practical. In that dusty root, the humdrum and the fabulous are joined, and, furthermore, we shared it.

Emerson said: "The poet's habit of living should be set on a key so low and plain that the common influences should delight him. His cheerfulness should be the gift of sunlight; the air should suffice for his inspiration and he should be tipsy with water."

Have we packed our lives with such a frantic pace in search of elusive happiness that God cannot get a word in edgewise?

The religious experience is the attaching connection that we make between the homely and the fantastic, both metaphorically and personally.

Our reasoning, sorting, scientific inclinations keep the heavens and the earth separate. We have come to believe that the profane and the sacred, the ordinary and the extraordinary, cannot meet. That schism prevents us from the experience of wholeness. In fact, we cannot find our religious nature outside the setting of our human experience. The flesh-taking of the spirit, the incarnation, is a mystery made new in our daily efforts to be fully human.

The voice that calls us out of the burning bush is the awareness of our own selves and our humanity. It is the awareness, the perception of the divine in what is so human. Heaven and earth are one. Or as Elizabeth Barrett Browning said: "Earth's crammed with heaven and every common bush afire with God."

CHAPTER THREE

The Art of Living

Life on the Freeways

We are pulled along, mesmerized and almost automated, going 65—over the speed limit, but we keep up with the flow of traffic. We take in our fellow travelers and learn what they want to teach us about themselves by noting the make of their cars, perhaps the ornament that hangs over the dash, the identity they announce on their vanity plates and their convictions and beliefs professed on bumper stickers. "I heart Jesus." "I heart poodles." "Eat your garbage; 50,000 seagulls couldn't be wrong." "One nuclear bomb can ruin your whole day."

Despite all the efforts, I still register a fear. It feels impersonal. Streaming along here, we do, indeed, seem "a fragmented society," each of us isolated and sealed into our tins, each of us vaguely aware that we want something more, something to live by and a way to live it fully and in community, something beyond the business of mere survival.

For this we pull over and re-form how we live—in fact, we want to develop an art of living.

Aidan Kavanagh, professor of liturgics at Yale Divinity School, describes his field as "perhaps ... little more than a craft that attempts to reflect on and practice the sundry arts of life where all these converge at their most critical mass—in the act of endowing with sanction and worth ('worship' is worth-ship) those persons, places, things and values in which a whole people have found existence to run strong and constant."

In liturgy, we recover the value of ritual, rhythm and the richness of symbol which in turn give back meaning to our human experiences. In developing an art of living, we value our individuality, but beyond the emptiness of individualism, we seek to build a family, a community where we are united by our common roots, where we can search for meaning and truth, where the engagement of our joys and sufferings, our successes and failures renews us and inspires us to grow. In family and community, we can find and, better yet, create those rites and celebrations which nurture our children and lend us identity, an identity that is founded in the transcendent.

So beyond my friend's "freebies"—those accidental, unconnected experiences which, however marvelous and blessed, have no container, no pattern and no rites of ratification—we can introduce into our way of being, both personally and communally, a "ceremonial discipline" which will satisfy more fully and make more sense of our experiences. Here, too, we might touch on the quality and nature of the ceremonies and rites which already are a part of our lives. Bringing consciousness and design into our approach to the important phases of our lives can teach us to address, express and satisfy the longings of our unconscious which get stuck in the neurotic structure. Spurred on by the unplanned-for hints of transcendence which come our way, we undertake purposefully to create our lives so that we can suffer legitimately and live joyously and that in the right proportions.

Before we take up the feasts of the Church year which lead us through the great life issues, we want to look at what the history of religion, anthropology, psychology, personal experience teaches us about the art of living. We cannot begin to exhaust this broad and rich topic here but hope only to introduce some of the principles that make a ritual and ceremony work for us. How might conscious planning enhance the quality of life as we experience it? Once we understand the paradigm, individuals, families and communities can make their own rituals.

The Making of Ritual

Forming the Formless

The making of ritual is a creative act fundamental in human life. It is also a divine gesture. Genesis tells us the first purpose of such creative action is to give form to what is formless: "In the beginning God created the heavens and earth. Now the earth was a formless waste, there was darkness over the deep, and God's spirit hovered over the water." Then God proceeded to create a world of order with space, matter, time, life, and humans in his own image. Through ritual and ceremonies we people in turn make order out of chaos. In endless space, we create a fixed point to orient ourselves: a sacred space. To timelessness we impose rhythmic repetitions: the recurrent feast. And to untamed or unbound matter, we give a shape, a name, a meaning.

What is too vast and shapeless, we deal with in smaller, manageable pieces. We do this for practicality but we also do this for high purpose: to relate safely to the mysterious, to communicate with the transcendent.

Recently I saw some small children playing at the beach. I watched them stand with considerable awe before the grand ocean as it rose up in huge waves repeatedly and crashed on the beach. The powerful water was not to be rushed into lightly or with abandon. They regarded the whole drama in silence as they clung to their mother's legs. Then with a little daring, the oldest launched an age-old ritual which we can all remember having performed ourselves and which we can see repeated over and over again wherever there are small children at the beach. The child turned her back on what was too awesome, and she began to dig a hole. Her brothers joined her. They dug and scooped the sand until they had a sizable hollow, and slowly they allowed something of the great sea to enter and fill their hole. It became their mini-sea. It was a body of water that they could easily encompass and control. In time they stomped in the puddle and splashed with abandon in a way that they were not yet willing to do in the surf. Then the surf rose higher and swished into their hole, wiping out one of its walls. With a delicious mixture of thrill and horror, they repeatedly rebuilt their walls, and the ocean repeatedly washed them down. Their manageable sea always let in something of the unmanageable. This was a game that they were able to play at for a very long time. For them it was a religious experience. They had created a hole to catch something of the transcendent.

In the same way we cannot head straight into the awe of the Almighty. Like the child before the ocean, we turn our backs on what is too much and slowly create the form that will contain something of the uncontainable. In faith, we make such ritual and are grateful for the discipline that form lends. That ritual is the "transformer" that makes communication with the awesome safe.

Without faith, we walk the same beach and are bored. We are not filled with awe; we have been walking this beach for years and nothing new ever happens. Boredom comes from taking for granted what is around us. We are numb. We do not allow ourselves to be touched and quickened. Then for the reverse reason, ritual begs us to perform the same act that the person, over-awed, is required to make. In search of faith, indeed, in hope we make ritual. The power of the Almighty needs, sometimes, to be guarded against but it also needs to be beckoned, called forth and wooed. In need of faith we empty ourselves and make ourselves vulnerable to the nature of things.

We ask to be touched again by what seems to have long vanished from our lives. We succumb. We make a ritual in a longing for faith. Perhaps, at first reluctant to get wet and sandy, we imitate the children in the sand and end up building wonderful structures. We start to take it seriously . . . and we end this play curiously refreshed and rejuvenated. Or we take a walk in our own neighborhood and try to see it for the first time. Or we dig a garden plot in the corner of the yard and resolve to grow sunflowers. "Unless you become like little children, you cannot enter the kingdom of heaven." Ritual is like play: it requires something of the childlike.

Making Sacred Space

Since the beginning of time, people have always known the necessity for a sacred form or space, even if it was only a circle drawn in the dirt. The important element is that its purpose be separate, sacred and safe. "Come no nearer," said God to Moses. "Take off your shoes, for the place on which you stand is holy ground." This holy ground is both container for and protection from the *tremendum* that lies beyond. It is the very business of religion to invite the great creative power in *and* to create the barriers that protect from what is too powerful. These forms and barriers are sometimes spatial, or temporal. Sometimes they are found in the form of rules. Sometimes they are literally structural or architectural.

After the simple barrier of the circle in the dust, enclosed space for sacred functions can be more developed. The Pueblo Indians build the kiva for ritual purposes. It is a hollowed-out space with the entry through a hole at the top. The participants in the sacred rites enter through this hole, send the smoke of their sacred fire out through it, call the spirit to visit and heal them through this hole and are finally "reborn" as they emerge, transformed and changed, through this opening.

This sacred hole is also characteristic of the Pantheon in Rome. It is a huge, sophisticated piece of architecture, an enormous circle, vaulted over, but with a hole in the center of the ceiling where sun and rain are not sealed off. Through this opening all the gods have a chance to enter at some time or other. This hole is a very graphic expression of the opening where the communication back and forth between the human and the divine takes place.

The Gothic cathedral, though it has no such hole in the roof, was built in proportions of many heights to one width. It encloses vast space above, while the people occupy the floor space far below. In between, its pillars are decorated and ornamented well out of reach and almost out of sight of those who worship. This "useless" space is difficult for modern pragmatic people to understand. Who could afford to heat all that? But sacred space is not practical space. It is enclosed and set apart for the transcendent.

In the baroque and rococo, we see an infatuation for appearances develop. Perspective and illusion become an art form. Baroque exuberance brings heaven into the church. There were rites at Pentecost where burning straw was dropped through a hole in the ceiling and a white dove was released into the church. That probably had some dramatic side-effects because later the "Holy Ghost hole," as it was called, was sealed off and, rather than risk missing the Holy Spirit, a dove was dramatically painted into place. Surrounding the Spirit-dove, amongst a tumble of puffy clouds, are God the Father, the angels and saints, in perfect perspective and showing us the soles of their feet as they float away into the beyond. For the faithful gathered below, there was little left to the imagination. It was all there before them, real as could be and just as glorious as the artists and technicians could possibly make it. Perhaps when belief falters, technology fills in as a god? Or perhaps when technologists become god, belief falters?

We have a long tradition of trying to paint the transcendent in, or of sealing the wonderful out. Impatient for a *tête-à-tête* with God, and unable to detect his revelations in the clouds of unknowing, we have been known as a people to fashion a god as we would like him to be and he turned out to look like a golden calf. Or, in a hurry to penetrate the heavens, we have built ourselves the tower of Babel, which after a countdown and blast off only made us more aware of our babbling breakdown in communication and our inability to understand or speak a common language.

Custom and ceremony require a holy space, set aside, that also works as a shelter. But while we must shore up and make firm our container on all sides, our remaining "open to the Spirit" means allowing some opportunity for the spontaneous and unexpected to enter. We cannot control everything in our experience with God, so we leave openings.

On a domestic level, our homes also have a ritual opening or hole. It is the fireplace. A fire built in the middle of the living room rug would be disaster, but a fire built just a few feet away in the fireplace is not only safer, but it becomes a good and warming thing. We may not always need the fireplace for its heat, but everyone appreciates its ceremonial warmth. The hearth may have lost its practical center but its religious center is still apparent. We know it from the centrality of the values we choose to display on and around the mantle. There we find our household gods, guardians of the hearth who, for the ancient Romans, could ward off evil spirits and dangerous occasions. Our household gods are our possessions. They cannot guard us; on the contrary, we tend to guard them. But they provide us with the comfort of the familiar; they are holy to us as standing for something stronger and longer lasting than we are. This is especially true of those possessions that, however tarnished with age, and however little of value in themselves, have come down to us out of the past and give us some hint of who we are by reminding us of where we came from. At the family fireplace we also celebrate our Christmas traditions with Christmas stockings and the yule log. One of the few truly American traditions we have has a god-man hero, Santa, enter through this hole and bless the household. The fireplace is often the religious center of the home, whether its focus is conscious or unconscious.

Holy Time Out

Holes are created in time through the creation of holidays—or, indeed, holy days—where the ordinary and everyday stops and time is set apart and not *used*. Every seventh day (sabbatical) since the story of the creation is a day of being, a "day of rest." That is what a feast is. The feast has its origin and its justification in its dedication to celebrating and worship. It belongs to the gods.

Plato put it this way: "The gods, taking pity on mankind, born to work, laid down a succession of recurring feasts, to restore them from fatigue and gave them the muses and Apollo, their leader, and Dionysis, as *companions* in their feasts—so that, nourishing themselves in festive companionship with the gods, they should again stand upright and erect." He describes celebration as the very act which makes the transition from crawling beasts to the upright and con-scious human, a transformation which makes what is human equal to and a companion (comrade) of the gods.

Such a hole in time, the holy-time-out, is not only what the contemporary work ethic would have us believe—a coffee break so that we can return refreshed and more efficient at the job/assembly line. A work ethic (and I sus-pect there have always been workaholics) makes religion of work when the ordinary has lost meaning and where there is no memory of the extra-ordinary.

The feast day, with its roots in divine worship and tradition, feels to be the most satisfying of all our feasts and holy days. Holy days refresh, replenish and ratify our common experiences; they make what has become ordinary extraor-dinary.

Taking sacred time out is a giving of equal rights to being over doing. It gives the sacred "no-thing" a value equal to the sacred something. It is the fem-inine aspect of a mystery which is open and willing to receive the value of mas-culine creativity without which the masculine value would remain unformed, uncontained and without a place of incubation or becoming.

There is the old nursery rhyme where each day of the week is named with a corresponding duty: "This is the way we wash our clothes, so early Monday morning." The maintainence of a whole household is completed by the time Saturday rolls around and on Sunday it's off to church. On Monday, we go 'round the mulberry bush and—the cycle repeats itself. There is comfort in routine, no doubt. Each day has a separate character. Studies show that people are relieved to have time divided into manageable increments. Structured time is not only more productive but less stressful, but by the same token, people are destroyed—if not in body, then in spirit—when there is no time out from the routine, no special time where "God can come down and dance with us."

Then the routine is deadening. Furthermore, the rhythmic repetition of feasts and fasts gives time a shape and life a balance and purpose.

It is in the very nature of culture to superimpose a cycle of celebrations onto time, forming a great reparative circle, or, better, a spiral, out of a more frightening linear time. Linear time has no beginning and no end. Worse, it has no repetition. I cannot get used to the new digital watch which shows me only the present moment and not its place on the whole circle of the day. When time is cyclic, it repeats, it looks forward and backward and gives one the opportunity to reflect on the past and look forward to and prepare for the future.

I know several people who share with me the same experience: when I pack up the Christmas tree ornaments at the end of each Christmas season I feel more reflective about the past and more curious about the year upcoming than I do even on New Year's eve. I always wonder what life will have held for my family by the time I unpack these little ceremonial objects again in a year's time.

Not only do the major feasts of the year give us that opportunity to look forward and backward, but occasions like birthdays afford us that special chance to assess and renew. Family ceremonies that are especially tailored to that moment of transition, out of the old and into the new, make birthdays extra-special. In our family life we make a special ceremony for the birthday person which includes the presentation of two envelopes: one marked "New Responsibility," the other marked "New Privilege." One envelope contains a task and the other a corresponding freedom. At age six, for instance, you might have the responsibility of scouring the bathroom sinks on Saturday mornings but you have earned the new freedom of widening your adventure radius. From now on you may ride your bicycle as far as Maple Street and back. (I can remember a time when the privileges and the responsibilities were more interchangeable and our Sara wailed, "Somebuddy already scrubbed the sink and it was my *privilege!*") At age sixteen, you might receive a key ring with a key to the family car. But then you are required to oversee the oil changes or provide a periodic wax job. At some point in the development of time, it is always enlightening to invite family members to write up their own privileges and responsibilities and to read them to the rest of the family at the birthday ceremonies.

As privilege has its counterpoint in responsibility, the feast always has its corresponding day or season of discipline. Later, when we consider the feasts of the Church year we will discuss this relationship further. But for the moment, it is important to notice that while the great sabbath of Easter has its Lent, our Sunday has its day in the week where tradition located our official bad day. It was Friday. Naturally, our bad day in the week does not always fall on a Friday, any more than the Lents of our lives always have the grace to fall during the season of spring. But the concept of organizing and accepting our "lumps" into a day that we consciously designate as our difficult day may actually protect us from having bad days, randomly, when we don't expect it and are not ready. The neurotic structure urges us to avoid all pain—only to discover pain everywhere. With consciousness, we are invited to suffer legitimately. Having a place to officially engage our sorrows is a healthy way to suffer: do the hard stuff first, fully engage our bad feelings, all the way down to their depths. Only then can we be transformed, resurrected, and ready to celebrate a life renewed.

So Friday in the old tradition of the Church was meant to be the day that we abstained from meat, atoned for our excesses, contemplated our human failings or undertook some form of personal discipline. That tradition was in danger, at one time, of being "inflicted" or followed automatically. Churches have often suffered under such automatic expression of what is sacred in character and made of form a formality (which leads so easily to righteousness or hypocrisy). I remember well the days when Catholics abstained from meat on Fridays. Too often, instead of engaging the mystery of "mortification," death to one's ego, death to one's selfishness and excesses, or the simple truth that the body and the soul could meet in the disciplines of health and diet, Catholics would quibble, for instance, about that magical lump of fat found at the top of a can of pork and beans. If I fished it out and discarded it, could I eat the rest of the can of beans and still be a candidate for eternal salvation? (What were we doing messing with those wretched beans in the first place, I ask myself now.)

There, we made a religion of the law and the rubric and avoided the ritual that was meant to engage an inner mystery. And when the magical law failed to make sense to our rational intellect, we simply absolved ourselves of the whole issue and allowed fasting and abstinence to slip into past history. But we cannot deny that even those prohibitions, automatically followed, once gave us an identity. And we would also have to question the meaningless formalities that have entered our lives to fill that void. The Jews of the Old Testament set themselves apart and created their identity through the use of prescriptions and prohibitions in their devotion to an all-powerful God. Their devotion gave them strength and meaning even in times of dreadful misery. Identity and communal strength are qualities which we miss today.

It seems time to reconsider and reinterpret the old rituals of the Church, rather than react against what has remained unconscious and without meaning. Suppose we take up again the original meaning of the Friday and consciously choose our "bad day." Imagine that we would choose a day in the week to undertake all manner of chores that required our discipline, that we would not procrastinate here but would undertake to do what we found difficult in the name of all that is bigger than ourselves, bigger than our egos, in the name of the Almighty.

We might fast that day and dedicate our discipline to all in the world who are starving, adding to our collection for world hunger relief. Or we might resolve to create a mealtime so thoroughly satisfying and thoughtfully partaken in, a time of family nourishment that so satiates body and soul that it would leave us free of further gnawings and cravings that cause us to nibble and graze between meals. We might make a reconciliation with a person with whom we have been in conflict, in the name of furthering peace and resolving differences in the world. We might engage fully and bravely what depresses us, weeping and mourning and writing it all out in our journal or risking to share it with a friend. We could engage some habit we have and look at it for what it might want to be telling us. Smoking is a habit which people are often desperate to break. If smoking, at least anthropologically, has aspects of taking of a thing of value and turning it into a vapor, it would seem that there is some human need to offer sacrifice (*sacrum facere,* to make holy) which our culture does not satisfy. Could the habit of smoking be translated and eventually satisfied in the making of conscious sacrifice—say, the burning of incense, the burning of a candle?

The point is that suffering and discipline are a part of every healthy life. We can choose to undertake them as consciously as possible and avoid contaminating all our days with our compulsions and the pesky agitations and gnawing anxieties that come of ditching and dodging the reality that life is hard.

If Friday was once the official "bad day" of the week, can we ask every other day of the week to be a "good day"? "Have a nice day" has become a common, friendly greeting. At the week's end we groan, "Thank God it's Friday," anticipating the glories of the weekend. Have we made any real distinctions between the nature of these days? Sunday, that day of holy time out, is in danger of becoming the watershed day of a successful or unsuccessful week-end where we merely congratulate ourselves for having packed in so much fun or bemoan the paperwork we never finished. Sunday becomes a muddy mix-ture of an obligatory hour in church and a rush to finish off the unfulfilled plans of the weekend. What happened to the "festive companionship" with the gods? "Holy time" and "good time" are sought out in mixtures that all too often yield up neither. Church, though we sang snappy tunes and clapped our hands, wasn't fun *or* holy. Cheery services that are meant to appeal to the broadest cross-section of the congregation are produced at the mortal cost of any sense of mystery or the sacred.

There is always the danger that the happy escape from engaging the dark side of our human nature on Friday comes up to greet us unexpectedly on Sunday night when we are about to make the transition back into the work week. Here we go 'round the mulberry bush and we might start all over again, with a "blue Monday." We seem, as a people, to have as much trouble creating our joy as we have suffering legitimately.

Sacred Symbols

The elements we find in "mere child's play" are often the same we find in the rituals of high consciousness. Both are carriers of religious experience. I watched my daughter Sara transform a whole array of crayons into a fleet of characters and march them around in a drama that contained unbelievable emotion. Each color represented a very real personality to her. Every day for a week, until her emotional drama was played out, the same colors were the same characters. Sal, Dan and Naughty Tom were the heroes. They were not crayons for coloring. Rather they were transformed into *real people*.

Joseph Campbell points out that play and ceremony often begin with just this sort of fun and then teeters on the edge between fun and earnest. Some-thing holy, something sacred, happens which makes the symbol, the object used, become indeed holy. Through a consecration the holy enters into the object used and the object used becomes holy.

We who have rationalized our way out of the symbolic world often forget how to allow simple objects or actions to become the container of the sacred. Incarnation is the flesh-taking of the sacred. The rational person, the scientist treats a sign as pointing away from itself to a reality outside it. STOP is a sign that points to a danger, out there, of cross-traffic. The stop sign has no other value than to get your attention focused on a reality beyond the sign. The religious person, the artist, sees a sign as symbol with a reality enclosed within. In the Eucharistic celebration, the priest with great solemnity and earnestness takes bread and wine and says: "This IS my body, this IS my blood," and it is no longer just a sign to get us to think of a deity far out in the space beyond us. Rather, the simple objects used are now Christ himself, real and incarnate in the simplicity of bread and wine. Matter and spirit become one. They are united within the symbol used. No object is too humble for the incarnation. Symbols and objects play a part in our religious experience or our ceremonial action. They are set apart and become holy through their use in the sacred action and through the transformation of our consciousness.

In our daily world, we are attracted to the power of symbol. From wedding rings to birthday cakes, we all value the symbolic in our lives. Some symbols indicate the sort of transformation we yearn for. Baking your own bread may not be an economic saving anymore, but it still satisfies as a powerful rite and expression of yeasty growth and conversion. Making wine or setting up jam out of your windfall plums is a gesture that holds all the power of an elegant transformation. Planting a garden and tending to the chemistry of your compost pile can become a therapy that lets you know in your very bones that life's rejections can be transformed into a blooming and rich new growth. All of us have known the delight and satisfaction that such work brings when it is transformed from tedium to conscious rite. First there is the process or the "consecration," and then the accomplishment or transformed symbol holds a power. I wonder how many times I've taken my patient husband on rounds to see my symbols for the day: "See this fat bouquet, opulent with larkspur and foxglove, and see, I used the parsley that bolted and bloomed for these marvelous umbrellas of lace. Come, let's pull carrots in the garden. It's such a pleasure to hear them separate from the soil as you pull." Or he, to me: "Come, let's make the rounds of the new fruit trees. See how I staked the grapes? Look at that peach tree! It's exploded with new leaf since I transplanted it to this corner of the garden."

No matter that you don't have a garden. You can make an art of any of life's tasks. Wash the windows of your apartment, settle under the reading lamp and sew all the loose buttons back on your shirts, rub suds over the car with soft cloths and feed it with a creamy polish, lay a ceremonial fire in the fireplace.

Or engage the mysteries of the season, with wreath and tree, with eggs and bread, with folk custom and creative imagination. The process contains the possibility of a "Zen" experience—the art of living. The sign and symbol used will contain something of the divine.

Transition

Most of the important ceremonies in our human cycles have to do with transitions, getting from one level to another. During transitions we are vulnerable and in danger. Like the creature who has outgrown an old skin and can wear it no longer, we shed what is no longer fitting. But thus exposed, we are in a state of crisis; we feel soft and unprotected and unsure of a future "skin" that is still unknown to us. In times of transition we are tempted to turn back to our old ways; these are at least warm and familiar to us, because the new is frightening and unfamiliar. But we know how unsuccessful are our attempts at crawling back into an old and worn-out skin.

Times of transition by their very nature bring conflict. Conflict which is not dealt with and recognized only mounts and increases the dangers. To help us engage the loss of the old and to give us the courage to embrace what is new, cultures have devised endless rich ceremony that occurs at times of transition: birth/initiation, puberty, marriage, the making of the healer/priest, sickness/health, death, mourning, life, resurrection or transformation. Many of these life cycles are connected with and celebrated in conjunction with the seasons, with agrarian cycles, which have myths and ceremonies for planting and reaping, for sun and for rains, for pests, famine, plenty and thanksgiving. The major life issues of birth, life, death and rebirth are addressed also in the feasts of the Church year which we will examine more fully later.

Meanwhile, in our secular circles, we often misunderstand the significance of the feeling states that we go through at the great moments of transition in our lives and miss the opportunity to point up with consciousness these times, lending courage and communal or individual support. A ritual or a celebration of the moment will invite a feeling discharge and offer safety to the person at risk. While we shed our old ways and embrace a new way, a ceremony will make the sacred experience taste both bitter and sweet. Good ceremony continually deals with both sides of a question in order to arrive at a place that can contain them both.

Colin Turnbull, in his marvelous accounting of the Mbuti peoples of Zaire, passes along to us their understanding of the dangers in transition. The Mbuti see the person as being in the center of a sphere. In moving from here to there, the sphere moves too and offers protection. If movement in time or space is too sudden or vehement, we risk the danger of reaching the boundaries of the sphere too quickly, before the center has time to catch up. When this happens, a person becomes *wazi-wazi,* or disoriented and unpredictable. If you pierce through the safe boundaries of the sphere into the other world, you risk letting in something else which takes your place. If the Mbuti know of and guard against such violent and sudden motion—and that without the experience of automobiles or jet planes—what do we, the so-called civilized people of the world, know of our transitions in space and time? I think we are a whole society in a state of *wazi-wazi,* beside ourselves, and possessed by impostor selves.

I was taken recently to visit a huge aircraft carrier. It was a world so foreign to me that I couldn't retain a single statistic—in fact I couldn't even comprehend most of what I heard. I was introduced to these giant proportions, and at the same time my host's living quarters had little more space or glamor than a large, tipped over shower stall. But he had a TV set—not to watch programs, but to look at the weather and see the out-of-doors, so deep is the isolation in the belly of this beast. I was told how the aircraft are thrust from the carrier, as with a catapult, into space with a mind-boggling force of power and speed. My heart was in my mouth. Talk about *wazi-wazi.* All the elaborate military ritual and form necessary for safety in this operation was outlined with the awe of a sacred rite. And yet, it didn't seem sufficient in the face of the whole operation. I wanted even more ritual. I viewed the whole, powerful, gray atmosphere of this masculine world, the thrusting design of the planes, the lack of any visible feminine value. I wanted to bring in some pots of dirt—mother earth with growing plants. My mind raced with fantasies of what the men in such an operation needed to "keep their feet on the ground." I wondered, when *wazi-wazi* prevails, who are the impostors who run the show? My mind buckles under such fantasies. I return to the world I know better, and I find that we have plenty of occasion to be "beside ourselves" without the help of powerful catapults.

I find that we miss a great opportunity, as families and as communities, to engage and celebrate as fully as we might any number of major and minor transitions in our lives and the lives of the people around us. Times of transition are moments of crisis and crisis is a part of change. Those compulsive habits we have employed may be our efforts to deal with the dangers and discomfort of the change we hope to make. "Neurosis," said Jung, "is a transitory phase; it is the unrest between two positions."

I think it is terribly difficult for people to spend all day in the office and then return home to a different pace, another set of faces, stories, demands, crises, delights, surprises. Perhaps because I do most of my work at home, I feel especially unsettled and touchy when I return home to my family after a period of being away. I come in the front door carrying my parcels or my overnight bag, give my greetings and hugs all around and head straight for the kitchen. I survey what I take to be my territory. Inevitably someone has made a sandwich at the counter; the crumbs and butter attest to the fact. I have lost control of the kitchen during my absence. Still in my coat, I am compelled to mop up. First the floor. It's a mess. Will I forever have to clean up in the wake of these troops? Do you think they might learn to sweep up after themselves? I bustle about making order. Some clever child groans from the doorway, "There she goes again, riding her broom." Now these counter tops. The crumbs encroach on the pile of mail that has stacked up in the corner, mail which unsettles me further—bills mostly, notices that need attention, sometimes letters from several corners of the world and corners of my past which don't fit together. Just one of these letters would be enough for me to focus on, but the small pile of paper, with its wide variety of levels, scrapes against every complex I have. And here, this pile of newspapers. Out. I don't want to look at past history. To one youngster, "Please, take your books to your desk." To another, "Why are your running shoes in the kitchen? Does this belong to you? Then please deal with it." I ride all my borders and try to gain control of my realm. I am in a state of *wazi-wazi* and beside myself. The family, one by one, recedes to the far corners of the house. An impostor mother has taken over.

Such habits examined and translated into a conscious "ritual of return" may do the job better for us—do less damage and offer greater satisfaction.

Then there are those popular customs or folk traditions that our culture offers for some of the major transitions in life; these may need to be reexamined and made worthy of the occasion. From housewarming parties to baby showers, from weddings to funerals, we have traditions which merit our further consideration. Is the passing out of cigars by the new father just a Freudian joke? What of this transition into parenthood? How can we engage its significance and how can assembled friends and family help to express ceremonially both the joys and the disciplines that parenthood will now hold for the new mother and father? Their feeling level will be running high. I know no other experience as miraculous and as exhilarating as childbirth. Recent medical wisdom has given back to parents the fullness of this experience. Because there is no denial of pain and the hard work that labor is, one is also present for the euphoric joy. It's quite wonderful to see the involvement of fathers in the birth of their children—their reactions of wonder and awe. How could this experience be further ratified and supported?

Transition plays a part in major life issues and also concerns itself with the simple fare of every day. The list of domestic and communal transitions that deserve our attention is long and interesting and challenging. I cannot cover all of them here, but I offer you a few examples to prime the pump of your own imagination and urge you to apply your creativity to those issues of transition that are a part of every human experience. Consider the day children leave for their first day in nursery school or college, bedtime rituals for children who find it difficult to leave the activities of the day and give themselves over to the dark. How can we celebrate the day our income tax forms are completed, or a deadline is met? What are our ceremonies for meeting a plane, the welcoming of visitors into our house, going on vacation, returning home after being away, leaving work or office and returning to the family? What might we do for the onset of menses for our daughters in the family, or how can we introduce shaving for the first time to our sons? Can we address with a ceremony the issues of midlife? How can we help friends or family deal with the feelings that accompany sickness, going to the hospital, areas of conflict and disagreement, the making of amends? On a personal level, how can we engage a depression and coming out of a depression? When you think about your personal experiences with these moments, do you remember the feeling tone, the success or failure of the transition made, the help you got or didn't get?

This list of transitions is as long as life's conditions will make it but it is important to know that no moment of transition is too small or insignificant for the nourishment of rites or ceremony. The following story is a case in point.

The Story of Paul

A young woman I know called me recently to tell me this story of her youngest son, Paul. Paul has been sleeping in a portable crib the whole of his two and one-half years. As can be expected, he has gotten rather long for the little bed, but plans for transferring him to a larger one were met with wailing resistance almost a year ago. His alarm and resistance to the change looked like something that couldn't be taken lightly. After two days of Paul's crying, his parents chose to delay the transfer until he looked more up to the occasion—or, indeed, until the bed would have him no longer.

In the past, we had joked that he might turn out like one of those Japanese watermelons we'd heard tell of that gardeners set, while small and still on the vine, into a crate to grow big, and, due to the constraints of the crate, square. This was to make them easier to pack and to keep them from rolling around. Well, his mother was ever so pleased to inform me that Paul was still his roly-poly self but that the bed had finally given way and he was now poking through its sides in several places at once.

This new state of affairs had now brought them around to face squarely the crisis at hand. Little Paul was still very attached to his bed. He'd known it all his life, after all, and it had served him well as cozy resting place and warm haven. It smelled like him. It was his. A change of beds was still not something he looked forward to. It was somewhat of a crisis issue for the whole family. They were apprehensive, each one of them, remembering Paul's anguished howls and the fitful nights when they had tried to force this change. His brother who roomed with him dreaded it. His sister across the hall dreaded it. His parents didn't look forward to it, but they knew this was it; they were brave and determined. Wisely his mama knew that the transition would have to be surrounded with some awareness and ceremony.

She explained to Paul exactly what was going to happen. For two or three days she told him over and over again what he should expect. She also showed him the broken places in his bed. And every night and nap time, she showed him how he poked through. More than that, his mama was not afraid to talk about his angry and sad feelings that the change would invoke.

"Finally with the third child," she said, "I'm getting the courage to admit to the negative feelings that kids have about things. And I'm discovering that rather than brushing them away and distracting, when we bravely name the bad feelings for what they are, they don't build up to so angry a crescendo later on. And afterward, there's always a good side to look for too. It leaves us all feeling refreshed at the end. There's such satisfaction after you've discharged and safely survived a whole array of feelings."

Therefore she frequently reminded Paul that he wasn't going to love the change and that he might feel sad. He responded with drooping head and lowered eyes and said, "And I cry."

On Wednesday his mama took him shopping and allowed him to pick out a bedspread. One caught his fancy and he clutched it to himself with delight. He hurried over to the cash register and pushed it toward the lady, saying, "This for my big boy bed!" And they took the package home and left it in its wrapping until Friday.

Each Friday this family has a special family night. It's their tradition. So Friday was the day of the great bed exchange. Paul's mother planned a special meal and she made Paul's favorite dessert. She carefully thought through the process.

After dinner the family gathered around Paul's old, little bed. They touched it and smelled it and patted it and thanked it. They said it was a good, fine bed, but now it was old and tired. Now it needed to be brought away. Oh, they said, how sad they all were with Paul, to see it go. They took off the sheets and unscrewed its sides and piled up the parts and brought it out to the garage and said goodbye and covered it up. (At one point, my friend thought she might leave the old bed handy for the children to play house or dolls with, but, on reflection, it seemed wiser to "bury it," to put it well out of sight so that the transition would be clean and there would be no ambivalence or mixed message.)

Then they carried in the parts to the "big boy bed." They all helped screw it together and put the mattress in place. Then they all circled around it and each took a corner of sheet and "sprrread the sheet and smooothed the sheet" with exaggerated gestures and chanting voices. They made a big game of it. They made the bed and put on it his wonderful old pillow and his bright new spread and his toy lamb, and then they piled Paulie in the middle of the big boy bed and cheeeered! Paul wanted to crawl in right then, so they readied him for the night and he was tucked in by all of them and prayed with and sung to.

This woman had worked out a ceremony, a ritual to help her little son make a transition which was more important to him than one might ever have guessed. His mother was conscious of how important the moment was and how difficult for Paul—difficult for the whole family.

The ceremony she devised was a little bridge for Paul, a safe path to take as he went from something old and warm and familiar to something new and cold and big and unknown to him. Furthermore, it struck her suddenly, how fraught with feelings the whole occasion was for her and her husband. It was another little transition marking the end of Paul's babyness, another transition in a whole long line of graduations to come.

"What a lot of time and feeling and imagination I've put into this! Just for something that shouldn't take more than ten minutes—if it didn't mean so much. It feels so right to spend that kind of time. Really, what else is there, after all? What's so important out there that I ought to hurry on for? I don't think there is anything more important than something this simple, this sort of awareness."

That's Reason To Celebrate

Ceremonies abound whenever a people mark and make an important new transition. For centuries peoples have made ceremonies for birth, the transition into this world. They have created elaborate initiation rites, to usher the adolescent safely from a happy and familiar childhood into an unknown and responsible adulthood. Wedding ceremonies mean to bridge two single people together into a new, social partnership which the whole community gathers to witness and bless. Sickness, death and burial rites bring us from our mortality to our immortality. There are ceremonies and rites and customs and folk practices for every major human event and for plenty of smaller ones.

The core of a celebration speaks to the hearts of all humankind—in all times and in all places. It speaks the symbolic language of the soul and is hardly ever practical, but more poetic, playful, prayerful. All good ceremony asks us to engage and make real the problem at hand and to feel and express fully both the dark and light sides of its reality, its joy and its fear or pain. Ceremony makes the ordinary extraordinary.

When we make ceremony and celebrate the nodal points in our life, we make an art of the life we live. When we undertake to polish our shoes with such consciousness that the experience hints at the transcendent, then we are creating a work of art. When Genesis says we are made in the image and likeness of God, I think that our very similarity to God lies in our ability to create. We are like God when we use the matter the Creator has already given us and further shape it to become the instrument through which he blows his song.

44

CHAPTER FOUR

The Elements of Celebration

W e mark the major moments in our human existence with a rite or a ceremony. Sometimes even the smaller events in our lives need the recognition of a celebration or the consciousness that a ritual brings. In our creative ritual making, we draw a circle around that place and that event so that we can be more fully awake to the magnitude of the moment. When we set out to mark these moments creatively, it is important to consider the elements that enter into the making of a ceremony. This short chapter will offer an overview of the elements of good ritual making.

A Leader

Ritual making and ceremony always requires a leader, someone who is not afraid to recognize his or her talent, insight or ability and who will step forward to use it. Collective ceremonies don't just happen. An embarrassment at stepping forward or a misconception that leadership is the enemy of democracy allows whole communities to remain unconscious and bereft of real richness. Families who have someone willing to mark occasions with rituals or traditions develop a unique identity and have a healthy format for a full, human expression. Making ceremony requires the vision of one who is willing and ready to take the leadership and to be as conscious as possible. This person takes responsibility, be it for the spontaneous moment, or on a regular basis, to respond to the greater good of the community or the family.

The minister, the priest, traditionally has this role for the community, but today the priest will consult and use the specialized talents of community members wherever his own talent or training is limited, but also in order to involve more people into the workings of the ceremony. The priest, furthermore, lies in the heart of every conscious, sensitive human being. In a community, wise people take turns with this kind of leadership.

In schools, the teacher has the occasion to create a vital community in the classroom with the creation of ritual and ceremony. Some schools appoint a gifted teacher to help the whole school with collective celebrations.

In a family, either the mother or the father will take this role of leadership and will engage each of the other members into participation as gently and wisely as possible. The parents between themselves will know who has the imagination and insight for this leadership and the other partner will willingly assist, suggest, encourage, implement and participate. In a single parent family, that parent may find it helpful and less lonely, on some occasions, to join together with the extended family or with friends and plan celebrations with their help. As children grow, they learn to become responsible and lead or carry this or that aspect of the planning and preparation. Everyone's input and feelings are to be taken into account and honestly aired and respected. But, always, there must be a conscious leader.

Participants

Ceremonies require at least one person, at least the leader, to be as conscious of the meaning, theme and goal of the celebration or rites as possible. Many, especially the children, will simply go along with the sights and smells and sounds and be fulfilled, enriched and fully satisfied by the simplest and earthiest participation. Some few may feel suddenly deeply touched and somehow changed by the experience. And others may remain untouched and removed from the action and the mystery. The more, however, each participant is involved in the preparation and the action, the more each has the possibility of being especially touched by the experience.

A Theme

It is not enough to have a vague feeling that we stand at the edge of a moment that needs recognition. We need to define the moment. What is it? What calls for celebration?

A rite or ceremony must have a central core or theme. Defining the character and feelings of the moment gives us the theme we wish to celebrate. Birth, life, death, loss, good news, partings and meetings—celebrations answer our most basic human needs, great or small. This is because they invite us to engage fully the feelings that accompany the occasion. The birth of a new baby into a family is an occasion for a wide range of emotions—everything from pain to ecstasy, from fear of the unknown to wonder at the mystery of new life. At the birth of a new baby, we need to celebrate the gift of a new creature to the whole human family. And we ask the community, in turn, to lend us courage in the face of our new responsibilities.

Transitions

The theme of a ceremony will most often center around a moment of transition, that is, a situation or moment of crisis where we must make the next developmental step—the move to a new house, graduation, retirement from a life's work. Here we are vulnerable. The new is fraught with the unknown and the past no longer works. Our step into the new is made safe when it is surrounded with the care and awareness of a ceremony.

Modern young people don't have nourishing rituals to mark their puberty or to usher them from childhood into adulthood. Instead, adolescence seems to have no clear beginnings, and without a clear ending it seems to drag on to embarrassing lengths. Even though we don't have the collective ceremonies that we learn about in primitive cultures, it is appropriate to mark the stages of our children's adolescence with family ceremonies.

One mother I know designed a ritual to mark the event of her daughter's first menstruation. Together they had visited some exhibits about puberty rites in primitive societies and talked about these rites of coming-of-age. They noticed that girls were often required to undergo a period of isolation or a painful exercise, or they were marked or tattooed with a visible sign. They planned that a part of this girl's rituals for coming-of-age would include getting her ears pierced for her first earrings—"ear marked," they called it.

Three Jewish women I know each told me that at the onset of menstruation, they received a slap on the cheek from their mothers. Each of the three was given a different reason for the gesture. That folk tradition, however, reminds me of "the blow on the cheek" we received from the bishop when we were confirmed, back in the days when that gesture was still a part of the rite of confirmation. This blow seems to signify the end of the carefree days of childhood and mark the entry into adulthood with its responsibilities and the difficulties that we now will have to stand up to.

Routine Cycles

Our human developmental stages are often remembered and celebrated in conjunction with the moon and sun cycles or simultaneous to the changing seasons in nature. Each day we experience a little birth, life, death, and rebirth. Every day gives us the opportunity to engage the routine rituals—rising and dressing, eating and leaving, relating and working, recreating and sleeping—with greater care and awareness.

Seasonal cycles offer larger repetitions of the birth, life, death and rebirth of nature. The mysteries of the Church year coincide with the mysteries of nature. Being in touch with nature's transitions allows us to engage our own inner transitions.

Celebrations which recur at regular, rhythmic intervals become a tradition when they work as affirmation of our most human qualities. Then they become worthy of repetition. The cyclic form helps us to look backward at where we were and forward to where we want to be as we grow.

At its core, a rite or ceremony points us, through our humanity, to the transcendent. Through rites we raise what is happening to us to a level of conscious awareness and in doing so we actively seek to be transformed.

A Container

When the moment to be celebrated has been clearly identified, a container of proper size and dimensions must be selected. *Time* and *space* appropriate to the moment must be defined and circumscribed. A good ceremony will have a clear beginning, middle, and end. The space we choose or create to celebrate in will be remade for its special purpose. In this space we experience a regeneration. In this period of time which we have set apart from ordinary time, we regain the creative and touch the sacred.

We all know the occasions that fall apart because the space we meet in is too open and undefined, or because the gathering which has been called comes to no clear ending. A party, for instance, can proceed very well, until later when an undefined moment arrives and it is right to bring the party to a close. Then the evening may fizzle out, and the guests, with ambivalence and discomfort, try to depart. Here, a thoughtful host will sense the right timing and with an artful action bring the evening to a close.

Models

When we set about making a ritual, our action can be utterly natural and supremely simple and spontaneous. A friend has received wonderful good news. This calls for a glass of wine to be shared, and we mark and celebrate the joy of this good news. But for larger situations, we may wish to draw on deeper stores, involve the whole family, or include our community. Then we ask ourselves: What resources do we have to draw from in planning a ritual or a ceremony? Where do we find our models? We have the traditions that folklore and religion offer us. These are enhanced and clarified by the science of anthropology where we can study the traditions found in other cultures. We have the insight of psychology. And, of course, we have our personal resources, such as our creative imagination and our intuition.

Tradition

Both religious tradition and folk tradition are a rich fund to draw from when we create a celebration. Often these traditions are a wonderful mixture of religious belief and basic human values. Traditions point to the past and in that way include all who went before us. Sometimes we have lost touch with a symbolic meaning behind a traditional gesture. Then it is rewarding to ask around, do a little research and dig into history, or anthropology, to discover what we are looking for.

A priest friend of mine has the marvelous task of creating a new parish. As yet he has no church but borrows space for Sunday worship in a local club. The public room is blessed and incensed to set it apart as they begin the celebration of Mass. Only four Sundays have passed and already the first child has been presented for baptism. My friend planned the baptism. He introduced the child and his family to the community and explained that on the next Sunday they would all celebrate the parish's first sacrament of initiation. To begin with he set up the simple implements necessary for this baptism: oil, candle, and water. Since he has sprinkled this room and assembly each Sunday with water from a large, fine, bowl, this bowl was chosen to become the font for the baptism. But he wanted to find something special to pour the water with. Remembering the folk custom of presenting a newborn child with spoon and cup, my friend learned that these gifts originate in the sacrament of baptism. The spoon was once used when the rites asked for the administration of salt to the initiant, and the cup once poured the water. So my friend found a very fine cup to pour the water with. At the end of the celebration, he presented the cup, inscribed with the child's name and the date of this occasion, to the child's family in the name of the whole assembly who had witnessed this moment. He explained to the assembly that this will be a part of their parish tradition, to present a fine cup to each newly baptized member. The cup will become a family treasure, a memento of a sacred occasion, a sacramental which symbolizes the moment this new Christian has been bonded to his larger family. The folk custom has been returned to the realm of the sacred symbol.

Psychology

Our psychological understanding of the human condition revitalizes our understanding of religious ideas, because religion celebrates the human condition as an integral part of our relationship to the transcendent. Both the Church and psychology understand our need for rituals and the importance of our feeling relationship to the archetypes. Both are vitally interested in the cycles of our human development. The rich symbolic language of the Church's mythology is a language which psychology can clarify or illuminate.

Imagination

Ceremony and celebration must have imagination expended on it. And when a ritual is old and rich, it has had years and years of imagination spent on it. We use our imagination when we choose an appropriate ritual and apply with a freshness what is old, tried and true to our own lives or to the uniqueness of a given situation. Our imagination is called on to create a compatibility between the moment to be celebrated and the container and resources employed to celebrate it.

The Tools or Properties

Rites and ceremonies use the ordinary and earthy elements of our existence and, by encircling them, render them holy. We consider the following properties when we make ritual.

Sounds

In making ceremony there will be chosen and spontaneous sound: stories which recount ancient mysteries and sacred times, myths, readings, wisdom or instructions from the past, old sayings, traditional music, new music, songs, chants, calls, cries and periods of the denial of sounds—silence.

Gestures

Ceremonies will use gesture and movement: processions, recessions, comings and goings, dance, hugs, kisses, handshakes, joined hands, clapping, plantings, harvestings, offertories, receivings, denials, blessings, burials, tears, laughter.

Gesture is an important part of sacred drama, and often these gestures need to be practiced by the priest and the other major participants. Gestures can become hasty, muddled and meaningless unless they are done with generosity, proper timing and care. Embarrassed blessings, hasty offertory gestures, muddled or unthought-out movements of all kinds weigh down a ritual drama, take from its power and rob the occasion of meaning and impact for both the priest and the participants.

I have seen a confirmation class glow with enthusiasm and confidence after the participants learned how to make a firm handshake and look the bishop in the eye. They practiced their gestures beforehand, and when the moment came, they did their part with grace and great good feeling.

The complex liturgies of the Easter Vigil Service, for instance, cannot be pulled together on the spot. A practice for all the ministers is necessary to make certain that they can serve with confidence and grace. With every detail attended to, and the timing carefully thought out, the ministers are freed to enact the sacred drama and be fully present to the mystery of the moment.

Elements from Nature

Ceremony is sure to use or honor some basic and elemental materials: earth, water, fire, air or wind, and bodily sustenance or nourishment.

Earth

Often when we celebrate, we bless or use: plants, trees, branches, flowers, fruits, seeds, rocks, oil.

Water

Water's mysteries are celebrated in the sea, the river, the fountain, the spring, life-giving waters as in the Easter water and the waters of baptism. We celebrate the water of life-giving rain and remember the destruction of floods and the new beginnings that emerge from them.

Fire

Fire gives us light. It gives us warming and sacred bonfires, but also destructive fires which need to be remembered and guarded against. Striking fire from flint and steel for the Easter fire reminds us how precarious and precious the spark of flame. On the candlestick, fire is contained and safe. Light passed from one candle to the next fills the darkness with light and sharing the flame never diminishes it but only multiplies its gift. In our homes warmth and light calls us together. The kitchen draws us by its warm oven where we cook and bake our nourishing meals. At the hearth we gather around a fire which is safe and comforting, or roaring and dramatic.

The greatest life-giving fire, the sun, is cause of many celebrations as peoples have marked its smaller cycles in the day and its greater cycles in the year. The moon, the gentle reflector of the sun's fire light, is also a part of our rites, and the marking of our time. It represents for us our feminine nature, in its reflective mode and in its rhythmic phases. Christmas is a feast based on the sun's cycle and Easter's date is set by the spring moon.

Winds and Open Space

We encounter air or wind and celebrate it in our open space, or we encircle an area of space and enclose it for special purpose when we build a barrier or form to protect against elements that are too raw.

The Spirit is often represented by wind and blows in to move and touch and ripple and churn up what has become complacent and staid. Outside in the open, we build windmills to harness the wind's energy and put it to work.

For celebrations, we like to use banners, flags, wind socks, streamers, mobiles, balloons, kites, pinwheels, all which react to and demonstrate the wind's action.

Once we planned a confirmation for out of doors, because the community was too large to fit in our little church. We staked out a great circle—a sacred space—in the middle of a grassy field. We set the altar at one end and stretched behind it a long, hand-woven fabric of reds and orange to provide a backdrop. We arranged chairs in semi-circles around the altar. All around the outer edges of the circle we planted tall poles from which hung long streamers in flaming colors of reds and orange, fuchsias and pinks. Tied at the bottom of each pole was a large bunch of yellow mustard. These posts provided the perimeters to our space, and the flowing, flying colors told of the Spirit's action among us in wind and fire.

The Work of Our Hands

Ceremonies so often call for the things we are able to make ourselves or which we ask an artist to make. Sometimes we are able to buy just what we need from a shop. But all that we use should be as dignified and worthy a piece of *materia* as the ceremony requires. These material objects do not need to be expensive, just honest, strong. The cups and chalices, the images and statues, the hangings and banners, the vases, the cloths, the baskets, the wreaths, the painted eggs and festive cakes, the vestments and clothing—all that is the work of human hands is made worthy by our conscious use.

The vestments that a priest uses allow the priest to step out of his ordinary role and put on the garments that designate his sacred role for a sacred purpose. Vesting with care and awareness helps the priest make that important transition from the profane world to the place of the sacred. All of us dress in certain ways appropriate to each occasion. Our "Sunday best" at one time had the very same purpose.

Nourishment and Food

Rites and ceremonies so often provide nourishment and food for our bodies. Christ himself created his feast around food. Eating together is a most satisfying and significant setting for human relationship. In ceremony we use bread and wine, cakes, eggs, meats, and all sorts of traditional dishes for traditional events.

The Celebration of Feelings

Rites and ceremonies will release, make conscious, affirm and celebrate our most human feelings: anticipation, waiting, longing, hope, receiving, giving, wonder, surprise, joy, gratitude. They also take into account our most painful human experiences of loss, grief, hunger, pain, sickness, jealousy, guilt and sinfulness. Slowly and in good time, ritual time, our painful feelings are transformed into the feelings of reparation, repentance, hope and salvation.

The Presence of Paradox

Ritual acknowledges contradictions and allows the ambiguous. When we have touched or been touched with a mystery we will always find ourselves at the point of paradox because we have seen a whole truth. We cry at weddings because we witness the end of an era. We rejoice at weddings because we witness the beginning of a new era. The core of celebration is at once bitter and sweet.

Part Two

CHAPTER FIVE

Advent

The Start of a Cycle of Feasts

By celebrating through the structure of the Church we actually are given the forms we need to become whole and we are given the formulas to make whole every human experience. This effort requires our rediscovery of the themes which the cycle of the Church calendar offers us and the application of our creative imagination to the rites and folk customs already available. Then, through the celebration of the sacred mysteries, we will find new meaning in the inexplicable and a worthy container for what we realize in our hearts.

In the Dead of Winter

Advent begins the Church year. And the first mystery we are asked to engage in is waiting. The Church cycle flows into the natural rhythm of the season and we enter the dormant, waiting time of winter. Nature seems asleep. The season is dark, and all that is becoming is hidden from our sight. The ancient combination of natural phenomenon with religious symbolism is still operational in our feast of the winter solstice/Christmas. Nature and mystery join and invite us to recognize our hopeful longing for the return of the sun and the birth of the Word made flesh. When nature and mystery remain combined there is great power.

It is Advent and, along with nature, we are a people waiting. Far out of the south, the winter light comes thin and milky. The days grow shorter and colder and the nights long. Try as we may, we cannot fully dismiss the fundamental feelings that lie deep at our roots, a mixture of feelings dark and sweet. Will the sun, the source of our life, ever return? Has the great light abandoned us? We are anxious from the separation and feel an obscure guilt. We know there are vague disharmonies that keep us at odds. But our longing for union is passionate. This year we want our Christmas to be different. We want to be touched this season—moved at a level that lies deep in us and is hungry and dark and groaning with a primal need. Like the receptive fields, we lie fallow and wanting. The dark, feminine, elusive quality of our receptivity is not helpless passivity. We are willing to receive the Spirit. We wait to be impregnated. "Drop down dew, O heavens, from above. Let the clouds rain forth the Just One. Let the earth be opened and bud forth a Savior."

The Marriage of Heaven and Earth

Gently, relentlessly as fine dew, the Divine soaks into a wanting humanity. And we celebrate the marriage of heaven to earth. The great opposites unite. God the heavenly Father has through his Spirit impregnated Mary, woman of this earth. Through the mystery of the incarnation, the flesh taking of the spirit, matter is made *equal in value* to the spirit. Our humanity is made Godlike and God expresses himself through what is thoroughly human. Creation is made worthy and perfected through God's presence within it. The ever-approaching kingdom of God continues as the mystery of Jesus absorbs all flesh and time and every human experience. Through this mystery we are reminded again of the value of material things—of the earthly—of the feminine.

Matter is given a rightful place, alongside God, equal in value to the godly, container of the godly, but not a God, not deified. It is our lack of belief in the equal value of our earthly matter that misleads us to make of matter a god, false gods, the aberration of materialism which so contaminates our understanding and celebration of this season especially. For God's purposes, matter was not too humble. Woman was fully worthy to bear his Son. Straw and animals, peasant-shepherds and the smells of the barnyard, all that the world deems inferior and worthless was the setting for God's self-disclosure amongst us. "The stone which the builders rejected has become the cornerstone."

God's design for our salvation is expressed through generativity, just as the history of humankind has always expressed itself. Through the incarnation, God underscores our human, adult sexuality, and sexuality points beyond itself, to every place in our human experience where spiritual and material factors intersect. God involves himself in the physical as part of his plan for salvation. The great mystery is expressed through what is utterly natural. By sharing our flesh he allows us a hand in creating and bringing about the fullness of time. Indeed, aware that we once "walked with God" and then lost that innocence only to be given a new hope in the incarnation, we become responsible for healing our brokenness and bringing him to birth in the everyday challenges of the human condition. We struggle to live out the same truth and make it conscious and real; in marriage we confer that sacred mystery on one another and know what balance it takes for husband and wife to become one in mind and heart and body. In marriage—in essence, in the joining of every split in opposites, as much as in the mystery of the incarnation—masculine and feminine, matter and spirit, darkness and light, are united and equally important in the creation of the new, the redeeming.

The coming together of opposites is the great mystery of the wildly impossible made possible and salvific. How many ways can we tell the truth of such mystery? Paradox is the place of mystery, the point of intersection which we enact and celebrate in Advent. And paradoxes are the theme of the Scripture readings during this season. A virgin shall be with child. The blind will see, the deaf hear, the lame leap, the dumb tongue sing. The wolf will be the guest of the lamb. The calf and the young lion will browse together. The cow and the bear will be neighbors. The lion will eat hay with the ox. The baby will play by the cobra's nest. Only the poet-prophet can describe such truth.

Pregnant and Waiting

It is Advent and we are a people, pregnant. Pregnant and waiting. We long for the God/Man to be born, and this waiting is hard. Our whole life is spent, one way or another, in waiting. Information puts us on hold and fills our waiting ear with thin, irritating music. Our order hasn't come in yet. The elevator must be stuck. Our spouse is late. Will the snow never melt, the rain never stop, the paint ever dry? Will anyone ever understand? Will I ever change? Life is a series of hopes, and waitings, and half-fulfillments. With grace and increasing patience and understanding of this human condition of constantly unsatisfied desire, we wait on our incompleted salvation.

Waiting, because it will always be with us, can be made a work of art, and the season of Advent invites us to underscore and understand with a new patience that very feminine state of being, waiting. Our masculine world wants to blast away waiting from our lives. Instant gratification has become our constitutional right and delay an aberration. We equate waiting with wasting. So we build Concorde airplanes, drink instant coffee, roll out green plastic and call it turf, and reach for the phone before we reach for the pen. The more life asks us to wait, the more we anxiously hurry. The tempo of haste in which we live has less to do with being on time or the efficiency of a busy life—it has more to do with our being unable to wait. But waiting is unpractical time, good for nothing but mysteriously necessary to all that is becoming. As in a pregnancy, nothing of value comes into being without a period of quiet incubation: not a healthy baby, not a loving relationship, not a reconciliation, a new understanding, a work of art, never a transformation. Rather, a shortened period of incubation brings forth what is not whole or strong or even alive. Brewing, baking, simmering, fermenting, ripening, germinating, gestating are the feminine processes of becoming and they are the symbolic states of being which belong in a life of value, necessary to transformation.

Waiting could use a fresh new look. The discipline of delayed gratification—not celebrating Christmas until the twenty-fourth of December—and the hope-filled rituals of our Advent preparations will give new value to the waiting periods in our lives.

The Advent Wreath

Pre-Christian peoples who lived far north and who suffered the archetypal loss of life and light with the disappearance of the sun had a way of wooing back life and hope. Primitives do not separate the natural phenomena from their religious or mystical yearning, so nature and mystery remained combined. As the days grew shorter and colder and the sun threatened to abandon the earth, these ancient people suffered the sort of guilt and separation anxiety which we also know. Their solution was to bring all ordinary action and daily routine to a halt. They gave in to the nature of winter, came away from their fields and put away their tools. They removed the wheels from their carts and wagons, festooned them with greens and lights and brought them indoors to hang in their halls. They brought the wheels indoors as a sign of a different time, a time to stop and turn inward. They engaged the feelings of cold and fear and loss. Slowly, slowly they wooed the sun-god back. And light followed darkness. Morning came earlier. The festivals announced the return of hope after primal darkness.

This kind of success—hauling the very sun back: the recovery of hope—can only be accomplished when we have had the courage to stop and wait and engage fully in the winter of our dark longing. Perhaps the symbolic energy of those wheels made sacred has escaped us and we wish to relegate our Advent wreaths to the realm of quaint custom or pretty decoration. Symbolism, however, has the power to put us directly in touch with a force or an idea by means of an image or an object—a "thing" can do that for us. The symbolic action bridges the gulf between knowing and believing. It integrates mind and heart. As we go about the process of clipping our greens and winding them on a hoop, we use our hands, we smell the pungent smell that fills the room, we think about our action. Our imagination is stirred.

Imagine what would happen if we were to understand that ancient prescription for this season literally and remove—just one—say just the right front tire from our automobiles and use this for our Advent wreath. Indeed, things would stop. Our daily routines would come to a halt and we would have the leisure to incubate. We could attend to our precarious pregnancy and look after ourselves. Having to stay put, we would lose the opportunity to escape or deny our feelings or becomings because our cars could not bring us away to the circus in town.

But to sacrifice our wheel means not so much "to do without" wheels as it means to "make holy" this stopped time. *Sacre ficere* means to make holy, and holy means hale, healthy, whole. We want to make this time holy and be made whole. And it is not easy to make this time holy. We recognize that the search for the Holy is so urgent and real that we are vulnerable to the lure that the commercial world offers in its promise to fill in the gaps that we so painfully feel. Materialism has contaminated the truth that "things" indeed can be carrier of the Divine. We do not want to fall for the ruse or Christmas becomes just another expensive disappointment.

During Advent, we are invited to be vulnerable to our longing and open to our hope. Like the pregnant mother who counts the days till her labor and prepares little things for the child on the way, we count the days and increase the light as we light our candles and prepare our gifts.

As a family we gather under the fragrant wreath. "Let's turn off all the lights in the house and first see how dark it is," says one of the children. Then we watch the growing light penetrate the darkness as we light the first candle on the first Sunday of Advent. Then the wreath is blessed: *O God, by whose word all things are made holy, pour your blessings on this wreath, our sacrificed wheel, and may it remind us to slow down our hectic pace and make our hearts ready for the coming of Christ your Son and our Lord.* The smell of the pine boughs hints at what is soon to come. "O come, O come, Emmanuel." We sing our songs and find comfort in the feelings and familiar sounds they bring back from other years. The very sounds and smells help us know that Advent is here again. The story of Adam and Eve, the readings from Isaiah and the words of John the Baptist are familiar to us by now. We think about the days when humankind had fallen from intimate "walking with God," each of us aware in some way that we are preparing for him again to "come down and dance with us."

We work our way toward Christmas. With quiet excitement, we go about those simple gestures that ratify the mystery about to take place. In ceremonies we deal directly not with thoughts but with actualities. We help ourselves to see again, in the outward sign, the inner truth. If we are awake and if we live the earthly process, we will feel what is inner and hidden. We make the wreath and light the candles, and we gain the courage to stop the wheeling and dealing of our outer life: to sacrifice the wheels that grind away in our heads, the endless rationalizations . . . the wheels that grind away at outward "progress" at the cost of peace and justice in this world . . . the wheels that dial and roll and spin and whirl and drive us to distraction. The sacrificed wheel of the Advent wreath encourages us to stop and wait. The symbolic life offers us a way to live those feelings which we might otherwise avoid or deny or rationalize away. The symbols speak directly to the heart. Intuitively we still know that truth; our children know it beyond a doubt. That is why we search for ways to prepare for Christmas together and look for the actions and the things that can adequately hold and carry such great mystery.

I Can't Wait

Small children say it all the time. "I can't wait!" Indeed, that's exactly the urgency we feel in this season. As parents we choose several ways to count the days and engage the waiting and prepare together for the big feast. We don't sing or play any Christmas carols unless it's music practice for the twelve days of Christmas coming up. We don't give any Christmas parties until Christmas begins. School and office parties which sidetrack us in our preparations make the feast itself anticlimactic. We don't eat the fruit cakes or put up the tree. We can wait. "We have to get our hearts ready," I'd tell the children. Would people make a beautiful turkey dinner for arriving friends and then, saying "We just can't wait," eat it before they came? Would a bride, so anxious to show her friends her wedding dress, wear it to the office? Would parents, awaiting a new baby, put up the crib, fold diapers, hang a mobile, and, unable to wait any longer, borrow the neighbors' baby? Sure we can wait. There's so much to do. How do we understand that our restraint might be different from that of the neighbors? Peter, at age seven, came home from visiting a friend in the neighborhood. We had only just lit the second Advent candle and he burst in to announce: "Michael's heart is ready! He has a Christmas tree. I'm not ready; I still got lots to do."

We inch up to Christmas—prepare, count days, keep secrets, watch for the signs. A red evening sky, every fleecy cloud on fire for a last few minutes before the winter night falls, still brings a shout, "Look! Christmas is coming! The angels are baking!" Hope and the exuberance of getting ready makes Advent not so penitential as it is anticipatory. Advent is full of comforting hints and tastes and signs. Our Advent wreath has the original red candles and ribbon. We save the color purple for Lent. We cook and we bake and everything is stored away in tins. But St. Nicholas breaks the rigor on the eve of his feast and brings a small sampling to spur us on.

While delayed gratification is almost a lost art and needs our ceremonies to reinstate it, it is important not to use the disciplines of waiting as a moralistic or manipulative tool as so many adults have experienced it in their own growing up. It is actually a tool meant to enhance life's joys where you learn to "pay now and play later." You take the cake out of the oven when it is fully baked and not, simply because you feel impatient, when it is still runny in the center. Waiting for the right moment is certain to produce a more delicious cake. Waiting is the ingredient necessary to a life of quality. Many adults have to learn this value before they can pass it along successfully to their children because their own early experience with waiting was punitive and perhaps rarely rewarded. But children can learn the art of waiting, and learn it most easily at an early age. Children can learn to wait in small increments, and waiting is worth it only if, in the end, the rewards really materialize. Advent projects and the commemoration of some of the Advent saints' days lend us courage in our waiting process and offer little rewards along the way that detonate some of the excitement.

The Advent Calendar helps us count days. "We await a Savior, the Lord Jesus Christ." Making the calendar is a project for the family to undertake during the Thanksgiving weekend or just before the first Sunday of Advent. A cardboard cut to a house shape is the general idea. It has a window cut in for each Sunday in Advent and a door for Christmas. Shutters close over the window and keep secret the picture or message hidden inside. With the passage of each Sunday an additional window is opened and the contents revealed. On the window's shutters one can write a prayer chosen from the text of that Sunday's readings at church. Inside will be a corresponding drawing in bright colors.

Each family member can be responsible for a certain window, pasting it in place on the back behind the shutter doors and keeping its content a surprise until the day of its opening. Hung against the window, the light shines through the picture emphasizing how darkness gives way as time passes.

A Pyramid of Light is created out of four fine apples joined with six dowels or chop sticks. Three apples form a triangle for the base. A fourth apple is held aloft by joining it with the remaining three sticks to the apples at the base. A candle tucked in at the stem of each apple and fresh greens make it a fine pyramid and table centerpiece. This can be used as an alternate to the Advent wreath, when the wreath hangs elsewhere and we need something to light during the family meal. The same custom holds of lighting one candle more each Sunday of Advent. The Adam's apples, however, will need refreshing from time to time. This pyramid prefigures the Christmas tree.

Gathering Straws to soften the waiting manger bed is a custom just right for small children. For every good deed—a sacrifice, a brave waiting, a job well done—a straw is placed in the manger as graphic sign of growth and preparation for the Christ Child we await. On Christmas Eve, the little manger, now soft with straw, is brought in procession to the waiting stable where the figure of the Child is placed during the night. In parish communities, this custom can be extended to an offertory procession each Advent Sunday where the children bring up some of the straws they have earned during the week. Where straw is difficult to obtain, wood shavings or similar materials can be made available.

A Reverse Suggestion Box is useful when "being good" is too abstract a concept for a child. We used a tissue box, decorated with signs of Advent, and we filled it with plenty of good suggestions to draw from. Write a letter to someone old or lonely. Brush the dog. Set the table tonight. Share a toy kindly with your little sister. Read a story to your brother. Plan an Advent meal prayer or reading for the family tonight using the missal or anything else that you've been reading and want to share. Take out the trash. Because we had three children with different abilities and needs, we color-coded the slips of paper; one got all the orange slips, one the blue, and the third, yellow.

The Jesse Tree is made from a bare branch or twigs or a potted house plant, and it is decorated with symbols of all those who went before us and prepared the way for the coming of Christ. Starting with Adam who obviously will have to be represented by an apple, and ending with Mary, we look up and read about the characters from the Old Testament and find or make an appropriate symbol to hang on the tree. Moses gets a burning bush, or the tablets of stone. Noah gets a rainbow or an ark, Joseph a coat of many colors, David a harp, and so on. The whole can be as simple or as complicated as you want to make it. Addressing one character a day is as much as we could handle at a time. One at a time and over the years, you will have made or collected a good representation of the patriarchs and prophets. (One of our friends checks out the miniature shops all year, keeping his Jesse tree symbols in mind.) You will also have given the children a good background in the history of the Old Testament. This is a great project for the classroom as well.

A Mama-and-Papa-Night was our solution to helping each child with his or her gift preparations. Each child had an evening alone with both of us and we gave that child our undivided attention. (Sometimes, however, one parent was excused from the event so that further secret undertakings, which were none of their affair, could be hatched out.) As well as planning and making the gifts, we often made time for a special story and a cup of hot chocolate. The success of Mama-and-Papa-Night caused it to spill over into ordinary time and it became a regular solution to getting the specialized time and attention that children in a family are likely to need.

St. Nicholas Day on December 6 is treated separately below.

The Feast of the Immaculate Conception on December 8 warrants a special dessert, and night prayers at the Advent wreath will include a hymn to Mary or a reading of Genesis 3:9–15 in which we become aware of Mary as the new Eve.

St. Lucy's Day on December 13 is the day when the oldest daughter wakes the family with music, candles and a special breakfast. Sara, who these days is just back from college for Christmas break, chooses an Advent passage from Handel's Messiah to play on the stereo and gathers the family to the kitchen for a candlelit breakfast of hot chocolate and special buns. The traditional Swedish Lucy wears a crown of real candles on her head and brings the family breakfast in bed.

The Christmas Crèche, if you don't have one, is something that someone in the family or the whole family together can plan, design or make during these days. If you are searching for a manger scene to purchase, you may find some especially good ones in museum shops during this season. An artist or folk artist will bring dignity to the figures. Better yet, you may become inspired to try your hand at making a manger scene yourself, discovering the hidden artist inside. It is in our creative efforts, I am convinced, that we are most like God. Art is a simple virtue of our thoughts directing our hands. It belongs in our homes to be enacted and lived with before it belongs in the museum to be guarded and looked at. The process and the effort is just as important as, or even more important than, the product.

As a child I was delighted with the crèche my mother made. She made it before she was married during a time of illness when she was bedridden. I am certain, from the stories we loved to hear about it, that her creative experience was deep and healing. It continues to heal. I wonder how many neighborhood friends, little boys, mothers, fathers, she turned on to making their own manger scene after a simple demonstration? It caused all of us in the family to take seriously our artist inside. We loved that crèche because it was not static, never boring. The heads, hands and feet of each of the figures were carved in wood and joined together with wire to form the body. The wire was wrapped with cotton, fleshed out, covered and stitched with cotton stockings and finally dressed. Because of their wire bones, the figures could be bent to sit and kneel and stand and hold. The manger scene was always changing and could tell us each of the Gospel stories as we heard them. Mary and Joseph appeared first on Christmas eve, searching for a place to bring to birth the Savior. Mary wore a bright red woolen travel cape, and Joseph a rough brown cloak. The shepherds lay on a distant hill with their flock. There was an angel, a strong guide and messenger who moved amongst the scenes, announcing good tidings here, appearing in the dreams of kings, and later guiding the holy family out of Bethlehem. I loved especially the shepherd's wife who brought a pot of soup and attended to the new mother. One shepherd always brought his young son. They were all of them shy, at first, these shepherds, and as they approached the stable, the son was lifted to peer in the window and report to the rest of them what he saw. Another shepherd had an apple to offer the Child; a third looked especially rustic in a real leather vest made of an old glove cuff. The glorious kings, from three corners of the world, marched for twelve days over side-boards and book shelves, following the star. As they arrived, in procession on the eve of Epiphany, the shy shepherds drew back. But Mary in silent wisdom held high her tiny Son, as though to make manifest to the world, the divinity of her Child.

You can imagine the stories we spun around this scene, grounded in the Gospel message and enlivened with our own imaginations. It made me certain that my children, too, would have a crèche that lived and breathed and was not just a show piece.

The crèche need not be carved of wood, if carving intimidates some of us. Papier-mâché saves us from carving, and the craft stores have all manner of materials that inspire simpler solutions. Neither do we have to make all the figures at once, but can add to the gathering with time.

Nor should cost inhibit creativity. We have made manger scenes entirely out of paper: paper figures folded double and cut to shape that can then stand on their own, paper rolled and tubed and taped, cardboard cut and slotted and fitted together. We have a whole Bethlehem of rock and pebbles from the beach—shapes that spoke for themselves and needed only a little paint to bring out an identifying feature here and there, twigs and greens softening the whole into a landscape.

The Christmas crèche is a worthy art form and deserves our efforts and consideration.

Choosing Rituals and Making Traditions

It is a doubtful thing to introduce an action or custom independent of a living experience. The rites and folk customs described here may seem too particular or too general or too elusive to meet a definite need. The idea behind including them is more to remind us of the paradigms that make ceremonies the dramas of our inner selves. By *doing something,* no matter how simple, we allow the earthly process to carry, once again, our hidden grace. I know no other way to help the family or our culture endure.

Many families have some Advent rituals but look for something more to enrich and lend courage to their waiting. There are dozens of customs, and though we mention only a few, only a few of these, in turn, will appeal to you and work as a repeated tradition. Best of all are those rituals and folk customs which husband and wife glean from their own backgrounds and gather from parents and grandparents to weave into a family life of their own which they create together. A search into our ethnic heritage will yield a rich store of customs which can affirm a family name and lend us a stronger identity.

At the core of our major rituals, it is wise to keep a character which is broader and richer and deeper than a too narrow personal piety, or a disjointed array of spontaneous actions and reactions. We use forms that carry to some extent a symbolic essence and that are rooted in the past and are yet a living expression, that have helped many people to know themselves and express themselves. A broad approach in the actions and words we choose will, like good liturgy, transcend the personal, the immediate family, and connect us with the rest of humankind, giving a sense of unity and purpose that will not leave us caught in our own narrow world. Then, when children grow up and express their spiritual independence and reject the narrow familial realm, they will have yet available to them a spiritual heritage that will continue to nourish.

For this reason, we have to keep looking at and talking over the visual shape we give to the sacred world and its hidden events. Parents, and later the children as they grow, might start by talking about the meaning of the season, what they feel worked in years past and what needs to be changed according to whom each member has grown to become, what needs more imagination expended on it and what, of course, is basic and remains the same. Family members can volunteer for some aspect of the preparations. A big burden is to leave everything to the mother, although experience often indicates that she is the natural coordinator and "mistress of ceremonies."

Once, when I gave a talk to parents about family celebrations, I was happily caught up telling of some tradition or other and a gentleman near the back row broke in to ask if my husband happened to be somewhere in the crowd, because if he was, he'd like to ask a question of him. It happened that Jerry was there and the young father wanted to know of him just how much he participated in "all these processions and things." Didn't he feel foolish? Jerry admitted that it hadn't been easy at first to get into the flow of ceremonies as we first threaded them into our family life but that progressively it had gotten not only easier, but more deeply satisfying. He said that more than anything, having children had reminded him of the mysteries of life. One Advent, he had watched Sara, perhaps four or five, repeatedly act out the wonders of a virgin birth. (Her own baby sister was certainly part of the mysteries.) With a tea towel over her head and her doll tucked under her skirt, she set up house under the kitchen (s)table and would wait with incredible quiet for the arrival of the baby. Watching how play and worship were one and the same thing for a child reminded him that this was a value to be kept alive in his children and to be regained as an adult.

As grown-ups, we can't expect to feel comfortable at first in introducing rituals. We may struggle with self-consciousness. While it is important not to be artificial or force a manner that doesn't fit our temperament, it is also just as important to dare what is uncomfortable at first until we find our own way. So often I have heard people express surprise and gratitude after they extended themselves into the other world and not only survived but felt enriched for it. It takes some risking to engage and put into action that hidden, childlike self, the playful person tucked inside, for ritual making is akin to play. Our children, in turn, are great ones for cracking through our caution. If you like to play with your children and you like to tell them stories, you will learn to love making ceremonies with them and you will also give legitimate expression to your own unexpressed feelings or undiscovered self.

Then there are those legitimate dark feelings that come at this time of the year. Take them seriously. When a family member balks, or sulks or feels left out or awkward, take him or her seriously. Get that member to talk out these feelings. Don't be surprised if, as an enthusiastic parent, you are the first and most handy target for accusations and attacks. You just happen to look strong enough to field these feelings. Not all these accusations are to be taken personally but they should all be taken seriously. The uncomfortable family member may simply be having feelings that he or she is clumsy about naming or understanding. We can celebrate with each other only when we have talked ourselves out and understand and forgive each other. While you won't gloss over negative feelings, it isn't necessary to drown in them either.

Men have a rather more difficult time "being pregnant" than women. But they aren't exempt. The dark feminine ferment of the season affects them too, and they can find it difficult to be at ease with so much feminine feeling in the air. Their discomfort might show up in moods and withdrawal or feeling as though they are being pressured into production. Patience helps. Relationships become rich and rewarding if a man will risk describing his feelings and talk them out. In that way he honors his forgotten feminine side and his inner feminine will deal kindly with him and not bring him into a mood.

And if a man can find a way to be creative with his hands, perhaps in making some of his gifts, lending a hand with the baking, becoming involved in the preparations with the children, it can become a viable way of enacting his spiritual labor and coming to birth. Stringing up the lights for the Christmas tree or serving drinks isn't adequate involvement in the rites of the season. The symbolic life demands its due. It does not ask the literal removal of our automobile tires—indeed, we do have our "shops to mind"—but the symbolic life demands that we keep our balance. Religion is not an intellectual concept; it is a deeply felt and utterly human experience.

Matter, *mater,* and mother are related words. More often than not, the mother of the household deals with all the material things of the season. (But the *materia* belongs to the feminine side of the man too.) Probably she is the one who knows where the ornaments are stored, finds the recipes, bakes the breads, knows how to make the wreath, sets the table, adorns the hearth. She is a wise woman if she also remembers that these material objects of the season which she sets out are to be beautiful and worthy carriers of what is holy. But they are not God. She can prepare and put forth a form to catch something of the spirit, but she cannot also go ahead and supply the spirit. The woman's responsibility may be a big one, but she takes on more than she need if she tries to reproduce heaven. Like the kiva, the ceremonial holy place of the southwest Indian ceremonies, there must be a "hole" in her material forms. Prepare, organize, plan, shore up, make firm, but remain open to the unexpected; do not seal out the spirit and do not think you can provide it. Trying to supply the spirit manifests itself in bossy behaviors rather than in wise leadership. Mostly it spoils relationship. I remember the time, when, because of my anxious perfectionism, I swooped down like a squawking raven on my children who were about to test out a new paint set where the Christmas tablecloth was laid. I could have gently moved the offending children to a clear space in the kitchen without all that harping. No cloth is worth that. The woman (and the feminine in the man) must not fall into believing she can or must be in control of everything and everyone. We do a very poor imitation of God and are better off avoiding it.

St. Nicholas and the Meaning in Myth

Our modern inclination to give a scientific explanation of the mysterious, even if it is "true" or factually correct, robs mystery and myth of its rightful place. In fact, we have equated the word "myth" with the word "lie." We seem to have forgotten that myth refers to a part of reality which cannot be described in ordinary words.

A young couple, expecting their first baby, told me recently about the prenatal classes they were attending. They said that the teachers of the course were very efficient and incredibly thorough. Every possible eventuality was considered and discussed. Everything that could go wrong or cause distress or pain was warned of and its reason explained. My friends felt rather uneasy about what was to befall them, and I thought they were somewhat more afraid and cautious than they deserved to be, given the other half of the truth: Marvelous! They were going to deliver their first child. The manifestation of "truth" was to take away all fear and question and put them at ease. But the other half of the truth, the sheer mystery of it, had all been forgotten. All the mystery had been leeched out of the experience in the name of scientific fact and truth.

From the "facts of life," the facts of birth, to the truth of Santa Claus, we stand in conflict about what we believe ourselves or what we should teach our children. A desire to be truthful with our children has made many people uncomfortable with one of the few myths retained in our cultic celebrations at Christmas time, the concept of Santa Claus or St. Nicholas. On the one hand we know in our very bones the power and magic of this figure—or certainly he would not be such a persistent force in this season—but on the other hand we don't know how long we can or should allow children to believe in him or what it is that they should believe. How will we deal with them when the "truth" is out and what will we all be feeling then? Is there a Santa Claus? In fact, we want to know if the church's St. Nicholas, the original Santa Claus, was ever "real." What do we do with him so that he does not upstage our celebrations of the birth of Jesus?

I don't want to get rid of Santa Claus. But I think that we need to give our Santa Claus, who has evolved out of a very ancient St. Nicholas, a closer examination. A myth is an exceptionally difficult thing to kill, for it continues to be devastatingly revealing even when we have tampered with it and changed its form by our rationalizations or our moralistic applications. A figure who can endure with such tenacity ever since the fourth century, and with a stunning continuity of legends and similarity of iconographic representations in so many countries, has got to be real. He may well be the most popular saint the world has ever known, whether he was ever real in history or not. His legends cannot be brushed aside as "mere" myths because they live on into the present and refuse to die while stories in history, on the other hand, deal with what is dead and past. Santa Claus is the father figure we all dream about and share in our collective unconscious. He is a type of God the Father, primal and powerful and, yes, real.

When my daughter Annika was four or five, she was tested by a school psychologist; I think it was to see if she could go into kindergarten. The psychologist was curious about her verbal skills, so he asked her some questions trying to trace the origin of these abilities. He phoned us to tell us the story of their exchange. He had asked her, "Do your parents read you stories?" "Oh yes," she told him. "My Papa tells us Piggle-Wiggle stories and my Mama reads us Greek myths." "What are myths?" he asked. "Oh, you know, mythology— those are stories," and she paused, "stories who aren't true on the outside. But they are true on the inside."

The mythology of St. Nicholas is the manifestation of a great inner truth. We do not lie when we share that sort of truth with our children, so long as it is not distorted or contaminated by our own lack of belief or distorted in allowing it to be a whole truth. We cannot apply to our children what we are not willing to "believe in" ourselves. And if we separate ourselves so far from the inner truth that we no longer believe, then our attempt to make our children believe is an exercise in our own sentimentality. And sentimentality is a lie.

Sentimentality and Reality

Sentimentality is the emotion we feel when we scoop off a part of the truth, that part which we are willing to accept, and slather it like syrup to cover what we do not want to see. Usually what we don't want to see is our own responsibility to the remaining truth. A half-truth is a very dangerous thing, because it is a lie. An example of sentimentality is those feelings of nationalism, often fostered with rousing anthems and speeches, that allow citizens to promote their own country's interests over the common interests of all nations, and to see themselves as superior and blameless. Sentimental are those paintings tourists bring back from Mexico done on black velvet which depict a haunted, great eyed waif with a rhinestone tear rolling down, as though human misery were cute and quaint. Our Santa Claus is a valuable mythic image, but he is often distorted into a father image without dignity or authority or mystery. Real myths and sacred occasions invite us to engage both sides of our fundamental psychological condition—the inner truth which is always both dark and light.

If Santa Claus is a God-the-Father figure for us, we will have to examine just what it is that we believe about God and what we know and believe about fatherhood.

Santa as Type of the One God

Primitives and children relate to primal truths as pure and unfragmented powers. They are able to attribute to a single being light and dark qualities. They also spring freely back and forth between inner realities and outer truths, and have no trouble relating to such opposites as to a whole. The "primitive man" in my life, who also happens to draw pictures at my kitchen table, taught me another lesson about the wholeness of God which I have had to think about and grapple with ever since. When Peter was around four he scrawled a large picture on a piece of paper and shoved it across the table with a sigh of immense completion. "This is God!" he announced. "He has a wing to fly with, and a fin to swim with. He has a hand to pat with and a claw to scratch with. He has a black face for the night and a bright face for the day." Peter had made a kind of *yin-yang* God. Such a whole and unsplit concept of God brings to mind what Isaiah spoke of: "I am Yahweh, and there is none else. I form the light and create the darkness; I make good fortune and create calamity. It is I, Yahweh, who do all this." Surely this is a God who is a source both of the unspeakably terrible and of the strength to withstand such terror.

It is our objective as healthy human beings to engage and embrace the whole of reality, not as we would like it to be, but as it is. If we want to live honestly and responsibly, we have to constantly repair our abilities to perceive reality and know that it is our human inclination to escape it.

We know the light side of God's creation as one half of reality in the wonders of nature, in the sun and its predictable cycles, in the mountains and forests and seas and rivers, in flowers and creatures, in the natural balance of nature. We know it in his marvelous creation of us, his people. This side of God fairly bursts with life and a creative love, with justice and order.

The light side of every reality is the *yang* in life, the positive, the masculine, the conscious, the tangible. We know it as white, as opposed to black, as day as opposed to night, as right as opposed to left, up as opposed to down, the creative as opposed to the receptive. When we refuse to integrate what is light with what is dark, we create an imbalance and a lie. Joy, as long as it is not an escape from legitimate pain, is an integral part of reality. We can always be certain that the marvelous qualities we admire, even worship, in our heroes are exactly the beauties and virtues which we fail to acknowledge and bring to consciousness in ourselves. We need to name, admit to and take responsibility for our ability as human beings to grow and evolve and learn. We are capable of great charity, selfless concern for our brothers and sisters, empathy, insight, patience, peacemaking. The light side of reality is one half of a whole truth.

The dark side of God's creation is as equally deserving of our attention and recognition as the light half of reality. We know the dark side in the unpredictable wrath of nature, natural disasters, earthquakes, volcanic explosions, floods, famines, unspeakable human suffering, the death of loved ones. We do not know yet if creation is ultimately good. That is an ineffable mystery, unclear, shrouded in unknowing, ambiguous. But we cannot deny that there is cruelty in nature, and in human nature, and this is not all due to the sinfulness of humankind. All this about God belongs to his dark nature. The untidy truth is that God's dark and mysterious nature is also the place of those feminine attributes of tender mercy, nurture, and gentleness which we attribute to God.

The darkness in every reality is also what is the *yin* in life, the negative, the feminine, the unconscious, the mysterious, the elusive. We know it as black as opposed to white, night as opposed to day, left as opposed to right, down as opposed to up, the receptive as opposed to the creative. How quick we are, when we observe "difference," to further infer a pejorative value. Darkness is not demonic until we refuse to allow life to be a harmony of opposites, where the dark side of life reveals the light by contrast. Evil comes into the world when we fail to include the dark side of existence along with the light—that is when, as an escape from reality, for instance, we seek after pleasure to avoid pain. We fail to see the dark truth in our own human condition when we avoid the work it takes to suffer legitimately and be disciplined, to work through depressions, to risk changing, to grow. Pain, as long as it is not a neurotic escape from reality, is an integral part of reality. When we refuse to recognize or integrate what is dark, natural qualities turn counter-productive or evil. Anytime you stand on the manhole cover of your unconscious holding something down, it either seeps out slowly and disastrously, or it simply explodes. Feminine qualities of waiting, for instance, turn impatient and forceful. Acceptance turns into passive submission or conversely into aggression.

We can always be certain that the qualities we so vehemently condemn in our enemies are exactly the insincerities we refuse to acknowledge in our-selves. Scapegoating is our own darkness and propensity for evil denied and projected on others. Any inequity which we suppress invites the suppressed to become dangerous, distorted or evil. We have to name, admit to and take re-sponsibility for our own ability to be agents of real evil, as in our avarice, man-ipulations, aggression, greed, lust, deceit, cunning. Darkness cannot be split away from our reality, hated, denied and projected without grave danger to human culture, especially now where it has horrendous technological power to hurl against its deemed enemies. Our capacity for unspeakable inhumanity toward one another should still be fresh in our memories and a lesson about what a sentimentalized world view can lead us to.

As the whole truth about the one God unfolds before us in our lifetime, we begin to see that his qualities are not simplistic, except insofar as he binds all opposites into one whole and is Ultimately Simple. The fatherhood of God has equal doses of the feminine principle. His further disclosure in our own humanity invites us to take a hand in our own redemption—indeed to heal our split of light and dark power. It is difficult to be sentimental about the Fatherhood of God, but it would be even more difficult for us to engage him at all without bringing him into the range of our human experience as the mystery of the incarnation allows us to do.

Santa Claus as Father Figure

Santa Claus, as a type of the Fatherhood of God, is another step in bringing God "down a notch" to semi-human levels so that we can grasp more easily what is too large and awesome and distant—taken down a notch, indeed incarnated, into a father figure to whom we can relate.

But the Santa that we meet in the department stores is in danger of being relegated to a powerless father. Often he is neither mysterious nor inspired. Any vestiges of the numinous or the serious are drowned out with a chuckle. Patronizingly he teaches us to beg for what we want, and he will be the provider. He teaches us nothing about how to give—how to take a hand in being co-giver and co-creator with him. He is a father for children who have to remain dependent, sometimes manipulative, if they want to relate to him. Of course any one of us is tempted to remain a child, to abdicate our responsibilities, even to a clown, if we can get by with it. We often look for the father figures who "know if we've been bad or good" and who will tell us just what is bad and good so that we never have to make up our minds and live with our own choices. We like the idea of a father who will sneak about in the night and while we sleep keep the world afloat and our enemy vanquished. Santa Claus as our hero for fatherhood is in danger of looking foolish or anemic or patronizing. Sentimentality wants the look of a jolly provider, a father who is buddy and pal.

How can we reconsider his image in the light of the whole truth? How does the Santa you know hold up as a father hero you can look up to and never outgrow? Without a new awareness and some restoration work on Santa Claus, we might be tempted to continue to turn a blind eye on the art of fatherhood. I think that in the process of scraping down the layers of paint that have coated our Santa over the years, we will recover a stronger, wiser, more dignified father figure who involves us in a process of growing and changing, who requires that we take a part in "creating all things new."

For, actually, our Santa Claus at core has the mythological basis of a powerful type. He is a capable symbol who might well carry the type of God the Father, Creator. He carries a father image that imbues all fatherhood, and leadership and authority everywhere with dignity and a powerful creativity. He is certainly that great Papa, a grandfather, who has given us so much and continues to nourish us out of his endless store of gifts that knows no end, who knows us so well, and who rescues us from our own inadequacies. But he also lends us the courage to grow and change, and helps us to see the world as it really is and requires that we do our part.

The Restoration of Santa Claus

Some people, uncomfortable with the distortions and unwilling to allow Santa to upstage the celebration of Christ's birth, have relegated him to the position of a jolly postman who delivers packages at Christmas. That certainly is a viable solution. It leaves Santa something to do, but that's about it.

Another viable solution is to return to Santa Claus his original role as a sainted father figure. We have a long tradition of seeing the Godliness in the person of our saints and we have traditionally turned to them to inspire us and point us in the direction of the heavenly mysteries. Like St. John the Baptist who teaches us how to "make straight the way of the Lord" during Advent, the saint effaces himself for the sake of what is coming that is more important. "He must increase, I must decrease," says the Baptist. The saints and prophets have taken the humble role of bringing us closer to recognizing God, withdrawing their own egos from our ability to eventually face God ourselves as he appears in the uniqueness of our own human experience. A saint or a prophet helps us to grow into a relationship with the numinous, not outgrow it.

The historical evidence of a St. Nicholas, the original Santa Claus, is thin and sparse. We know only a few things out of history about him. He was bishop of Myra, Asia Minor (near modern Finke, Turkey) and is said to have lived around the year 325 A.D. In 1087, Italian merchants and sailors took his body from his tomb in Asia Minor to place it in a new shrine in Bari, Italy where he is still venerated today. His traditional feast day comes early in the season of

Advent, on December 6, as though this gift-giving father image came early in our Christmas preparations to prepare the way for *the* Father, giver of *the* Gift at Christmas.

From there, the evidence of his archetypal reality—his reality "on the inside"—fairly bursts into a host of legends, icons, songs, plays and folk practices out of eastern and western Europe. The stories find a strong parallel to many stories of Yahweh in the Old Testament and to Christ in the New Testament, and they tell of a person who knew, more than anything, how to give. He was the ultimate gift-giver who did his work so that no one ever saw him. He never expected a return for his good deed. That very selfless giving is a big part of our being parents. We know, in the urgency of doing what is right for our children, that our ego does not often get the credit.

If you believe in the Santa Claus who is worthy and "real on the inside" he does not necessarily have to materialize in the shopping centers as proof of his existence "on the outside." For when myth is confused with historical reality, it no longer applies to inner life. Myth is only a "revelation" as long as it is a message from heaven, from what is beyond time and place. Myth does not tell of what *was* true but what *is* true, always. Such a message one need never outgrow; in fact I would say that at my age I am still growing into that reality. A reassessment of the Santa or the St. Nicholas who blows down your chimney can enlighten your understanding of him. Remember that you can enrich the Santa you already have with some added stature, through pictures and stories. Or you can adopt St. Nicholas into your traditions. I hope that these stories out of my own experience will not intimidate you, but will give you new ideas and that you will find, enriched and deepened, the holy man you already know.

A European Tradition Tailor-Made

In our household, because Nicholas was already a rich part of my growing up and German heritage, we never questioned his part in our Advent ceremonies. He continued his mysteries from many past generations into the generation of my own children and they found their engagement with him real and satisfying so that they never worried about the absence of a Santa as other households knew it. In our house we celebrate the feast of St. Nicholas on December 6 as it is celebrated in many countries. We keep this celebration separate from our celebration of the birth of Christ at Christmas.

What we taught and believe is that St. Nicholas is real on the inside. He comes back to this earth from his place in heaven and relives his holy actions. One way in which he functions is through any person willing to continue his work of generosity, justice and creativity. He lives in the hearts of mothers and fathers who know about him and understand his ways. He lives in the hearts and actions of children who catch on to his message and, now wise to his ways, participate in his secret giving. He puts the ideas into our heads and the actions into our hands that further his work here on earth. The spirit of Nicholas rises up every Advent and fills the house with his mysterious and unseen secrets. He inspires how we prepare our Christmas gifts during Advent and the spirit in which we give and receive. His gift-giving was such an art that he gives us the finest lessons available as we prepare our own gifts for each other during the Advent season. He teaches us how to give, "so that the right hand does not know what the left hand is doing." That has inspired the concept that we are each one "a little Nicholas," and during Advent the children creep and sneak about doing one another a good turn, never letting on "who done it."

I remember groping my way into the dark kitchen of a winter morning to start the breakfast and discovering, when I turned on the light, the table already set and a note in the center reading: "This tabel was set for you by saint Niklus." Later at breakfast, snorts and giggles and toothless smiles made me none the wiser.

Nicholas requires our self-examination and an illumination of our Advent spirit. The children kept Nicholas calendars for years on which they marked the quality of their day with their favorite color of crayon for the good events and their most disliked color for the bad. "He knows if you've been bad or good" becomes not a threat of moral judgment but an opportunity for the self-examination of the quality of a day and the development of conscience. A sheet of paper with a grid on it—with a square for each day from Thanksgiving until the sixth of December—was given to each child. They decorated the margins with their own illustrations of this fatherly bishop and the wonderful contents of his sack. More often than not, they showed themselves in bed, asleep while he came to visit. With a stunning accuracy they marked the calendar square for the day with just enough of a smudge to indicate some selfish act or bad experience. Bright colors decorated the day for any acts of kindness or happy experiences. Finally, during the night of the fifth of December, his ultimate visit was evidence left in a small but magical foretaste of the Christmas still ahead.

The mysterious nature of these ceremonies was so tenacious that when Peter was ten years old he still had not asked us some of the usual questions that we parents figured might be normal to ask about Christmas and about our St. Nicholas celebration. Although my husband and I had made a very conscious presentation of Nicholas as that mythical figure who lives and works out of the hearts of those who know him and understand his ways, I still was curious that inside truth and outside truth weren't more ruptured in Peter's understanding. For once I do things right, and then I still am filled with doubt. I expected him to ask questions like who reeely is St. Nicholas—or how does he get cookies to us and also to the cousins in Michigan, but none to Micky, the guy next door. Peter simply went about his job of being a "little Nicholas" with his secret actions, and he always was delighted and surprised on the morning of December 6 at what Nicholas brought him. Well, I needed some ritual way to involve him even more tangibly in these Nicholas mysteries and I invited him to stay up one night with Jerry and me to bake the traditional Nicholas cookies that we found each year on the plates around the table on the morning of this feast. (Besides the traditional St. Nicholas cookies, we try to get all the Christmas baking finished and stored away in freezer and storage tins during the days between Thanksgiving and St. Nicholas day. This not only frees up the rest of our Advent for other projects, but it supplies Nicholas the necessary "foretaste of Christmas" to give us as samples on his feast.) My husband and I always worked at this baking during the night when the children were asleep, and some of it I did when the children were off at school. They had never been involved in this process, so it was now for the first time that I invited the first of the children into the process. I told Peter that Nicholas always worked through his people and he needed our hands to further his work, much as the salvific work of Christ is hindered or furthered through our hands. Would he like to creep out of bed tonight after the girls were asleep and help bake? Peter was stunned and delighted. Standing there in his striped pajamas, flour on his face, he rolled out dough, and he kept absolute silence. Mystery hung in the air. He never snitched a scrap of the dough as he might otherwise, and he didn't ask for a sample as the cookies emerged from the oven, baked. Even in the midst of this direct involvement, the waiting-spirit of Advent still prevailed.

Then in the early morning darkness of December 6, the family proceeded—I think I could say, processed—into the candlelit dining room. The
smell of spices and tangerines hung in the air. We sang our songs and danced
around the table and finally came to a halt before our own plates which we had
placed there in ceremony the night before. Our plates were heaped with one
sample of each of the traditional Christmas goodies we would enjoy in even
greater abundance during the twelve days of Christmas. There were nuts, fruits
and a variety of cookies. At each place there was propped up a little book or a
small gift. The chandelier was hung with greens and special cookies—each
cookie formed in a different symbol for the family members and signifying
some charming traits, a weakness or a current passion: a cat for the cat lover,
an ice skate for the fanatic skater, a snail for the one who was always somewhat
late, a telephone for the talker. The central cookie was the image of St. Nicholas
with beard and mitre. In the candlelight, the whole thing *was* magical. Even
Jerry and I were struck with wonder. We looked at Peter for some sign of recognition or realization. Some of this splendor was of his own making, after all.
Finally, he drew me aside and whispered: "Good thing that Nicholas comes in
the night and puts all this out himself. I'm glad he keeps a hand in it, because
no ordinary person could make things come out like this!" And he clung to the
mythical truth.

When Peter was fourteen, he arranged a campout for his outing club at
school for the weekend of December 6. I thought, "Aha, now we will have to
experience a new phase of our tradition making in this family. Peter will have
to make a new choice." To our surprise, the outing was organized, everyone
in the club was in readiness, and Peter did not get packed to go. "Naw," he told
us. "They'll manage just fine without me. You didn't think I'd just go off some-
place on St. Nicholas day?"

Then came the year this Peter returned to the college dorms after Thanksgiving at home. He left equipped with a large lump of Speculatius cookie
dough (see recipe below), and my extra rolling pin poked out of his backpack.

On the eve of St. Nicholas, he and his roommate baked the traditional cookies until 2:30 A.M. and distributed them in great secrecy to every room in the dorm. (Later, I remember how I came upon Peter and one of his buddies, both returned from their respective colleges for the Christmas recess, discussing how *each* of them had baked his cookies and had made his secret deliveries. "Yeah," said Dan, "and then they wouldn't eat them because they liked them too much—they thought they were too beautiful to eat!")

The following year, his study break allowed Peter to be home for December 6, and this time it was Sara who was away at college. So we parents had this rather large son and his sister Annika left to dance with us around the table. That year, I confess, I made a mistake. We did dance around the table and deposit our plates on the table the night of December 5, and we did all enter the candlelit room the next morning to find our cookies and nuts. But something was missing. After the rituals, Annika and Peter took me aside. They "didn't want to sound greedy or anything," but they thought I should know that things felt "a bit skinny this year," as they put it. Indeed. Something was not quite right. I thought it was that we were all mourning the loss of Sara. That night Sara phoned us from her college dorm to tell us with excitement how she had been a secret Nicholas and had hung cookies on all the doorknobs of her floor. She wanted to know about our celebration, and I confessed that we missed her and that her brother and sister had expressed some disappointment. Promptly she put me through the third degree—had we done this, had we done that, had they each found the traditional cookie in their shoes when they got up? Well, no, I thought that an unimportant detail that we could now easily dispense with. "Wrong!" she scolded me. "You should know better. You can't meddle with the basics of tradition. That way you leave out important things. A tradition is a tradition precisely because you repeat it year after year, no matter what. And don't ever think that people grow too big for a tradition." She was right. That was it. It was wrong to leave out any vital part of the tradition. Here, we parents figured we might be pressing our luck expecting a fifteen year old and a nineteen year old to sing and clap and dance around the table. Certainly they didn't put out their shoes again, too? I checked it all out with Peter and Annika. That was it. "You *always* find a cookie in your shoe on St. Nicholas morning."

Jung said: "A ritual must be done according to tradition, and if you change one little point in it, you make a mistake."

Family Ceremonies for Santa Claus or St. Nicholas

So as you evolve a Santa Claus or a St. Nicholas tradition for your family, you will have to find the elements that will be strong for you and then abide by them—even if everyone has vanished off to college. At home, things have to remain the same.

Use elements out of your childhood or your family backgrounds that worked and add whatever will give strength and substance to this father figure. You might use December 6 as a Nicholas feast to give some relief from long waiting and incentive to carry on and prepare further.

This might be the time to put out a shoe before the door or hang up the stocking on the hearth or set out a plate on the table for some little sign.

You may wish to introduce the concept of being a "little St. Nicholas" and involve each family member in secret kindnesses to one another. You can include friends and neighbors into being secretly gifted. You might want to introduce anonymous gift-giving, even into your Christmas giving where gifts are given and received without a name. I had a women's study group for some time; we became quite interested in the process of gift-giving and receiving and the ego feelings that got caught into the action. We thought to take seriously the suggestion that the "left hand not know what the right hand is doing." We devised for ourselves an interesting exercise for the last day of our meeting. Each woman brought a small gift of no great monetary value but of some symbolic value. Without words or cards, the little gifts arrived on the day of our meeting, wrapped only in a brown bag with a white cotton string tied around the neck. This way each gift looked exactly the same on the outside. They were placed in the center of the room, like so many bag lunches. At the end of this final meeting, each woman picked up one of the bags and left the house silently. She didn't open her sack until she was at home alone with her little gift. If she didn't happen to choose back her own sack by chance, she had a little gift which she now had to as gracefully "receive" as the one she had given. She would never know who got her gift and whose gift she had received. It took away all ego involvement and left room for some powerful, new feelings. I see this as a lesson in gift-giving that might work in a classroom on St. Nicholas day and as a little prelude to the preparation of our gift-giving at Christmas.

The legends and stories (below) of St. Nicholas are delightful to tell and children can dramatize them and put them on as little plays for family or invited friends.

Nicholas ceremonies extended to the larger family, to include friends or neighbors, add to the festive spirit. It gives the children some company in what might seem too unique and individual.

Celebrating St. Nicholas Day as a Parish or Community

Secret Giving

In one parish where we lived briefly, we introduced the idea of secret giving to a group of teenagers in a parish youth club. It was already their tradition to collect groceries as Thanksgiving donations from the parishioners. They had always first sorted these into boxes and then made the deliveries during early December to addresses supplied by the local social services. It was awkward, their delivery to these needy families, standing about to give explanations and to accept thank-yous. This time, however, they would each take their deliveries and in groups of two go off and invent ways of making the deliveries anonymously. After what proved to be a series of great adventures, they collected again at the church hall. They were beside themselves with excitement and delight as each duo told the others of their adventures and their creative solutions to the mysterious deliveries. No one had been seen or found out and several had hidden themselves in bushes to experience the reactions of those who came to the door. Suddenly the "dark deeds of the night" had taken a new twist. Not getting caught and the deeds that involved sneaking about could also be benevolent actions. It seemed to fill a basic mischievous bent in the youngsters and it made me wonder if taking serious responsibility for "being a little Nicholas" could lower the incidents of dark and harmful actions.

An Evening with St. Nicholas

The Nicholas legends are great to tell children and give the material to create little plays and opportunity for celebration. In our community, we have taken to celebrating St. Nicholas day on December 6 or a day near it. It gives all of us, young and old, the opportunity to hear the stories of his deeds and to set the tone for our communal Advent. We gather in candlelight and before our parish Advent wreath. The program sometimes has the children put on a play depicting one of the legends; at other times it is the fathers of the community who become the storytellers. Since St. Nicholas day is a sort of father's day, we point up the theme of fathering. Fathers choose which miracle story they want to tell and come forward with their individual storytelling talents. Another follows up with a reading from Scripture which tells of a parallel miracle or lesson. In between, the community sings every Advent hymn and Advent round we know. For years, a retired priest, who was part of the community until his death, was delightful and dignified as a Nicholas in paper mitre and bedspread robe. His bishop's mitre and crook gave the children, who have never seen a bishop, an idea of what a bishop might look like in his official, fatherly capacity. A homily on fatherhood, on leadership versus authority, or on the nature of our Advent preparations is then directed to us all, no matter our age. All around the altar are baskets full of traditional Nicholas men—fragrant spice cookie bishops with pointed mitre hats and beards which the families have baked and contributed to the feast that follows. In solemn procession we all receive our Nicholas cookie and recess to the back room for apple juice and festive fellowship. Collecting the parish family or a group of friends to celebrate St. Nicholas day with you and your family extends the tradition making to a larger circle and lends support to those who want to enrich their Santa Claus.

Here is a recipe for a traditional Nicholas cookie that comes out of the Rhineland. The cookie is called "Speculatius" which means "image." In Europe, the "image" is the mirror-image of a Nicholas which had been pressed into a wooden mold and then turned out on a sheet to bake in the oven. As we don't have these molds, we roll out the dough and use a cardboard pattern (about 7″ tall) of a gingerbread bishop to cut around for the basic shape and everyone further decorates it as the imagination dictates.

Speculatius

Mix in order:

1	**cup shortening**
2	**cups white sugar**
4	**eggs whole**
3/4	**tsp. salt**
2	**tsp. baking powder**
4	**cups flour**
4	**tsp. cinnamon**
2	**tsp. allspice**
2	**tsp. nutmeg**
2	**tsp. ginger**
2	**tsp. cloves**

Turn out onto a floured board. Knead in about one cup additional flour or as much as you need until dough is no longer sticky and is easy to handle.

Put into a plastic bag and refrigerate until chilled and stiff. Then you are ready to roll out and cut the cookies. Cut off a manageable piece and keep the rest cool until you are ready for more.

For many little cut-out shapes, roll out the dough thinly. Thin cookies are tastiest.

For the larger, decorated St. Nicholas cookies, roll the dough to about ¼ inch thickness. Cut out cookie around paper pattern. Place on greased baking sheet.

Then get inspired. Use scrappy bits of dough to decorate your Nicholas. For a beard press a little dough through a sieve or a garlic press. Use little balls of dough for eyes or buttons.

The same dough lends itself to all sorts of shapes and symbols and is useful for making "St. Nicholas awards" to certain people on this special occasion.

Bake at 350 degrees until golden-brown. These keep forever in tins in the freezer or for two-three weeks on the shelf.

For presentation at the celebration, each family tied up their Nicholas cookies into individual plastic bags and tied the tops with a ribbon and brought them in festive baskets to place around the altar.

St. Nicholas Legends

The stories, like fairy tales, are great entertainment, whether they are Advent bedtime stories, or become stories for a larger group.

Of the Three Golden Balls

One story tells of the three golden balls or sacks of gold which St. Nicholas, during the night and with great secrecy, threw into the window of a poor householder. His three daughters lived without any hope of suitors and hence feared that they would be sold into slavery or prostitution for lack of a dowry. The three golden balls saved them from their poverty and shame. The pawn-broker's three balls have sometimes been explained as derivatives of the Medici coat of arms or as the byzants, or gold coins of the merchants of Lombardy. But it is plausible that perhaps these three golden balls may be the same ones that Nicholas is depicted with wherever this story comes up in image or iconography. Their charitable significance, however, is often in danger of crossing over into a sign of exploitation and profit.

One year the teenagers wrote and performed a drama in the form of a medieval miracle play using this story as a base and performed it for the rest of us at one of our celebrations. It was a thrilling affair with a dashing devil to tempt the girls' father as he was the only suitor that ever turned up. The fair damsels in question, named Faith, Hope and Charity, were rescued from their plight when Nicholas delivered three golden grapefruits to their window sill.

From this legend, Nicholas became known as "a protector of virgins" and patron of maidens in search of a husband. Because of Nicholas' secret gift we draw the parallel story from Matthew 6:1–4 where we are taught not to trumpet our good deeds, but to give our gifts so that "the left hand does not know what the right hand is doing."

Of the Miraculous Grain

Another story tells of a famine in Myra. The people were suffering from severe hunger. Merchant ships involved in grain exchanges between east and west passed through Myra, but Myra itself was without grain. As ships laden with grain stopped on route, Bishop Nicholas begged for some of this grain to feed his starving people. He promised the sailors that at the final weighing in on their arrival home not an ounce would be missing if they would only share some of their load. The story says that some of the grain he stored as seed. As he was a special friend to children, he used the rest and baked bread himself— sugar bread in his own image. I wonder if these were the first gingerbread men? Today, especially in Holland, Germany and Greece, there are beautiful cookie molds carved in wood, with the image of Nicholas on them. How can you avoid making a parallel connection with the story of the manna from heaven, the multiplication of loaves and fishes or with the Eucharist itself? We read the parallel lesson from John 6:28–34 which contains the passage, "It is my Father who gives you the bread from heaven, the true bread; for the bread of God is that which comes down from heaven and gives life to the world."

Of the Wicked Butcher

Another story out of this famine time tells of three wandering students, or three young boys, who are robbed, killed and pickled in a vat by a desperate and cruel innkeeper. Nicholas finds this out and restores these three to life. In many places in Europe you can see this miracle depicted on church walls or in carvings. The image shows three children rising from the vat and singing the praises of Nicholas as he blesses them. From that story, Nicholas is invoked as the patron of butchers and of vat makers, children and students.

This is the story which the children in our parish especially look forward to. Its gruesomeness is tempered when you hear it chanted as an old French folk song, sung in minor tones. But when the mode used is storytelling, the children will giggle and hug themselves and boo and cheer until the wicked butcher is finally brought to justice. Like a true fairy tale, what is inhuman and evil in the story is tolerable because it has a ritual, repetitious quality about it and the predictable and finally good ending.

We found another miracle play, a variation of this story, which the children in the community have also put on for the Nicholas celebration. It is called "The Sausage Maker's Interlude" and is in a book of plays by Henri Gheon. It is a wild story, no doubt from the beginning of the industrial revolution, which tells of a butcher who sells sausages at the fair. He is very proud of his marvelous new, food-processor-sausage-making-machine. He has a supply of pigs that, stuffed in whole at the front end of the machine, come out as sausage at the other end. Everyone at the fair is having a great old time of it. They love his sausages and soon buy up his supply. With no more pigs to convert, he has a little argument with his wife about supply and demand, and no matter how his wife protests that they'd made enough money for the day, the butcher becomes more and more greedy, convinced that an endless sausage production will bring him endless customers. The devil in an elegant disguise joins the arguing couple and convinces the butcher to find a quick substitute to convert into sausage. He argues that the wheels of machinery must never stop but must ever grind onward. Such, after all, is progress! Even the butcher's wife is at risk. However, when three juicy young boys happen by, the butcher quickly interests them in the inner workings of his machine. He urges them to check out the groaning and grinding cavernous mouth of the funnel and then stuffs them in, when, who should just happen by, in the "Nick of time," but the good bishop of this community, just back from the council of Nicea. He feels that he has lost control of his flock in his absence, and has a dread intuition of what is going on here at the fair. He asks the butcher to explain this machine. But the converted boys are already emerging as sausages out the other end. On a holy hunch, Nicholas grabs the wheels of progress and turns them in the opposite direction. The string of sausages are retracted and out of the feed tube emerge three bewildered little boys who think that they have just had a very bad dream.

The devil is sent away and the butcher brought to his knees with remorse and the resolve to make amends for the rest of his days.

You can imagine the delight the children had inventing a sausage machine that looked in some parts like a medieval hell with a toothy maw and in other places like a blinking, flashing, computer with a bicycle wheel. For sound effects, the children had made a tape recording of every household appliance imaginable switched on in succession. The sausages were stuffed stockings in endless strings and were produced in a fashion that greatly satisfied the pre-school contingent. It was a masterful production, and since we had to use the church as our stage, we quickly saw how the medieval miracle plays were banished from the sanctuaries and sent to the streets.

Of Deodatus

Even after the death of Nicholas, people continued to pray to him for special favors. It seems appropriate that this representative of the Father-Creator has special concern for women wanting to bear children. It seems that a couple, anxious to have a child, invokes St. Nicholas and they have a son whom they then called Deodatus (Given by God). The thankful father, having promised to offer a sacrifice of a golden cup at a shrine to St. Nicholas, waits to make his offering until Deodatus is old enough to accompany him on the sea voyage himself. Well, little Deodatus perhaps proves to be more of a handful than they had reckoned with. Whatever the case, when it is time to undertake the voyage, the father has changed his offering to a more ordinary cup of lesser value, and father and son strike out to sea. At sea, there is a tremendous storm and Deodatus is swept overboard. The distraught father arrives first at the shrine with his inferior gift and his dreadful remorse and then must return home to tell his wife of the tragedy. When he returns home and spills the whole sorry tale, his wife brings him in to the boy's bedroom where Deodatus is sound asleep. St. Nicholas had fished him out of the sea and returned him to his home.

There are many, many more stories and legends about the life of St. Nicholas and about more miracles after his death. Themes and variations of these legends spread throughout the eastern Church and were brought to the western Church, sometimes telling of these miracles. Sailors going east made it a point to visit his grave. Norman sailors brought the stories, as they heard them from the Sicilian sailors, back to Normandy and England. His name spread with the Russians trading in Constantinople in the ninth century, and before long he was made a patron saint of Russia, and many nobles and czars were named Nicholas after him. In Greece, he is also a patron. Bankers, pawnbrokers, girls hoping to marry, women hoping for children, sailors, butchers, boatmakers, vat-makers, thieves, prisoners and children all claim his special patronage.

CHAPTER SIX

The Christmas Season

Emmanuel, God-with-Us

The season for which we have waited with longing and diligence is finally upon us. It carries us with joyful exuberance through the twelve days of Christmas, to the feast of the Epiphany. What better news could we hope to hear but that Jesus and his saving grace is within reach and tangible to all who share in his humanity? The Gospel readings of the season unfold the story of his disclosure first to Mary, his mother, then to Joseph, Elizabeth, Zechariah, John the Baptist, and old Anna and Simeon in the temple (on the feast of the Presentation, February 2). From the poorest shepherds to the exotic kings from the east, from the uneducated to the teachers in the temple he reveals himself as the child who is also God. In an endless and always expanding circle of space and time, we are included in his continuous reaching out, his continuous revelation amongst us.

Emmanuel means "God is with us." Here, where myth and history intersect, he stands in our midst and we are none of us too poor, too broken, too sinful, too rejected by the world to know his glory. In the very depth of our humanity we discover the power of the Sacred and every human experience is transformed. For the Word is made flesh and dwells in our midst, dwells wherever we are willing to recognize him.

This is the feast where we celebrate the commonplace blessed and transformed by the flesh-taking of God. Straw and manger bed become a throne, ox and ass the gracious hosts, and humble, fumbling humanity the honored visionaries who come to look and, what is more, to see and understand. The old tensions between sacred and mundane ease, merge and grant us peace. It is our chauvinism, not God's, that contrasts the earthy to the heavenly and finds it ordinary, banal, and unimaginative. The divine contradiction is that we find him where we least expect it. The human condition: our peak experiences, and especially our sorrows, our successes and especially our failures, our "in loveness," but especially our struggling human relationships—this is the manger bed, these the places where we will know him, the Word in human vesture.

Because of the first Christmas we need wait no longer. *Hodie Christus natus est.* Today Christ is born to us. That word, *hodie,* means something special to me. It is eternal and it is now. The world's constant baiting of us with progress and a better future prevents us from living as best as we can in the now and for the creation of the future. Rather, we want to live ahead of ourselves in a future we don't even have in reality, disconnected from the heritage of our past traditions and robbed of our full presence in today. (Even heaven is consigned to the "better deal" ahead that we have no role in creating right now.) The other danger is that we leave the mysteries of the incarnation trapped in history, which relegates the incarnation to an event long past, its sacred action dead and irrelevant to the life we are living. The mythic reality tells us that what was true continues to be true, and we no longer have to wait for God's presence amongst us.

But we have to do our part. We all know that we do still wait; we wait for ourselves, our own belief. And that is up to us. His grace is there for us, if we will know it. How often does our sentimentality or the hardness of our hearts interfere with the mystery of his presence amongst us?

Sentimentality at Christmas makes the sheep of Bethlehem too white and wooly, the shaggy donkey quaint, the manger picturesque and sweet-smelling, the Virgin soft and melting. The real Bethlehem is more profound. But for all its pungent smell of hay and animals and the holiness of what is earthy, it also tells another side of the truth. The dark truth of Christmas is that Jesus is born in these conditions "because there was no room in the inn," because, the fact is, we gave and continue to give him no room. We open our doors but a crack and fail to recognize him in the request of a poor and nameless traveler and his wife, about to give birth. "The ox knows his owner, and the ass his master's crib; but Israel has not known me and my people have not understood." Our fears bolt the doors again. We don't have the time or the passion to expand our vision. We have nothing to share. We want no moochers. Whether our fear makes us withdraw or lash out, it is our inhumanity to one another, personally, communally, globally, that is the continuation of this darkness. "He was in the world and the world knew him not. He came unto his own, and his own received him not."

And yet we will sing our glory to God and joy to the world, nonetheless. The Lord has come despite us, despite our fears, our apathy, even our cruelty to one another. Beyond a thin and fleeting happiness is the flood of joy that comes when we feel and then survive the pain of our lost innocence and know that all this has been necessary to our redemption. Meaning and self fulfillment is affirmed and ratified in the mystery of salvation. *Hodie,* today and each day that we choose to live a whole reality, allows us to taste of the joy of heaven now.

Christmas Eve

It is pre-dawn. It is finally the vigil of Christmas. Families everywhere have worked toward this climax over the four weeks of Advent. Every action, preparation and restraint has led us to this moment. Outside, all of nature is quiet and dark.

I remember especially a Christmas when the children were small and we lived far north at the edge of Puget Sound. We had a small barn then and some animals which put us more in touch with nature than we had ever been. The barnyard chores were the only ones the children never complained about. Perhaps the gratitude of the animals was sufficient reward.

On that dark morning, I got up before any rooster called. From the upstairs window I looked out and I could see the barn; a yellow slice of light in the crack of the door told me someone was already out there. In the chicken house, too, a dim light shone. In the chilly darkness I groped and rustled amongst the Christmas parcels in the closet for my warm clothes and my thick shoes, and I readied myself and crept down to the kitchen. The light shone warmly, the coffee pot was already perking, and Jerry sat at the table with his trusty yellow pad, making the notes and drawing up the lists that are his talent for big days. Peter, I was informed, was also up and out already with the old horse, doing his chores, and Sara too, feeding the chickens and checking for any miracle eggs. The chicken coop had gotten too dark these days for the hens to lay. The dark trees at the edge of the pasture which never seemed to stop spreading had encroached on their already meager daylight. So beyond the possibility of fresh eggs, Sara, never one to procrastinate, felt that before the holy night descended, we must give the horse, the geese, the chickens, the wild birds, and the cat an extra ration of food in the Scandinavian tradition that honors the animals of the barnyard on Christmas eve. These two were too excited to stay in bed, so only Annika was still in, curled under her blankets, and the visiting uncles were also still asleep. Against the night-black kitchen window hung the cardboard Advent house. All the little shuttered windows were open, and they had already opened the little upper half-door which held the message: *Today you will know that the Lord is coming to save us and in the morning you will see his glory.* Inside were revealed an ox and ass. They munched hay and looked perfectly at peace. I hoped we could all stay as patient and tranquil today as these animals with the large, gentle eyes seemed to be. But when the two come in from the barn, the uncles appear, and Annika emerges to join us, the house is sure to be ignited and burst with accumulated excitement. So I poured some coffee and discussed the list quickly and in whispers before the day burst open in earnest. There were, of course, any number of last-minute things to fetch and preparations to complete. We always find that a careful schedule and family plan for the last preparations and the culminating cere-monies is essential and somewhat calming.

For all was not peace and tranquility. The uncles teased. The children were a bundle of energy and feelings ran at a high pitch. Ready tears and sudden laughter belonged to the tension of the moment. They jostled and poked at each other when they passed in the hall. They held meetings and whispered secrets and rustled paper and closed doors and posted signs: "Please keep out; the Christ Child needs this room for something." Sometimes they needed to consult one of us about a last-minute detail.

Whether it was years ago when they were small, or now when they return from university, whether we lived in the country or here in this town, certain things seem never to change on this day: the tenor of excitement, the whispers.

And still they insist and expect that certain details of our family tradition carry on. The mysterious curtains at Christmas are one of those issues. The living room for Christmas eve is always closed and curtained off, which confines us to a smaller living space, and the darkness beyond the curtains tells us that there is work going on there. The Christ Child needs that secret area all day, and every time you pass the mysterious sheeting that covers the archway, you get a funny thrill as it forbids your entry.

There, on our little farm, as the morning passed, the children had collected the gifts they had prepared. These they pushed under the curtain for the Christ Child to deal with further. My husband, with his yellow pad, parcelled out the tasks. Visiting uncles are never exempt from lending a hand here and a whispered encounter there. All morning we were sent our ways to wrap up details. My husband and I slipped away for an hour to select the Christmas tree.

Wherever we have lived, we have learned which tree lots still yield a good selection at this hour; usually we can get the tallest and fittest tree for a fraction of the original cost. Again we found a fine tree, its branches well spaced and safe for the candles we would clip on it. We brought it home and slipped it round to the side of the house where no one would see it too soon. I doused off the dust and freshened it with water spray and we plunged the fresh cut into a tub of clear water to drink deep until it would be contained in its stand.

At noon we gathered around the kitchen table for our fast-day lunch. We had a pitcher of cold water and some bread in the old fasting tradition. My husband read us some short passage or a little essay which he had found for the occasion. It reaffirmed our orientation and calmed down our bustle. The directives and plans for the rest of the afternoon were discussed.

The Posada

Before the afternoon had turned to dusk, it was time to hold the Posada. Latinos enact this Posada as a community play and bring the figures of Joseph and Mary from the parish Christmas crèche from home to home in the last weeks of Advent. Each family has the figures for a day. They put them in a special place and keep a candle burning nearby. They look after their guests and create an atmosphere of consideration and unselfishness in the family. At the end of the day, the family brings the statues to the next family and so on until they arrive at the church on Christmas eve.

In our case we did a variation. Peter played Joseph, Sara was the expectant Mary, and Annika had her choice of roles: an angel or the donkey. Sometimes she was both in rapid succession. They circled around the outside of the house and knocked at each door in turn, explaining their situation and asking for help. Father, mother and the uncles were the innkeepers inside who opened and listened and gave the poor trio a difficult time of it. Sometimes the response was abrupt and definitive, and Mary and Joseph held counsel with their donkey/angel about another approach at the next door. An uncle with a political orientation became an innkeeper with a barrage of social interrogations. "What's your lineage? You know, don't you have any famous uncles? What sort of job do you have? What sort of a car do you drive? What? You ride that scruffy donkey? You must not be very successful. You can't *afford* a family. Why did you get pregnant, lady? Or are you two even married?" Mary and Joseph and their donkey/angel worked hard to explain themselves. The interrogations and the bitter or frightened refusals made us all aware of the ways in which we refuse to recognize and shelter the Christ. A weary and frustrated Mary burst in, "Look, I don't really need your hotel. Don't you have any barns around here? I think I like animals better than people." And finally they were brought to their quiet corner. An uncle led the way, Joseph was given a lantern, and they ventured into a thick, wet mist and trailed up to the barn. An innkeeper waved a hand in the direction of the heavy barn door. "There is some fresh straw spread out in there. You can put yourselves up there and your donkey-friend too. But mind, when you open the door, not to let out the sheep." Oh, their wonder when they rolled back the door and there *were* sheep in there! Two pregnant ewes, huddled in the hay, started stumbling and baa-ing as Joseph, in disbelief, shone the lamp in their black faces. Mary clutched hold of the angel, and they hugged for joy. Indeed, this was a far better arrangement than any old inn.

When Darkness Falls

Robes and props were cast aside, and the children and the uncles were sent away for the remaining hours of the afternoon to make the round of friends and neighbors, to deliver Christmas breads and packages. They weren't to return for another two or two and a half hours. We agreed that when they returned they would go to their rooms to shower or nap or read in silence until they were summoned.

In the meanwhile, Jerry and I took on the work of the Christ Child inside the curtained Christmas room. It is always a delicious time, one of our favorite moments. We put on the music of Handel's "Messiah," poured ourselves a glass of wine and with dispatch we began the transformation of the room. *Comfort ye, comfort ye my people. Speak ye comfortably to Jerusalem, and cry unto her, that her warfare is accomplished, that her iniquity is pardoned.* The tired old Advent wreath was lifted down gingerly, refreshed with some new green and longer candles and placed out on the kitchen table. We brought in the tree, made sure it stood well in its corner and proceeded. All the boxes of ornaments, the Christmas crèche, tapes and scissors, lights and candles, pots of evergreen branches—everything we needed was already there. The tree, the hearth, the crèche, all would come together. *Every valley shall be exalted, and every mountain and hill made low; the crooked straight and the rough places plain.*

The action of the transformation worked its magic in us too; we whispered. "Do you remember which of the children made these clay ornaments?" "Yes, that's a good place to hang that one." "Shall I put this pitcher of greens to the left of the manger? What do you say?" We distributed the gifts which the children left behind the curtain for delivery and arranged them in individual piles around the room. Then we set the dining room table with a bright red linen cloth and the best dishes. I put out the baskets of breads, the cheeses and cold fish, and Scandinavian and German dishes, all prepared in advance so that there would be nothing heavy and no cooking to do. There was also a basket with some of each of the Christmas cookies. In the center of the table I placed the pile of straws that had been earned through our Advent efforts. On it I set a small flatbread we would share and the Child from the crèche. *Behold, a virgin shall conceive and bear a Son, and shall call his name Emmanuel, God with us.*

It was time; everything was ready. Jerry put the bell next to the crèche, the bell the Christ Child would ring when it was time for us to come into the room. The room was dark, the curtains put back into place. The house was quiet when the children and the uncles returned. In silence they went to their rooms.

On each pillow there was something special for them to read, using the

Advent and Christmas books that we had collected over the years. They showered, read or napped, and then dressed in their very best clothes. We parents did the same. When it was time, we went from room to room and gathered everyone to the kitchen table to sit in the light of our four Advent candles for the last time. In the gentle, hopeful light we waited for the Christ Child to ring the bell and invite us into the Christmas room. We sang our Advent songs and hymns one last time. I read a chapter from *The Christ Child in Flanders* by Felix Timmermans, a warm and human description of the story of the shepherds that corresponds with the Gospel we would hear later at Midnight Mass.

In the midst of our reading and singing, we finally heard it. The bell rang faint and clear from the far corner of the house. An uncle blew out the Advent candles and we began to sing the first of our Christmas carols. *Oh come, little children. Oh come, one and all.* We went through the darkened house and filed into the Christmas room. The curtain had been drawn back and all we could see was the Christmas tree with all its candles shining like one great light. It smelled of pine and cookies and warm beeswax. From the dim but growing light of the Advent wreath to this dramatic glowing of many lights we had a visual realization of the Light who is born to us this night. That is why we did not have this tree until tonight. It was right we waited. And we could look forward to twelve more days of candlelight and festivities and songs. We sang "Silent Night," "Joy to the World," "O Come, All Ye Faithful"; we sang one carol after another.

My husband sprinkled the tree and manger scene with holy water and began this blessing which we had prayed together, this time in its entirety, since the children were old enough to help with the readings and hold still that long.

A Blessing for a Christmas Tree and Christmas Crèche

Leader: Our help is in the name of the Lord.

All: Who has made heaven and earth.

All: Then shall all the trees of the forest sing for joy before the Lord, for he has come.

Psalm 96

Sing a new song to the Lord;
Sing to the Lord, all men on earth!
Sing to the Lord and bless his name.

Proclaim his triumph day by day,
declare his glory among the nations,
his marvelous deeds among all peoples.

Great is the Lord and worthy of all praise;
he is more to be feared than all gods.
For the gods of the nations are idols every one.

But the Lord made the heavens.
Majesty and splendor attend him,
might and beauty are in his sanctuary.

Ascribe to the Lord, you families of nations,
ascribe to the Lord glory and might,
ascribe to the Lord the glory due to his name.

Bring a gift and come into his courts.
Bow down to the Lord in the splendor of holiness,
and dance in his honor, all men on earth.

Declare among the nations, "The Lord is king.
He has fixed the earth firm, immovable;
he will judge the peoples justly."

Let the heavens rejoice and the earth exult,
let the sea roar and all the creatures in it,
let the fields exult and all that is in them.

Then let all the trees of the forest shout for joy
before the Lord when he comes to judge the earth.
He will judge the earth with righteousness and the peoples in good faith.

Glory be to the Father, and to the Son,
and to the Holy Spirit.
As it was in the beginning,
is now and ever shall be, world with end. Amen.

All: Then shall all the trees of the forest sing for joy before the Lord, for he has come.

A member of the family reads the following lesson from the prophet Ezekiel (17:22–24).

These are the words of the Lord God:

I, too, will take a slip from the lofty crown of the cedar and set it in the soil; I will pluck a tender shoot from the topmost branch and plant it. I will plant it high on a lofty mountain, the highest mountain in Israel. It will put out branches, bear its fruit, and become a noble cedar. Winged birds of every kind will roost under it, they will roost in the shelter of its sweeping boughs. All the trees of the countryside will know that it is I, the Lord, who bring low the tall tree and raise the low tree high, who dry up the green tree and make the dry tree put forth buds. I, the Lord, have spoken and will do it.

Leader: This is the word of the Lord.

All: Thanks be to God.

Let us pray. O God, who, in the midst of this holy night, did send your Word to dwell amongst us and be our true light, bless this tree, we ask you, which we have hung with signs of your creation and with lights. Let it remind all of us who behold it this season of the mystery of his flesh-taking and may we be ingrafted as living branches into the same Lord Jesus, who lives and reigns with you now and forever. Amen.

Bless also, O God, this Christmas manger, which we have prepared in honor of the birth of your only begotten Son. Through the mystery of his incarnation all creation and the works of our hands have become holy and the worthy birthplace of Emmanuel, who is God with us, now and forever. Amen.

We embraced and kissed and wished each other a blessed Christmas. Candles on a Christmas tree have to be watched constantly—or blown out. We blew them out and allowed our strings of tiny white bulbs to give us light. Someone pointed out a favorite ornament that dangled on the tree, one of an accumulation of years of creating and collecting. It induced a whole string of memories and blended one Christmas into the next. Shiny red apples hung there too, the apples of Adam and Eve. They drew a connection between the tree of knowledge and the tree of the cross: *The tree of humankind's defeat became his tree of victory; where life was lost, there life has been restored.*

The crèche was arranged on the mantel and showed the shepherds hearing the message from the angel. In the stable Mary and Joseph knelt waiting. At the end of our evening meal, we would bring the Child in the pile of straws from the table centerpiece and lay it before them.

But before our meal, we wanted to open a few gifts. Peter started a crackling fire in the fireplace, and in the light of the tree and before the fire we sat on the floor in a circle. All of us had to go and select a gift to bring to the person we were sitting next to. Around the room were little piles of gifts, one mound for each person. Papa mused over which parcel to bring to a squirming Annika. "Choose the blue one; bring her the one wrapped in blue tissue," someone urged, a dead giveaway as to the identity of the donor. We worked our way once around the circle.

The Gifts

We do not open all our gifts at once. We prolong and relish the surprises all the way through the twelve days of Christmas. We have worked too hard and waited too long and prepared too well to have everything over within an hour. The homemade gifts are especially wonderful. Our creative efforts are appropriate as we celebrate the gift of the Father-Creator in the person of his only Son. The material evidence of his action amongst us is pointed up in our gift-giving. What a pleasure to have planned, found or made something very special that is sure to surprise and please.

For this Christmas the children had drawn pictures for their Papa which I translated into stitchery and framed to hang in his office. They also made butter and cheese paddles from redwood lath, rasped and smoothed with sandpaper into fanciful shapes. Annika and I had made a fierce looking wooden puppet for Sara. It was the wicked witch, Baba Yaga. Finally, Sara could not contain herself a moment longer and insisted that I open an impossibly large box. I unpacked endless paper shavings and opened countless empty paper wads until I was almost at the bottom of the box. It was becoming clear that there would be nothing there to find! But Sara just sat there on the floor and giggled and hugged herself and rocked with glee. Finally she burst out, "You won't find anything in there, Mama. The present isn't in there. It's in my head! Ask me my times tables. Ask me any one. Richard taught them all to me and you didn't even know it, did you? Ask me the nines; no, ask me the twelves!" It was true. She knew them. With an uncle's help she had crossed over a great block which my own math anxieties had only made worse. This was indeed a triumph. "Oh, Sara, you're wonderful, and so are you, Richard!" and all three of us hugged.

Our gifts of self in the things we give each other are the places where the Word reveals himself, wrapped in the simple materia which is also our humanity. Only when we take our gift-giving and receiving on the wrong level and expect some literal salvation to emerge from the tissues and the ribbons is there disappointment. How many sins we commit against each other in expectations and the unconscious put-downs that surround gift-giving and receiving done in the wrong spirit. How many people mill around in the department stores "on the feast of Stephen," on the day after Christmas when their feasting has gone flat, and they return their gifts and start their longing search all over again because the Christ Child arrived in the wrong size and color. The art of gift giving and receiving needs a new look and new consciousness in the light of the incarnation. It takes some work and understanding to keep our balance here. Matter is equal in value to the Spirit, but it is not the same as the Spirit. When we are ready to believe that mystery in the incarnation, our gifts will bridge the gap between believing and knowing. Matter as matter will be the worthy carrier of the divine, but it will not be the divine.

Midnight Mass

We ate our festive dinner and ended with strong coffee to keep us awake, for it was time to join the greater family around the altar. Here, in community, we came together again, all with our varied backgrounds, unified by the common phenomenon of faith. *O come, all ye faithful, joyful and triumphant.*

After Midnight Mass, after we had sung and celebrated with all of our friends and greeted each other with the blessings of Christmas once again, we hurried pale and yawning children out in the dark chill air and home to bed.

Family Celebrations

Whether families celebrate before or after Midnight Mass depends on personal tradition and the special circumstances of the family. Some families make a ceremony of decorating their tree together before Midnight Mass. Some bless tree and manger scene at that time too, and then hang stockings at the hearth for Santa Claus to fill with little things in the night. Some parents prefer to decorate the tree while the children sleep. The German tradition that was my own experience and the years when the children were small seemed to dictate that we do some celebrating, as indicated above, before Midnight Mass. When children are very young, Midnight Mass is inappropriate or difficult for them and only becomes a possibility later. As the family grows, we can keep, as so many families do, the Advent spirit until Midnight Mass. For indeed the Christ-Mass is the center and apex of our worship together. *While all things were in quiet silence, and night was in the midst of her course, your almighty Word, O Lord, leapt down from heaven from your royal throne.*

Although we all celebrate the same central mystery of Christ's birth, we each approach the mystery with the traditions and the ceremonies which bespeak our own circumstances or backgrounds, and which arise out of the experiences that we have found—and continue to make—meaningful. Some aspects of our traditions do not change and do not need to change, and other aspects of our ritual-making depend on our creative adaptation to circumstances: small children, adolescent children, visitors, geography, climate. Different settings require new adaptations of the old. I have celebrated Christmas on different continents, in big cities, in the suburbs, in a small town, on a farm, and in the desert. I remember a Christmas night with thick frost flowers on the windows and a hot stone at the foot of my feather bed to keep my feet warm, but I remember a Christmas day that was 85 degrees in the shade. It was the city Christmas and the hot Christmas that I would have thought to be most difficult for me, but it wasn't so. In fact the challenge was to adapt old ritual to new circumstances and to hold fast the continuing and unchanging central mystery that makes mystery come alive.

It is with some ambivalence that I describe at all so personal or individual a Christmas celebration as our own, because it is always risky to give examples. What works for one family may not—indeed, probably cannot—work for another. If examples invite comparison and feelings of inadequacy, it means that the listener negates the validity of her or his own past efforts and experience or discounts the individuality of style. Examples, successful or not, are meant to show alternative systems at work, how some people handle the business of celebrating together as a family. Indeed, we share the stories of our traditions if for no other reason than to inspire one another to build and create a quality of life in our homes and families—a way of engaging and expressing in sign and gesture, that which lies in the hearts of each of us. In community, in the ceremonies of the Church, we come together again, each formed by our diverse origins, and are unified by the central mysteries we celebrate.

On the First Day of Christmas

On Christmas day, and during the festive days that follow, we like to extend our family, either through the inclusion of relatives, or by inviting friends, who, like us, find much of our extended family too far away. Christmas day brings friends to our festive table and swells the sound of our carol singing. Sometimes, during these holidays, violins, flutes, recorders, are cracked out and added to voices and piano. There is so much great music for this season and it's good fun to add new carols, ancient carols and carols from other countries to a growing repertoire. There have been years when a wise St. Nicholas has provided a new carol book on his feast, in time to practice something as a Christmas offering. It gives great pleasure to extend the parties and the gift-giving throughout all twelve days of Christmas. In the mornings after breakfast or just before dinner someone suggests we gather around the tree again and take turns opening another package. Sometimes a package will be marked: "Do Not Open until ... St. Stephen's day ... or St. John's day ... or Holy Innocents' day." Sometimes, even a few new packages suddenly appear overnight. (Some wished for or needed item can be purchased at a better price, now that Christmas is over for the commercial world.) In the evenings, we light the candles again and watch the tree and sing or listen to old stories that have become a part of the tradition in these days. Often there are new books to curl up with and read, or even to read from to the whole family gathered around; or there are special Christmas records to listen to.

The saints' days that immediately follow Christmas honor those saints who from the earliest centuries of the Christian Church were deemed to have had a special connection to the Lord.

On the Feast of Stephen, December 26, we remember the first martyr and we read his story from the Acts of the Apostles and sing the carol of the good king St. Wenceslaus, a royal saint, who on Stephen's day remembered to feed the poor. It is a day to send our Christmas offering to a special charity.

On St. John's Day, we honor the apostle "whom Jesus loved" and who was also the writer of the Gospel and of letters which give an outstanding summary of the teaching of Christ. He is the one who told us of Christ's words: "Little children, love one another." According to legend, John once drank poisoned wine and suffered no harm, so it became a custom to bring wine and cider to the church for a blessing. And later, at home, some of it was poured into every barrel in the wine cellar. We can extend this tradition into the family and bless wine at home on this day and propose the customary toast to family and friends: "I drink to you the love of St. John," or "Where there is love, there is God." It seems appropriate in a family, for all the times when we are poisonous to one another, to sweeten the lot with a reminder that we also love each other. Wine is the drink of adults, and it is the work of adults to know the spirit and quality of their love for spouse and children. We can only pass along to our children the qualities and feelings that live in our own hearts, for better or for worse. Out of our inner world we toast each other daily with poisons or with blessings. Let this cup of blessing give adults the courage to know their own hearts and pass on the saving quality of love to each family member. Even the children, then, are sweetened with a little sip of wine on this day and learn of wine's ceremonial value.

On the Feast of the Holy Innocents, December 28, we commemorate the flight of the holy family to Egypt and the children in Bethlehem martyred by the power-driven Herod who was threatened by a kingly child born in his land who would never be interested in worldly power himself. We read the story in Matthew (2:13–18) and mourn with Rachel her children and all innocent people who are put to death because of power and greed. *A voice is heard in Ramah sobbing and bitterly lamenting: it is Rachel weeping for her children because they are no more.*

It is also a mythic truth, a recurring theme in mythology, that the savior-hero must flee and that others die so that he may live and so do his work. (Otto Rank published a psychoanalytical interpretation of this same theme in the stories of about seventy folk and mythic heros, *The Myth of the Birth of the Hero.* The stories of Zeus, Romulus and Remus, Oedipus, Perseus, Krishna, Moses and Christ have strikingly similar themes. He points out several essential recurring constituents: that the infant-hero is born of noble or godly parents or even combined divine and earthly parents, that the birth is surrounded with difficulty and danger from a jealous father or cruel king, that the child must be sent away in order to survive, that the child is rescued either by animals or by simple folk, and that in the end the hero comes to his own people and takes his place, either overpowering the father or reconciling with the father and completing the father's work, as does Christ's New Testament fulfill the Old. There is an interesting discussion of this in Joseph Campbell's *The Mythic Image.*)

On a personal level we have all suffered the loss of "innocent good" for the sake of what is better. As an artist, I know it in a small way when I have to sacrifice a good idea, form, color or illustration for the sake of a better one. Writers and poets know it when a favorite word, or line, or chapter is deleted for the sake of a greater good. In our own lives we know the areas where fate has caused us loss, sometimes little losses, sometimes great loss. We contemplate our own divine heritage and the vocation we are called to in the work we do on this earth—"our Father's business"—to complete the work of salvation.

This is a day to celebrate the innocent among us. We make it children's day and have had parties for the children and their friends. When they were little, one time we all helped prepare everything tiny—little cookies made with canape cutters, tiny bundt cakes baked in small jello molds, tiny sandwiches, all served on little tea tables.

On New Year's Eve, December 31, we contemplate the year past and the beginning of the new. Mircea Eliade says that peoples of ancient cultures "tolerated history" with great difficulty and attempted periodically to abolish it. Defeats, humiliations, sins, diseases, loss of innocence—a vague and painful memory of when times were once ideal, when people walked with God, when God and people mingled—inspired peoples of all times to attempt to restore, even if only for a while, mythical and primordial time. Fire and water ceremonies were a part of the ancient rituals of libations, ablutions and purifications. The ancient Church, on the feast of the Epiphany (a few days into the new year), celebrated the blessing of water and baptism as the ritual death of the old followed by a rebirth. Every new year is a new beginning, a "pure" time of a new creation. The uproar and noise-making that still is a part of our modern New Year's celebration is an ancient expression of blasting away the devils and evil spirits, the faults and failings that represent "old time" and a purging and purification that allows a renewal and a regeneration of creation.

I'm not sure that we modern people are any more comfortable with time even if we are preoccupied with it. Our lives no longer follow the path of the sun or the pull of the moon. We can light up our nights and darken our days as we will. We can eat strawberries in the dead of winter if we want. Taming nature cannot eliminate the questions that all of us still have to ask ourselves from time to time, "Who am I and where am I going?" We are a restless and uncertain people. Our lives may not be centered anymore on plantings and harvests, but they will always center around buried failures and fresh undertakings. By celebrating and making conscious our endings, we take time out from our restless searching and allow ourselves hope for a new beginning. New Year's Eve can be one of the great washdays of the year. We can shed and give up the lost job, the old house, the missed opportunities, the tax forms, the political, economic, interpersonal regrets and anxieties, some good things, some bad things. Then we can announce a new day, a new year, a new creation which we resolve to participate in and to help form.

On New Year's Eve, we gather the short candle stubs from the Christmas tree and melt down the wax in an old coffee tin set in a hot water bath. Each family member pours a ladle of hot wax into a pot of ice and ice water. The casting that results is a fantastic shape and the inspiration for a "reading" of the individual's past year and future possibilities. At one time we chose the "seer" in the family to take the readings, but now all members share with the rest what they read into their wax casting.

Twelfth Night and the Feast of the Epiphany

Rise up in splendor, Jerusalem! Your light has come, the glory of the Lord shines upon you. See, darkness covers the earth, and thick clouds cover the peoples; But upon you the Lord shines, and over you appears his glory. Nations shall walk by your light, and kings by your shining radiance. (Isaiah 60)

The radiance of the light which has come to us at Christmas is so bright, the mystery so great, that we end our season of celebrations with a final, great day. Every major feast is heralded by a prelude which begins at sunset the evening before, just as the Jewish sabbath is introduced at sunset. Twelfth night is the fifth of January and is the vigil of Epiphany. Epiphany, which is historically a feast older than Christmas, is a major feast which has been often overlooked or even forgotten by the English-speaking world. Many countries save their high feasting and gift-giving for Epiphany. The eastern Churches call Epiphany "Little Christmas," though it is in no way little in its breadth and depth. And they have always celebrated it with wonderful festivity and special blessings and rites. Now that the western Church reiterates its importance by offering the readings of this feast on the Sunday between January 2 and January 8, it has the chance of being given its due.

Epiphania, the Greek word, means manifestation, revelation. On this feast we have revealed to us the other side of the mystery of the incarnation: this tiny helpless Child in the straw is also the God and Ruler of our universe. All our Advent prayers of longing for a king and ruler—"Wonderful, Counselor, God the Mighty, the Everlasting Father, the Prince of Peace"—have come true with a royal fullness on Epiphany. Beyond those simple people who happened to be in the area and who saw and recognized the wonder of this Child, beyond the provincial is the vision offered all the world and all peoples in the vision of those wise men who came from far-off lands to find him in a tiny town called Bethlehem. The Messiah was born to all of us, Jew and Gentile.

These wise men who studied the sky followed a great star they had seen in the heavens and asked about a newborn king whom this star announced. They set many people to asking and wondering, not the least of them the cruel Herod. King Herod, the Matthew narrative tells us, became greatly disturbed and with him all Jerusalem. He called together his own chiefs and scribes and asked of them where the Messiah was to be born. "In Bethlehem of Judea," they informed him. "As the prophet has written, 'And you, Bethlehem, land of Judah, are by no means least among the princes of Judah, since from you shall come a ruler who is to shepherd my people Israel.' " Then Herod called the astrologers aside and asked them about the appearance of the star and sent them to Bethlehem, saying; "Go and get detailed information about the child. When you have found him, report it to me so that I may go and offer him homage too." And the star led them to the place where the child was and they found him with Mary his mother and they bowed down and did him homage. Then they opened their coffers and presented him with gifts of gold, frankincense, and myrrh. At night, an angel told them in a dream not to return to Herod, but to go back to their own country by another route because Herod really wanted to do the child harm.

A Family Celebration

School usually reconvenes at about this time and it is difficult to slip back into "ordinary time" after our extraordinary celebrations, so it is a great comfort to have a final and culminating party. With the mysteries of Epiphany, the glad tidings are broken open to the whole world, and in the same sense we open wide our provincial family and invite guests and relatives from everywhere. Sometimes there are foreign students at a local school who enjoy being included and who expand our limited horizons on this day.

On Twelfth Night we perform an old ritual still used in many parts of Europe for blessing the family home. You might use holy water or incense and make a procession bringing the three kings from the crèche. *The kings shall walk in the brightness of thy rising. . . . They all shall come from Sheba, bringing gold and frankincense.* They have been traveling slowly over the living room landscape during these days and now, with a starbearer at the lead, we wend our way through the whole house singing "We three kings of Orient are." We sprinkle each room with holy water and finally bring the kings to the stable for the adoration of the Child, but the manger, with a few simple changes, has taken on the nature of a royal throne with brass candlesticks and a bit of velvet. The Child is set in a crown or wears a crown and is now a King for all to see.

Then we gather at the main door of the house for the blessing of the house entry or entries.

For this ceremony we use a piece of chalk which is either blessed at church in an Epiphany ceremony there, or one of the parents blesses a piece of chalk at home with these words or with words of their own choosing.

A Blessing for Chalk on Epiphany

Leader: Our help is in the name of the Lord.

All: Who made heaven and earth.

Leader: The Lord be with you.

All: And also with you.

Leader: Lord Jesus Christ, who by becoming our brother in the mysteries of Christmas and by taking flesh like our own made all human flesh and all earthly matter holy, make holy with your blessing this simple creature, chalk. With your blessing may it no longer be the ordinary marker we know so well as the tool that teachers use on chalkboards and children use to mark walls and sidewalks with their secret words or joyful games. Make it, for this Epiphany occasion, a special marker for those who use it in faith so that they can mark the doorways of their house with the names of your saints, Caspar, Melchior and Balthasar. And may these holy saints then be reminders throughout this new year that all who come and go in and out of these doorways will find your peace in the shelter of this home and seek your light as they journey forth to the wider world of their work and play. This we ask in your name.

All:　　Amen.

A Blessing of Homes

Leader:　　Peace be to this house.

All:　　And to all who live here.

Leader:　　Three wise men came to Bethlehem to honor the Lord, and opening their treasure offered precious gifts: gold to the great king, incense to the true God and myrrh for Christ's body which would suffer and die like our own.

Let us pray. O God, you used the light of a star to show all nations and peoples your only-begotten Son. Allow us also, who know you by faith, to recognize you in the epiphanies of our life experiences.

Be enlightened and shine forth, O Jerusalem, for your light has come and the glory of the Lord Jesus Christ born of Mary shines upon you.

All:　　All nations will walk in your light and kings in the brilliance of your splendor.

Leader: And the glory of the Lord is risen on you.

Bless, O Lord, this household and family and allow all of us who live here to find in it a shelter of peace and health. Inspire each of us in this family to develop our individual talents and to contribute wisdom and good works for the benefit of the whole. Make our house a haven for us all and a place of warmth and caring for all our friends who come to visit us. Enlighten us with the brilliance of your Epiphany star so that, as we leave house and family to go out into the world, we might clearly see our way to you and discover you in our work and play.

This we ask to your glory and in the power of your kingship—

All: For yours is the kingdom and the power and the glory now and forever, Amen.

House and family are blessed with holy water or with the sign of the cross. After the blessing the initials of the legendary names of the Magi, Caspar, Melchior and Balthasar are written with chalk on or over the main doors of the house and framed by the numbers of the New Year in this way:

19 C+ M+ B+ 86

(Because the names of the Wise Men are legendary, a recent suggestion has been made that CMB stand for *Christe, Mansionem Benedica* which means Christ, bless this house.)

The Bean Cake

Our blessings are followed with a special meal or most especially with a dessert which is a traditional "Kings' Cake." In this cake is planted or baked a dried lima bean, and the person who finds it becomes king for a day with a royal paper crown. We choose a favorite bundt-cake recipe, and in view of the size of our family we plant only one bean in the dough, but for a larger family or when there is a big group you might be able to afford three kings. The bean, when discovered by the new "king," can become the main jewel in the waiting paper crown. The crown is then fitted and the new king is crowned with much fanfare. The king in our house has the honor of ruling for the next twenty-four hours, chooses the menu and creates some new rules which are also effective for twenty-four hours. The king, however, must also prepare a small talk for the family on the lesson we can learn from the story of the three holy kings. Often the description of their dangerous journey and their encounter with the jealous Herod is enough to point out the perils of our own road in life and the need to keep our eyes ever on the star, the light of lights.

A friend who celebrates Epiphany in this manner with her family recounted this story:

> Several years ago my cousin found the bean and became king of our family Epiphany dinner. I'd hesitated to invite her for fear that would happen.
>
> The preceding year had been a grim one for her: she'd gone through a divorce, the first in our family. And I worried that it would be salt in the wound if she were made to talk about the God-awful journey the year had been for her.
>
> She entered into the frivolity of the evening with at least some of her familiar lightheartedness. Arrayed in a worn yellow bedspread for a royal robe and a construction paper crown with paper clip jewels, she accepted our ministrations: the choicest cuts of meat, the roundest butter balls, the wine glass that never was allowed to empty.
>
> Maybe it was all that wine, maybe it was the camaraderie, or maybe it was indeed the Lord working in mysterious ways, for when she finally rose to speak, what came out was worthy of a king.
>
> She talked, as she hadn't been able to before, about the divorce, about the lonely, painful days and nights of introspection. And, addressing the children around the table, she found the right words to share with them the great lesson that we all must learn, and learn again: that each of us is a person of value and that something awful can deepen our understanding, can enrich, not destroy us.

A Play of the Kings

A pageant or play of the kings' visit on the Feast of the Epiphany was a part of the liturgical service in church in the Middle Ages. Because of Herod's nasty role, the affair got to be a bit too boisterous for church, but the reenactment of these ancient stories, or at least the retelling of them, is appropriate where there are small children. Without many props, it is a good way for a story to come alive in the understanding of a child.

An Epiphany Parchesi Game

It is a great deal of fun to help the children design a kind of Parchesi game for this feast, only we would call it something like "Follow the Star" or "On Our Way to Bethlehem." On a cardboard make a path and little illustrations which lead to a Bethlehem scene. Along the way hazards and advancements await the players: "You have sighted the star, advance 10 paces." "Get cactus prickles out from between toes, stay put one turn." Sandstorms, an oasis, friendly shepherds, Herod's castle—the story of the magi's journey will whet the imagination. The winner is the first to arrive in Bethlehem. Use a pair of dice, some buttons as markers and the imagination and colors that make the kings' journey come alive.

Gifts from the Magi

It seems appropriate that the gift-bringing kings also leave a last box for the family to open on Epiphany. In our house, the kings seem to be so caught in the issue of the journey that they have left us items that enhance our family camping trips and vacations.

A Journey on Epiphany

Sometimes a feast and its rituals benefit from being taken out of their usual context. I tend to fear that without our usual place and props, it will be difficult or impossible to carry on a tradition. We have discovered that this isn't necessarily so. Our family and some of our friends went on a camping trip one Epiphany and we found that the mysteries of Epiphany followed us on our journey and filled it with meaning that we could never have fully planned for or counted on.

The family started out first and traveled over some very high mountains in Mexico and descended to the desert floor on the other side. It was cold, as cold as either these mountains or the desert can get. In the mountains a storm was brewing, and we were relieved to get over the pass and through the winding descent before the snows and sleet came. We set up camp at a designated place at the foot of the mountains: a high spot between huge boulders at the mouth of an alluvial plain that poured out of one of the many canyons that scored the mountain flanks. At our backs, the mountain tops seethed with storm clouds; before us the desert floor spread out in an endless flat plain under a cold, cloudless sky.

Bundled in warm jackets, the children scampered around the rocks and clambered over the boulders. They discovered hiding places, collected kindling for a fire, and poked around the camp finding this and that treasure that completed the furnishings of a safe corner in a huge landscape. We waited for our friends, four adopted uncles, to come over the pass and join us. They had left home several hours later than we had, and we worried that they were caught in the storm. Night fell early and quickly. We huddled by our fire, sipped soup, and watched the darkening sky over the desert fill with stars. The night sky enveloped us. We pointed out constellations and wished we knew more about the stars. Orion, a certain winner with amateurs, climbed high in the sky.

Still our friends did not arrive. We pretended we were shepherds and had heard there were kings approaching our country. Had they lost sight of the star? Had they lost their way in the moors or mountains? Would they find us here, this obscure X on the map where no one, absolutely no one else lived who could point out a direction? The light of the fire danced on the giant boulders. Smooth, heated stones wrapped in towels warmed our frozen feet as we kept vigil.

Finally we heard the drone of their car engine and listened to it for miles as it approached, coming the length of a sandy and dimly defined road. We welcomed them with hot soup and warming rocks. They were shivering with cold and weariness and told of a harrowing journey in freezing rain and icy roads. Sleeping bags warmed with the heated rocks were welcome reward, and we slept. The next morning it was Epiphany and the sun promised to be warm.

Epiphany, and there was no Christmas tree to mark the event. A palo verde tree standing in the middle of the camp, well formed and brave in its survival skills, offered its grey-green, leafless branches. It took no time to discover ornaments. A search through everyone's provisions produced a ball of string, a sack of tangerines complete with stem and leaf, and a bag of yellow and red apples. At the top we placed a star made of braided grasses. It was splendid. "Making do" actually produced a work of art.

After breakfast, we packed lunches into knapsacks, consulted maps and chose to explore a deep canyon that led into the side of the mountain. A stream came from it. Perhaps we could find the palm oasis that was its source. We scrambled over rocks and headed up. Hummingbirds found the desert season's first cactus flowers and buzzed at our bright clothing. Lizards scurried from their sunbathing and disappeared into cracks when someone came too close. Here and there a huge jackrabbit, frozen in place, the sun shining through its ears, broke its freeze and dashed behind the next bush. The sun grew hot and short legs grew weary.

The canyon cut its way into the mountain; the gorge grew narrower. Then beyond some boulders we saw the first palm trees, and set amongst them was a small shack. It was a crude, transparent structure, built of ocotillo branches, some of which had taken root and were in bloom again. Around it lay the dragged-in treasures of its resident's existence. Scrawny dogs with coyote ancestors rushed toward us and barked and bayed at their discovery. Beyond them, oblivious to their hubbub, their master, a small withered man, scratched at a tiny garden through which he diverted clear water channels from the stream—little rivers neatly lined with rocks. He continued to ignore us, and we concluded that he was deaf. It wasn't right to disturb this man, so at peace in his double isolation. We slipped back behind a boulder and decided not to alarm him. Instead, we rummaged in our packs and pulled out a large sack of oranges. One of the uncles wrote on it in Spanish: "A gift to you from the three holy kings." He crept around the boulders, worked his way between the frantic dogs and set it at the entry of the shack. Then we all flew off around the bend, cheering and laughing at this great Epiphany that had visited us in the desert where nothing ever happens.

An Epiphany Celebration for School or Community

When I taught school, we instigated an all-school celebration for Epiphany. It was much easier to send children off to their families when the Christmas recess began, still in the waiting spirit of Advent, if they knew that the first day back was going to produce a great party that wrapped up all the glory of the Christmas season and brought it to a close. Christmas pageants during Advent are avoided in this way and can become an Epiphany play on return to school. In this case, it became the tradition that the school children put on a wonderful pantomime of Menotti's "Amahl and the Night Visitors." We had three large "bean cakes," one for each section of the school, which produced us a small king, a middle-sized king and a big king. We sang our Christmas songs one last time. The kings made speeches to the assembly about the school rules and what changes they would make—if only their power lasted over twenty-four hours. Gift exchanges in the classroom, if that is the tradition, can be moved to this time and a variation of the game described below can become a part of the all-school festivity.

In our parish community we have a Twelfth Night Party. We choose an evening in the weekend nearest the feast of the Epiphany. Everyone comes, young and old, and we make it an ecumenical feast and invite the other church communities as well. The group is divided into small children, teenagers and adults, and we eat kings' cake and elect our three kings, one from each age group, by finding our royal beans. As the kings are discovered, they are labeled Caspar, Melchior or Balthazar, robed and decorated and cheered, most especially by the royal subjects of their own age group. The adult who finds a walnut in the cake becomes the wicked King Herod and everyone is duly appalled and emits all the jeers and boos he deserves. The smallest children are then dressed as shepherds and angels; there is a Mary and a Joseph and often the newest born is the Baby Jesus. Led by a glittering star held aloft on a pole, trailing bathrobes and glitter, the children and the robed and bejeweled kings lead the rest of the congregation into the church in a great and noisy procession. Loud music is played and all the rest of us royal subjects follow, beating on coffee tins, tooting or whining on kazoos, blowing horns and whistles, rattling and clanging car keys, bells and pot lids. In church, because we have no room large enough to accommodate our big assembly, we carry on with the rest of our celebration.

The angels and shepherds and the holy family have arranged themselves before the altar and are a living Bethlehem. A lector reads us the Matthew story of the visit and adoration of the wise men. It is followed by the telling of the story of La Befana (from Epiphania), an Italian legend of an old woman who is so caught up in her housecleaning and sweeping that she is unable to interrupt her work when the kings come to her door and want to know if she will join them to look for the Christ Child. Only when it is too late and she can no longer catch up to the kings does she realize that she may have missed her chance. In Italy she brings every child a small gift on Epiphany as she goes from door to door looking for the Christ Child.

Now comes the hard work of getting our kings "over field and fountain, moor and mountain" to bring their gifts to the Holy Child. The star has a spinning arrow which points to numbers and sets the fate of our three kings. From church pew to church pew, two steps forward, one step back, the kings wend their way toward Bethlehem. In each pew there stands a person ready to read the king his verdict. "You have lost sight of the star; go back one pew." "A sandstorm has covered your path. Wait one turn." "Kindly shepherds point the way. Go forward two steps." "You must water your camels; go back to the nearest oasis." "Bandits have stolen your gifts; go back and get more frankincense." (In a different setting these "steps" can be squares of paper on the path, each one giving a direction.) The subjects boo and cheer their kings along, but they set up a real hullabaloo when a king gets caught in Herod's castle and starts to listen to Herod's oily suggestions. Finally the kings arrive in Bethlehem.

We have a short homily then, perhaps about what it means "to go back to your country by another route" as the dream message to the kings instructed them, and then the priest blesses the chalk which each family will carry home to mark the lintels of their door with the Epiphany house blessing described above. We process out, singing one last refrain of "We Three Kings," and, blowing our kazoos and banging our tins, we bring to a close our joyous Christmas season.

CHAPTER SEVEN

Carnival and Lent

Thinking about Lent is not my favorite thing to do. In fact, I rather hate it. Every year, when the subject comes up, I see myself resist. I can think about Advent, about expectancy. It holds some concerns, but to be impregnated with new life is a rather hopeful subject. During Advent we rejoice as we open ourselves to the mysteries of the marriage of heaven to earth. But in Lent we come to know that the only way to our own healing and wholeness comes paradoxically through dismembering—an appallingly painful process which life offers us, ready or not, and which Lent gives us the form and meaning for. "They have pierced my hands and my feet, they have numbered all my bones." We engage dismemberment and atonement so that we may be transformed through the Easter mysteries and arrive at "at-one-ment."

It is a very old tradition of God's to pick his inept, reluctant, non-eloquent types to carry the message of change and atonement. Worse yet, peddling penance is unpopular. It doesn't sell. That makes anyone trying to carry this message home a candidate for painful ineptitude.

Moses had a speech defect. But try as he might, he wasn't exempt from becoming a great spokesman to his people. Elijah was dreadfully unpopular. He was run out by the people, and so he went off to the desert and slept a lot. Getting up to do his job was simply too unpleasant.

Jonah was an especially good escape artist, with every trick up his sleeve.

When God told him he was to go to speak to the citizens of Nineveh on the subject of repentance and reform, he first sold his donkey so that he had no means of transportation. Then he hopped a ship going the opposite direction. The sailors on board had a hunch that things weren't right with Jonah and figured that he was the carrier of bad luck, and so they pitched him overboard and got rid of him. That freed the sailors, but it didn't help Jonah.

A whale swallowed him up and kept him in the dark for three days and three nights, and Jonah felt as good as dead before he was sufficiently repentant and transformed to do his job. Then he was coughed up on the very shores of Nineveh and he had the task of convincing the king and the citizens of Nineveh to do penance and atone for their sins. They had to change their ordinary behaviors and put on sackcloth and ashes. They had to clean up their act—and they had only forty days in which to do it.

Jonah learns first that trying to avoid suffering by running away seems to serve up suffering anyhow. Far better he stand still and take what God has in mind for him, because he'll get his share either way and it seems to do less damage when you accept it. In the whale's belly, Jonah learns to accept suffering and death in his own life and recognizes that he can't avoid it. Then he learns that he has to help others effect change. In fact, he can only effect change and influence others after having experienced "the dark night of the soul" himself. That's the thing about prophets: they have to face the agonies of change in themselves before they understand it well enough to affect—to touch—those around them. That's true, too, in the relationships of spouses and lovers and parents and friends. It's true about the prophets and healers who stand before us as priests and leaders. We cannot hope for change in the other until we have changed ourselves. We cannot change without dying.

During Lent, the Church suggests that we engage our death and that we go about it as a community or as a family, "wearing sackcloth and ashes," making ritual gesture to engage the painful dismemberments we must undergo in order to become whole. Conscious engagement of suffering and death forces us to take stock of our gift of life and consider ways of reforming and living our lives more fully and passionately. We have the company of the rest of the family or community to take this pilgrimage with us, because we are, indeed, all in this together. The very least a communal Lent can offer us is the opportunity to understand mortification so that as suffering comes into our lives, we will recognize it for what it is and have some tools to find in this earthly pilgrimage its mysteries and deepest meaning. Our personal Lent may not always coincide with the communal season of Lent. But we will always have our Lenten seasons, one way or another, because we are always called to change.

Which of us, young or old, does not know we must change and fear it and in that fear come face to face with the mystery of death? We are all Jonahs. We are all the citizens of Nineveh.

The Church offers us the scriptural readings, the symbols, and the disciplinary forms necessary to surround ourselves as consciously and as creatively as we can with the business of transformation. Through our ritual acts of mortification, death to self, we are given the courage to enter into and experience sacramentally and creatively the "ordinary" experiences in our lives that call for little deaths, the mysteries that return meaning to our daily interactions. Every day, if we live passionately and risk, we are asked to give ourselves up, to break out of our old patterns of behavior, our interpersonal laziness, our habits to control, criticize or put-down, our selfishness, our fears and reticence—to give up our egos for the sake of something bigger—for something better in ourselves, for the sake of someone else. For the Church's offerings send us back to our human experience and lend us the courage to know ourselves more deeply and to fully engage ourselves in the human events, the relationships, the struggles that make up our days. Our suffering, in and with Jesus, is never separate from our daily struggles.

Misunderstandings, losses and failures, separations and loneliness, loving and longing, the fears we know deep down, all cast long shadows across our days because we cannot come to the light unless we are willing to enter into the darkness. Guilt—the sort that demands a change—suffering, death, are not hot items which the citizens of this world seek out. Rather, we have learned a hundred tricks to avoid those issues in our day and we have been told for years that we must avoid what will hurt. And still we know the sufferings which are self-inflicted and the neurosis which does not allow one to examine and understand the change that must be made. We think that we have sold our donkey, like Jonah, and have no means of transportation left to get us to what is unpleasant. We are so clever: we hop a freight going in the opposite direction. There are drugs to mask every pain and sounds to flood out every silence. But wisdom shows us that holding off painful feelings is a pain in its own right. We can hold off suffering only so long. Things go from bad to worse and we finally find ourselves in the belly of the whale.

Death, so contrary to our natural inclination, may seem like some grim mistake of nature, but the very name of this season, Lent, gives the name of the game away. Lent means spring, and we sing during the Easter Vigil service of the fall of Adam, which was the first taste of death, and call it a happy and necessary mistake which merited us Jesus as a Redeemer. We yield up, we fall apart, we die, so that we can bloom anew.

How do we approach such mysteries—death and Lenten springtime, form and transformation, dying and rising? How do we enter this Lenten period of fasting and dying properly?

How do we begin? By the opposite of dying!

Carnival

There is a dreamlike place that tradition offers that holds a wild pageantry of the dark, unknown elements of the soul: Carnival. Carnival precedes any efforts we might make at dying by allowing us to live in a compensatory period, briefly, in a kind of recklessness and daring make-believe way.

Throughout history, in every part of the world, civilized societies recognized the need to return for a brief moment to chaos. For every step into light and consciousness that a society is able to make, it must remember and honor what is dark and messy and disorganized and iconoclastic just the other side of our human consciousness.

Carnival sets free for a time our negative, irrational and unacceptable aspects and, by reminding ourselves of the dark and steamy side of our human nature, gives warning what global disasters the unconscious is able to create if left separate from our conscious selves. But through the ceremonies of its ritual action, it also allows us to recognize the vulnerable beauty of our human condition. Carnival is the ritual hint at what lies behind our desire for the Holy.

The unacceptable impulses in our human nature insist on being admitted into our awareness. Wherever an excess of one quality has been built to a towering height the impulse is to compensate and bring to bear its opposite, like a small child who has, with great effort and concentration, built a block tower; he admires it for a moment but is then compelled to knock the whole creation over with a glee surprisingly destructive for his earlier effort. Like messing up a sand castle so that we can start anew or like dumping out all the drawers before sorting and ordering them, Carnival offers compensation to the ordering of Lent.

Carnival itself went through the wildest pendulum swings in the course of history. Accounts tell of extraordinary excesses where the Church stepped in and condemned almost everything so that in turn the fun allowed was so tame as to give no release to the tumbling, untamed impulses in human nature.

The basic issue at stake, however, becomes clear. As the British psychiatrist Alan McGlashan points up, Carnival offers a reminder of the forgotten or rejected or suppressed Dionysian elements in our Apollonian life. Both attitudes—of creative tumult, and law and order—are valid if complementary aspects in life which need recognition and balance. Neither side must win over the other. Rather both sides enrich each other when brought into conscious balance. Constantly Carnival is connected with opposites. The figures and costumes and untamed shapes that walk the streets during Carnival in big cities show that: men dress up as women, women as men. Those who feel inferior tease and goad those who elevate themselves. Bigger than life political leaders are depicted for what the people see beneath their façades. The rich are made poor, authority is dethroned and fools rule. Anarchy and rebellion hide not only in the hearts of the "youth of today" but in all our hearts and can only be honored safely in ritual.

Carnival, for all its look of madness and its possible danger, is the wish to honor all that wells up from the forgotten level of our souls which, on every other day of the year we would rather not look at or recognize but which does need a period of consideration and celebration.

A Carnival for the Family

Just before Lent then, we can plan and celebrate a family or community Carnival. We enter into a day or a few days of relaxed rule, feasting and playing.

Friends told me of how they made their first Mardi Gras or Shrove Tuesday come alive this year for their family. Although a Carnival might well be celebrated with a number of families together and over the weekend prior to Ash Wednesday so as to have more time, they celebrated this Carnival amongst themselves on the day before Ash Wednesday.

While they waited for their dad to come home from work, the three children helped their mother make doughnuts. Mardi Gras means fat Tuesday, so it is traditional to make something fried in deep fat and wickedly rich. The oldest child rolled out the dough, the next one cut the doughnuts with the cutter, mother dropped them into the fat and fished them out. When they had given over their excess fat onto the paper towels, they were popped into a brown bag with sugar in the bottom, and the smallest one shook the bag until the doughnut was well covered in sugar.

During the process my friend told the children about the meaning of Carnival—that this was a big party before they began the season of Lent.

"I didn't go into great detail," she told me. "Somehow it was clear that the very process we were enacting was worth a lot of words. I told them that we could all dress up crazy and silly, that we were going to have a great dinner with our favorite foods. I told them we'd have loud music to dance to after dinner. Then, at the end of our wild time, we would take a few moments to think of what we wanted God to help us with during Lent."

My friend got down a box of theatrical make-up she had and told the children that they could make up their faces any way they wished. "Most notable was Joseph," she told me. "He has this marvelous way of understanding exactly what celebrations are all about and I wish you could have seen the way he immersed himself in the festivities and made up his face. He very cleverly painted himself to be a devil. He rummaged around in the garage and produced a costume for himself and swept into the kitchen with this flamboyant red beach towel for a cape, his shorts and tennies flashing out below.

"His evening chore is to set the table, which he did very nicely, but he added an extra touch to his own napkin and drew a 'devil's pitchfork' on it. Then he proceded to *be* this devil. He spent the rest of the evening teasing and scaring and shocking his little brother! He popped out at him from dark closets and corners at every turn. Joseph *was* a devil and Freddy was beside himself.

"For dinner we ate spare ribs. I thought: What do we all like that's juicy and messy? The ribs were perfect. We all got into it. Manners were dispensed with. Everything was messy by this time anyway. I think we must have had juice dripping off our elbows. For dessert we ate our doughnuts. After dinner my husband and I put on some silly hats and the whole family danced and tumbled to loud music in the living room.

"Then we got everyone settled down and we trooped out to the terrace and gathered round the charcoal broiler. We talked a little about the season of Lent and the need to change and what issues we needed God's help with. We had some little cards and pencils and we drew pictures or wrote out what those issues might be. Joseph wanted to know how to spell 'devil' and announced that what he needed most help with was not teasing Freddy—exactly what he'd been doing throughout the evening!

"We burned our little slips of paper in the broiler and watched them turn to ashes. Our daughter wanted to know if that was the same kind of ash as the priest used on Ash Wednesday. I told her I thought that the ashes were very much related. After all, every living and material thing on this earth will eventually turn to dust and ashes. We prayed an Our Father, said our good nights, and followed the plan of going to bed in complete silence. The silence was just as impressive as all the rowdy noise we had made earlier! We helped the kids wash and brush teeth and, except for Freddy who'd hoarsely whisper: 'What happen, Mommy?' the whole lot of us were absolutely quiet. On the morning of Ash Wednesday we really felt ready to begin our Lent."

A Carnival for Community

In our worshiping community we celebrate a Carnival where each person looks inside, perhaps even with the aid of dreams, and hauls up those aspects of personality which one might wish to bury. We unmask our carefully constructed egos and personas and remask with the best representation of our hidden self. "By masking, one unmasks a supernatural source." One year we all made masks together as a prelude to our party.

Dressing the Shadow

To discover or engage the most hidden shadow self within, we need only look amongst our neighbors, watch the TV screen, check out our public figures, and whoever arouses in us the most feelings—fear, disgust, disdain, avoidance, longing, admiration, adulation, positive or negative—that person is our shadow, our hidden and forgotten self.

In our community Carnival celebration, humor and vulnerability were mixed as each person arrived for the celebration in costume.

One conscientious woman who said she tended to take all things literally suddenly discovered a symbolic language as she looked for her hidden self. She felt that she was often too serious, reserved, prone to worry, so she appeared as a wonderful clown inviting humor to temper her list of concerns and considerations. Then she played out her clown role the rest of the evening.

Another woman, wise and full of creative ideas, who is also a natural leader, arrived as a general in uniform with a whistle and shouted all sorts of commands. She was leading our games and charades that evening, and she was afraid that every time she took on leadership, she might just emerge as this demanding general, so she wanted to engage that possibility with us.

One adolescent boy came in black tights and shirt with a stocking pulled over his face. At first I thought he might be a cat or a panther. But he explained that he was a dark shadow who would rather not be discovered, because he said in daily life he sometimes was "a sneak."

A man came dressed in a gray sweat outfit with a long gray sock hanging from his nose as a trunk and two pot holders for elephant ears. He explained that he was going to sniff out the feelings of others with greater care—and that he needed these large ears the better to listen to others.

A very gentle and thoughtful man came dressed as a two-gun rustler with a ten gallon hat and a swagger that was totally opposed to his usual reticence. His wife came as a queen. She said that her children decided that she made enough rules in her household to warrant looking the part for the evening.

A Theology of Dress

The idea of dressing up and clothing oneself in costumes has a kind of theology of its own.

Scripture makes special mention, in the story of Adam and Eve, that it was at the moment of lost innocence, after heaven and earth were split from each other, that the two of them sought to cover themselves, because they recognized that they were two sexes. While the first "clothing" may have been fig leaves or the skins of animals, donned as primitive man fell from innocence, we notice that the Church has used the idea of special dress at moments of regained innocence and fresh beginnings: the white garment of the newly baptized initiate and the white garment of the first communicant and the bride. All have the same overtone of purity and a new start: a transcending of one's fallen state.

Then, when it comes to the need for penance and atonement, we have a great reversal of form with the call to put on sackcloth and ashes—a custom that has a distant and pre-Christian past. We, too, on Ash Wednesday, put ashes on our outer face and look inward, contemplating our own inevitable bodily death. At Easter, however, we are asked by St. Paul to "put on the new man," to "put on Christ." And with that a folk custom has emerged on Easter with the Easter bonnet or the Easter outfit—a wholly other kind of dressing up which comes at the end of our six-week preparation.

Games and Skits

Our Carnival tradition of dressing up, which seems to ridicule our ego dressing and compensate for our religious dress, also inspired some dressing-up games. These involved relay races where everyone competed madly at opening trunks and luggage of the most outlandish get-ups, pulling these on every which way, racing back to their teams, stripping them off, each new team member adding another item of clothing until the trunks were empty.

One year, two of us did a skit for the assembled friends. The skit was something that I remembered my parents playing out for my sisters and me when I was about three. It had made a huge impression and so I had to try it out again many years later. I made a life-sized head out of stuffed hosiery with yarn for hair and affixed the whole to the top of an old, large umbrella. The open umbrella I draped in turn with bedspreads and shawls. I crawled underneath it and came waddling into the crowd on my knees under this very convincing fat lady. I rolled and wagged my way down the isle with great drama, weeping and crying because of my plight. I was visiting the "doctor" who awaited me and who with kind assurance helped me into his "office." I represented lady-excess who was looking for a quick fix for my problem. I wanted a pill or a magic elixir to end all my troubles. The silly dialogue between me and the "doctor" was designed to engage the excesses on any level that we all seek to curb and balance out in our lives from time to time. I was told that there was no hasty solution to my problem, but that I had to name each of my vices and be determined to change. As I gained the courage to do so in my discussion with the "doctor," underneath, where I was kneeling under the lady's skirts, I slipped the catch in the umbrella and ever so slowly I began to both close the umbrella and to rise up on my feet—until with quaking and shrieking I was finally a very thin and a towering tall lady, actually another exaggeration, looking down on my "doctor," eternally grateful for his good advice and help.

Farewell to Flesh

The very thin lady reminds us that Carnival means farewell to flesh, so we feast one last time on everybody's best desserts. In the old Church the traditional dishes that turned up during Carnival actually used up the ingredients that were being cleared out of temptation's way before the great fast.

After feasting and games and dancing, the last Alleluia is sung and sung in rounds and then buried in a deep chest. (The Alleluia we bury is lettered on a long piece of shelf paper and decorated with spring flowers by all the participants. We will not hear or use this expression of ultimate joy again until it is sung again, in full glory, during the Easter Vigil service.) We remove some aspect of our silliness and kneel down for community night prayers and face into tomorrow's Ash Wednesday. At the end of prayers, at a given sign we begin the great silence. We all move about collecting our belongings and cleaning up, but no one speaks a word. We are silently surprised at how well we can cooperate without the use of words. The families drive home in silence and wash off their paint in readiness for tomorrow's sign on the face.

Ashes

There are at least four major ritual fires in the history of seasonal celebrations, and our ashes, which are the burned palm branches of last year, may well have originally come from one of them. The only fire that is left in Church liturgy is the great fire of the Easter Vigil night. But folk custom cannot let go so easily of the elements in rites and offers any number of interesting celebration-fires for us to consider as we look for meaning in the ashes.

An Italian end-of-winter custom is to burn all the old junk one has accumulated over the year. The village square collects the whole community's discards. Rather than have a yard sale, or a garage sale, everyone simply had a good house cleaning and piled up the old chairs and mattresses. On top of the whole thing perched a straw witch—or, in Switzerland, a straw snow man. The witch, La Befana, is the old lady of Epiphany (Befana—Epiphania). Her end marked the end of the Epiphany season, the end of winter and the beginning of spring. From this came the tradition of spring house cleaning. We can reenact something like a spring house cleaning. Children can sort out the things of a childish past and put them away or give them to the poor. Adults could sort through their childish attitudes or haul out the inner witch, which may have to be put away or "burned" in a ritual at the family fireplace.

I think that spring house cleaning was an old way of introspecting. We clean house, inside and outside. We let in the fresh air, shake out the bedspreads, clean out the cupboards. We collect all the inner useless accumulations of our life style and contribute them to the dust and ashes that we take up again on Ash Wednesday.

Ash Wednesday

On Ash Wednesday we are signed with the outward sign of our humble beginnings and common end. The priest puts ashes on our foreheads, or perhaps we take them ourselves, take responsibility for this living flesh, notice everything around us—the possessions we hold valuable, the persons we love—and know that all will one day turn to dust.

Led by the Spirit

Lent lasts for forty days, and with that we enter that symbolic time of forty. After forty days and nights of rain and floods, Noah floated his ark out of bad times into a freshly washed new world. It took forty years of wandering around in circles in the desert until the chosen people knew where to find the promised land. Jonah led the citizens of Nineveh through forty days of penance and reform. Christ fasted forty days in the desert.

The American theologian John Shea points out that just before Christ's period of fasting he was baptized in the Jordan before a crowd. There was heard the voice of the Father saying, "This is my beloved Son; with him I am well pleased." With that revelation, it is clear he is the Son of God. Just as Christ's identity and life's purpose are made clear, he retires from the crowd and goes into the desert to be alone. He fasts for forty days and he is hungry. Then the devil tempts him: "If you are the Son of God, command these stones to turn into bread."

The clear identity and Christ's high calling that has just been proclaimed at the river Jordan is promptly questioned, and then he is tempted to play tricks with it—*if* you are God, and I question your identity, then play at being God, since you have such a great calling. Go ahead, use your special gifts and powers for your personal gain and satisfaction. Certainly it is our propensity as humans to fly off into playing at God. Who am I? And if I am called to an important vocation, then it is only right that I have some special privileges, recognition, acclaim, approval, all of which would help me to fulfill my vocation. Arrogance and pride blind us in that moment and we fail to see that vocation demands an emptying of ourselves. The primal sin of Adam was the same temptation. "No, you will not die! God knows in fact that on the day you eat it your eyes will be opened and you will be like gods, knowing good and evil." To be as gods, knowing good and evil is to function alone and independently, the relative trying to be absolute, man committing God.

The "fall" is always a fall upward: pride. The sin is putting the ego at the center of the personality instead of God. The result is isolation, loneliness, a separation from intimacy with the other, a hell that is not so much the punishment for sin but the result of sin. It is that dislocation, that ugliness and strife that indicate our being at odds with ourselves, because in our will to power we have lost love. And indeed, we no longer know who we are and what we are about. Beyond our ego-identity is the vocation and calling that is "to do the will of him who sent me." Adam's gift of free will is, at its best, the call to carry out willingly God's will by the power of love. We empty ourselves of our pride, for what is godlike in our humanity is not to be clung to, but invested. Personal power and influence, the gifts and the good things given can be used for God's will, but the inclination is to cling to these gifts as though they were a personal right and proceed to do a loveless and poor imitation of God.

What we cling to is the ego, protecting it, licking wounds, locking ourselves away in splendid isolation. Paul tells us about this clinging and tells us that we "must be the same as Christ Jesus: his state was divine, yet he did not cling to his equality with God but emptied himself to assume the condition of a slave, and became as men are; and being as all men are, he was humbler yet, even to accepting death, death on the cross." Only when we have accepted a great task and are open to the whole spectrum of our calling do we suddenly know also our weakness and human inadequacy, our selfishness, our conditional loves. Christ's temptations or questions, like our own, are not just tests, but revelations necessary to self-knowledge and to an understanding of our calling. They tell us who we really are and not just who we'd like to think we are.

Loss and Restoration

When I was a child, the words *Vacare Deo* hung in the kitchen over the sink each Lenten season and though I was told it meant to vacate—indeed to empty oneself—for God, it was not until very much later, when my developmental task to create an ego-identity was only just coming to a head, that I began to get a glimmer of the painful truth. As *children* it is our task—and it is right and necessary for our ability to love—to develop a love of self. That love of self must not die; what needs to die is self-love. Hardly have we established a sense of self, an ego, and the task of love asks us go a step further and give it up. We love, to a degree, but we fear that if we don't keep back the inner, secret place of the self, we will lose ourselves. If we let God have it all, there will be nothing left for us.

What needs to die is not the real self, but the false one, the self that thinks it is whole and complete when, in fact, it is all in pieces. Identity and calling are the first great uncertainties we question as we come to the deserts of our life. As we approach the age of forty—that mystical Lenten number—we learn the pain of the mid-life transition. Not so very long ago, people had the grace to die around age forty. That was about as long as one could physically hold out, having spent up all energy at survival. Today we live well past age forty. We live at least twice as long, and at mid-life we are asked to die on a different level. Identity, vocation, motives, judgments, relationships all come into question again. We reach a vantage point, like standing on a mountain top, where we are given the opportunity to look at our past and look into our future all at once. We look back and see the roads not taken, the strokes of luck, the missteps, the relationships failed or avoided or taken for granted. We see the path that we have slashed through life in some blind groping to reach the point where we now stand. We look at the downhill side and are challenged to complete our journey, this time with vision and design and conscious choice, correcting and evening out what has gone awry in the course to this point. We are asked to make some new choices about the quality of our daily lives and the world we participate in creating around us.

Our fall began earlier in life with the scrambling of the self to a place of autonomy, and is now followed by the dissolution of the personality into questions and confusion. And so it must be or we are not willing to be "led by the Spirit" into a place of self-revelation. The opposites come forth to meet us and demand a balance. The simplified good and evil that we knew earlier no longer holds. Playing at God can no longer be our defense against growing and changing. We must love God, which is easy as an abstraction, but what is more we must love our neighbors with the sort of self-love we have indulged ourselves in for years. Furthermore, we must love our enemies and pray for those who persecute us. We must take seriously the well-being of every person, even those who for years we excluded from our responsibility as being in the wrong camp, who vote for the other party, our spouse, when we know he or she "is simply wrong," the person at work who is constantly in competition with us.

Suddenly we meet a situation at our most vulnerable place and we know this is the test. We head into the downhill side of our life and are aware of our death. On the road, we die a hundred little deaths. We die when we reach out to others, and there is no hope of recognition or repayment. We give up our control of others and we give them the life they are meant to live. Our children are not our creations. We forgive and ask forgiveness. We realize and accept that our marriage may never be the fantasy dream we planned out for ourselves. It has its own reality and its own fate which we can only commit ourselves to with a renewed vigor. We give up the dreams of "in loveness," the love we "fell into," and take up the hard work of loving which has nothing to do with romantic ego-demands: it is the love we make. This love is stronger than death. This love is the only solution where we fail to be trusting, where we disappoint. Love overrides the imperfections of this world. There are no more simple excuses or judgments. This love is not the sort that fulfills and completes us. Rather, it is so centered on the other that our own ego is pulled apart.

We know what it is to be torn in two directions, no, in four directions. We know now why the cross is the Christian symbol of suffering necessary to wholeness. So this is why it has been held up before us all these years, so that we recognize it when its mystery becomes a reality in our own lives. Now we have to remain very still at the center of life's paradoxes, nailed in place between the opposites out of which we once built our lives.

Restoration must reverse the process of the fall. Only after we have gone to the depths of self-knowledge and known the hell we have fashioned for ourselves, only when we can love with an identification with the other, can we begin to rise again. Perhaps wearing ashes as we launch our Lent is not so much a statement that we are "nothing but" ashes, as it is the gesture that brings us "down to earth." The fall of Adam, his awareness of death, allows a new consciousness. Consciousness always seems to bring us back to earth.

Prayer, Fasting, Almsgiving

To help us engage the reality of our need to be transformed, the Church suggests a threefold form of discipline for our Lent.

Prayer, we have been told, is for the good of our souls, fasting for the good of our bodies, and almsgiving for the good of our neighbor.

This trilogy of disciplines, it seems to me, must be seen as a holistic journey into reality, and not so much as separate and private exercises that we undertake with heroic determination. I think we have a wrong picture if we think of our Lenten sacrifice as greater mastery over the materials of life, or a challenge to execute elegant schemes of asceticism of our own design. Daily life seems quite able to offer us a broad variety of trials which we don't seek after and which we feel free to grumble over nonetheless, while we proudly take on our heroic feats—until we fail.

Prayer, fasting and almsgiving, as parts of a whole schema, are disciplines that pull spirit and body together again and thrust us back into the context of our relationships and the human condition, where, indeed, our "spiritual exercises" are truly put to the test and validated. Prayer is not meant as a detachment from the world, but is an integration of the Gospel message with our human experience. Self-denial is completed beyond the self in its reinvestment of service and ministry to others. Almsgiving is not just a monetary paying-off of our guilty conscience but a challenge to love our neighbor with unselfish concern. It is taking a position of responsibility for how this human life unfolds beyond my ego-concerns.

Prayer

Prayer, which separates our spiritual life from unity with the personality, is perhaps an old approach which perpetuated the split that we have suffered as Christians for years where we continued to hold heaven and earth apart and continued to see the spiritual as a greater good over this earthly, human existence. For that reason a great deal of the guilt and inadequacy that many Christians feel with regard to their prayer life comes because they have only learned a kind of prayer that is quite outside the context of life as they know it. Rote words, petitions, concentration, the desire to "raise heart and mind to God" seem a splitting off of the spiritual from the flesh and blood of life's experiences. Perhaps prayer is less an exercise to get God, out there in never-never land, to hear us, as it is our hearing and responding to God as he reveals himself to us in the ferment of our interactions with others in this life. Then the human condition will make sense through the workings of the Spirit and needs to be quickened by the life of the Spirit. When we are in union with ourselves and with our neighbor, we are one with God.

All of this is not to say that praying is, hence, simple, or that there is no place for the rites of public worship, private prayer, spontaneous prayerful expression, petitions, praying for friends and enemies, or rote prayer. Thank God, I say, for the form and those words already written and well said which I can reach for regularly and with devotion. They say so well for me what my heart knows in faith: that this creation is also my creation, that my neighbor's concerns are also mine, that my enemies' failings are not separate from my own, that my agony and my joy is shared by my brothers and sisters.

Common Prayer

The eucharistic celebration is our community response and witness to the reality that religion isn't a private matter. We are the Church, "a people set apart," and at the same time marvelously similar in our imperfect efforts as we try to help each other along. We are a Church, alive because of our very relationships in a real world, brought together in the mystery of Jesus and the sharing of his body. Family prayer, during which we read the psalms or the Gospels especially during Lent, points up our interdependence and mutuality and gives us the words and the inspiration to live out what we hear. It is appropriate to create an evening ritual for the family, a form, that is led by one of the parents with grace and presence and intelligence.

Private Prayer

Private prayer allows us the time—that precious commodity that we say we cannot take—to think about ourselves and know ourselves better. Thinking deeply about oneself is difficult. There is a way of thinking, a concentration, which is not idle day-dreaming or wishful thinking but a relaxation of control over our thoughts as we allow them to unfold before us unhampered by our "shoulds" and "oughts." It is a revelation of self to follow a line of thinking as far as it will take us, and to pull ourselves back to the issue that comes to light every time we want to flee it, to veer off just to the left or right of it, to avoid some as yet unclear and uncomfortable issue and to engage it fully with all the attendent feeling. Some people do this by thinking, others by writing every day in a journal. Sometimes a dream gives us the starting point from which to launch a day's inner journey. This work is truly a private affair and fully a form of prayer, when we are not afraid to turn over the stones in our souls and see what lives under them. And it brings us back to our relationships clearer about who we are and aware of our individual uniqueness.

Fasting

Fasting is a form of self-denial which traditionally involves the limitation of foods we take in or an abstinence from meat. It is a discipline which some Christians have felt "freed" of lately. This may be because the Church's earlier emphasis on this discipline as law has been changed and the prevalent view that suffering and self-denial were absolute goods in themselves is becoming vaguely redirected. Hardly was the emphasis on fasting as law changed that fasting was all but discarded. The size of the void that this created may be measured to a degree by what rushed in to take its place. Weight watching, diet fads, guilt-ridden calorie counting and a multitude of eating disorders rushed in to fill the vacuum. It seems to me that the human condition struggles as much with a respect for what is flesh and blood as it does with relationship to the Spirit. What we do not undertake with consciousness overtakes us as a neurosis, an illness, or a bad habit. While mortification, a dying to self, is thought of today as sick or foolish, it is replaced by exactly the same disciplines we once disdained, and with a plethora of attendant self-help books.

There is, however, a difference between dieting and fasting. Dieting is done for the health and beauty of our bodies, and, as we are beginning to see, there is nothing inferior about bodies, nothing that does not warrant our utmost respect and reverence and care. But dieting also tends to feed the ego;

seldom is it done in honor of something beyond the limits of ego. Fasting on the other hand was viewed at one time as a value in itself; it was often punitive: a put-down of the body and a fight against "our base nature." A person was put at odds against himself or herself rather than set into harmony with the nature of things. It was a form that often lost touch with its real value: a denial of self for the benefit of a larger truth and something to reinvest to the advantage of another. Self-denial leads to a healthy love of self, which is not the same as self-love.

Balance and respect seem to be the real issues when we consider what benefits the body. Certainly, where there is excess, where indulgence and our affluence drive us to seek comfort and pleasure beyond all else, fasting is a discipline that means to bring us back into perspective. It might be helpful to see a discipline like fasting as something we do *for* our bodies rather than *against* our bodies. Imagine that we would use this Lenten discipline to see what our real attitude is toward our bodies—that "housing of the Spirit," our own incarnation. This may be the season to invest in a bicycle, get the family an exercise machine or undertake a health and diet program or a yoga or exercise program. It may be appropriate to go off for that physical exam that one keeps putting off, that visit to the dentist. Imagine we would consider the effects of our workaholism on our body, notice when and why and in which parts of our bodies we feel tension and stress. How does our state of health affect the rest of the family?

I rather think that many of us find it very hard to know our bodies and to attend to the needs of the body, because, deep down, we think them inferior and not worthy, whether we over-indulge or neglect them. It may be as great a penance for some to relax in a hot bath or to ask someone else to rub their tense shoulders as it is for another to turn down a dessert or a drink. For some, it would be a good Lenten project to get a new haircut or to spend some time and thought on the way they dress. The Easter outfit, which can be given some thought in the last days of Lent, is another celebration of our new attitude toward our bodily selves. How we treat and respect our bodies is some measure of what we think of all matter and the persons with whom we share our life and health.

Self-denial is work and is difficult and irksome, and only love can make it a joy. Fasting and other forms of self-denial seem easier to undertake if they are dedicated to something or someone beyond the ego—easier than if they are simply a contest against oneself rather than for the benefit of the true self. We can creatively balance out the omissions and commissions of sins against our bodies. We can transfer our new healthy respect for the body to a respect for everybody: for all who are hungry in this world and deserving of a share in our great wealth. Between the old slavish following of rules and the uneasy disregard of an official fast lies the choosing of a fast that one undertakes to honor one's body and to benefit one's neighbor.

Almsgiving

Almsgiving is a disciplinary form which so often stops at a hasty or half-hearted solution for the guilt we feel about the world's poor and hungry and an embarrassment at the good things in our own lives. Trapped in our own ego, our alms become grim, stoic, gestures. It is not *I* who fast twice a week, *I* who give a tenth of all I possess to the world; again, it is not the ego from whom I am ripping this heroic contribution, giving to those who can't get it together as *I* have—but beyond the ego. We have what we have knowing our dependence on the Father who gives us all and we return it, transformed into love.

What we give to others comes best out of a joy and thankfulness of what we have and a desire to share our good fortune. In that spirit we notice all our excesses and learn to balance them. We notice what challenges our love of comfort. What we share with our brothers and sisters in this world does not always have to be monetary; it does not have to be what we find hard or costly. We can translate our mortifications into actions that are useful and creative and beneficial to those who live with us. For even if we did have the monies to give the world and continued to make our family life miserable, it would be worth very little. We can look to where we are unloving, make the effort to overcome our natural distastes and take the extra step to do things for those who irk us. We might look at and make the effort to curb our own irksome mannerisms, our habitual naggings, our eccentricities which make us difficult to live and work with. We give "alms" to those around us when we attend to those qualities in ourselves that make family life richer rather than poorer, in our renewed efforts at patience, our empathy, our understanding, our tolerance, our creative contributions, our sense of humor and joy.

Outward Signs and Family Practices

The following suggestions are meant to jog your own family creativity, for children benefit especially from active participation and tangible expression of what may otherwise become too abstract or boring as a long Lent draws itself out.

To give an outward sign to our Lenten efforts, we can make and hang something over the hearth or, for that matter, the kitchen sink, which will encourage us and make us mindful of our resolutions.

A *Banner or Poster* with that threefold theme of prayer, fasting and almsgiving is a fine place to begin. Illustrate their symbols next to them and draw out a discussion at dinner time about how the family might interpret these disciplines during the next six weeks.

Lent Means Spring, another theme for this season, can be lettered on a length of shelf paper and illustrated with everyone's signs of springtime. Guests and visitors and the children's friends can be invited to add to the illustrations as they come to visit.

A *Mask* or a drawing of a face with two halves, one side cheerful and one gloomy, can illustrate Christ's suggestion to us that Lent not be a dismal affair but actually something that contains its own rewards, shining out of a happy face. *When you fast, do not look glum as the hypocrites do. . . . When you fast, comb your hair and wash your face. In that way no one can see that you are fasting but your Father who is hidden; and your Father who sees what is hidden will repay you.* (Ash Wednesday's Gospel)

Valentine's Day and Lent often converge. Then we make a banner or scroll, *I will take away their hearts of stone and give them hearts of flesh.* Or, *A clean heart create for me, O God, and a steadfast spirit renew within me.*

(Responsorial Psalm for the First Sunday of Lent) The scroll can be decorated with hearts, and with flowers that grow from the hearts.

A *Simple Cross* made of two twigs can be planted in a desert pot with cactus. Add the inscription: *If any man love me, let him take up his cross and follow me.* Or make an arrangement of bark and twigs and dry weeds, and as Lent progresses make some changes by adding spring greens, pussy willows and new life to the dry collection.

A *Flower Garden Chart* is a help for small children. With each day that passes, or with each good deed or experience, they can add a flower and watch Lent bloom.

An Alms Box or a tin to collect up your money for the poor can be set on the mantel or prepared as a table centerpiece. We decorate ours with the inscription: *The Fasts of the Rich Are the Feasts of the Poor.* Omitted desserts, cheaper cuts of meat, meals at home rather than eaten out, movies not seen, miles not driven, unessentials not bought all add pennies to the mite box.

Meals themselves often do not need to be more austere. Some families need to learn to honor the body by eating wisely or more slowly and interacting with dignity and caring. Family mealtime is essential to the life of the family and warrants time together and genuine, caring interaction. This is another form of nourishment, well beyond the food that is served. Time yourselves and see how long the family generally stays together at table. Why? Is the TV competing for attention? Do you tend, as parents, to use mealtime to make constant corrections on what you see in your children? If decent family mealtimes are a problem for you, begin by designating one day of the week where everyone will be at home and on time for dinner. Serve a meal that everyone enjoys. Then go about helping the interactions between family members to be warm and caring. Take time to enjoy the food—even if you have to serve one item at a time with space between each course. I remember thinking I had eaten the most brilliant potato of my life when, at a dinner in France, the potatoes were served alone, in their jackets, with a bit of sweet butter.

Meal Prayers need variety and our creative attention to avoid becoming boring. Meal prayers are necessary if for no other reason than that they give a clear beginning and end to our family interaction and help us focus on what we are about.

One family shared with me their process of making Lenten meal prayers which seems wonderfully satisfying. All family members wrote down their favorite quotations on a card and slipped them into a box. These came from psalms, from Scripture, from the reading they had done in school or at work, out of literature or from the daily news. They took turns reading these or drew them at random from the box at the start of each mealtime. The theme presented sometimes became the theme of their conversation. It wouldn't be wrong for an inspired family member to "stuff the box." These were some of the shorter quotations, mostly from the psalms, which they shared with me.

"Great Spirit, fill us with the light. Give us the strength to understand and the eyes to see. Teach us to walk the soft earth as relatives to all that live." (Sioux Indian prayer)

"God, grant me the serenity to accept the things I cannot change, the courage to change the things I can, and the wisdom to know the difference." (from Reinhold Niebuhr)

"I thank you, Lord, with all my heart,
because you have heard what I said.
The day I called for help, you heard me
and you increased my strength." (Psalm 138)

"Trust in the Lord and do good.
Live in the Lord and be safe.
Seek your happiness in the Lord
And he will give you your heart's desire." (Psalm 37)

"The Lord will give strength to his people;
The Lord will bless his people with peace." (Psalm 29)

"It was you who created my inmost self
And put me together in my mother's womb.
For all these mysteries I thank you,
For the wonder of myself, for the wonder of your works." (Psalm 139)

"I am listening. What is the Lord saying?" (from the Psalms)

"Walk cheerfully over the earth, answering that of God in everyone."

Create a *Prayer Corner* in the house for the family to gather around for evening prayers or for the individual to use as a place to read or as a place of peace and recollection. Prayer can take many forms.

Discover the psalms and perhaps memorize a favorite one.

Teach the children a new song or hymn.

Get yourselves some books for Lenten reading. These can be helpful in getting to know yourselves better; it might be a scriptural commentary. They can be something to read individually or as a family.

Read some Bible stories to your younger children.

Create a little booklet of the Stations of the Cross for the family. Relate the sufferings of Jesus to the sufferings we all know as members of his body. Perhaps the children can illustrate it over the days of Lent or find pictures from the newspapers of the suffering of Christ as his people share in it. Be certain to end the story with the mysteries of Easter, the goal of our Lenten considerations.

Invite the children to take turns contributing a reading or a song to family prayers.

Discover and discuss with the family the ways that we pray without using formulas or words.

Give of your time to someone who is sick or old or alone or sad.

Take a child for a walk.

Help a friend with a project.

Forgive someone against whom you have been holding a grudge.

Dare to ask someone's forgiveness.

Make mutual forgiveness a part of your family night prayers, being careful not to force children to forgive each other until they have had an opportunity to work out their differences.

Prepare yourselves for a Lenten penitential service. Children sometimes need extra help and encouragement here.

We can *Fast and Abstain* from more things than food. Discuss with the family the ways we can fast, as from a prime weakness, impatience, unnecessary talk, specific vocabulary, disorder, fussiness, irksome habits, social whirls, over-work.

What we "give up" can free us for a new, positive action: patience, listening to your spouse, or hearing what your children are trying to tell you in their inexperienced way.

God doesn't need us to pray, fast or give alms. We need it, to put our bits and pieces back into a single perspective and give us a renewed sense of our vocation and responsibility. Virtue is negative only in the sense that what a sculptor takes from a block of wood is negative; it is necessary for making a thing of positive beauty.

154

CHAPTER EIGHT

Holy Week and Easter

The sacred mysteries of the coming week, the very apex of the Church year, are brought into our homes. Actually, we move gently back and forth from the sacred rites at church to folk and family traditions and then back again to the richness of the Church. The tangible signs of our inner transformations are found in *materia:* in the ordinary and daily things around us, renewed and charged with meaning. During Holy Week our celebrations are especially rich in those material symbols. All of us—our every sense and fiber—is involved. Bread and meats, kiss and cross, oil and water, water and fire, passion and praise, candles and eggs and dress and chants, primal laments and bursts of thanks, fasting and feasting, silence and sounds, all these mix and point up the poetry of paradoxes which the sacred mysteries celebrate.

The simple objects are within our reach at home. The simple gestures done at church and then at home with reverence and consciousness can bring the mysteries straight to hearth and table and chair and bed.

Palm or Passion Sunday

A paradox greets us directly on Palm Sunday in the voices of the children of Jerusalem. They cry Hosanna one day and crucify him shortly thereafter. Too often we are like one of these children of Jerusalem. How easily we join a crowd to shout the fashionable slogans of the day and forget our individual responsibility a day later.

Christ had a special love and empathy for the people of Jerusalem. He knew their weakness. He saw the future of his city and the tragedy of his people. We would rather slick over our fate, and in our happiness refuse to see or to engage the serious tragedies that lie just the other side of a truth. We are told how Jesus wept for the people of this city and said he wished he could gather them under his wings like a mother hen gathers her chicks. Perhaps from that story comes a folk custom out of the Netherlands which we have adopted as our own.

For the Procession

The day before Palm Sunday, we make little bread-dough chicks from a favorite bread recipe. We form a little bun, pinch out a beak and poke in a currant or raisin for an eye. These little bun-chicks we then hoist on a stick or dowel and decorate with streaming ribbons and palms or branches indigenous to our gardens. We also make a larger mother hen with tiny bun-chicks under her wings, with current eyes for Sunday afternoon "tea."

In our community many of the families make these processional Palm Sunday chicks and take them to Mass that morning. I know another community where it has evolved into tradition that the children bring their bread chicks, the teenagers make banners and fluttering flags of Lenten purples, reds, pinks and fuchsias, and the adults bring leafy bows decorating a little pole, or branches of olive and palms.

This way the participants take responsibility for waving their own greens, whatever grows near at hand, just as the people of Jerusalem were certain to have done it. In some climates, however, it may not be possible to find greens in the garden yet, the branches still being bare sticks. Then the churches provide the palms and olive branches, and they can be tucked into the chicks or added to the ribboned poles. The banners, sometimes with symbols from the days of Holy Week, become the decorations in the church until the stripping of the altar after the Holy Thursday ceremonies.

With our branches and banners, we collect outside the church. There is a stir of excitement and fervor and the ceremonies begin. A whole week of the holiest celebrations in the year are about to begin. The palms and branches are blessed, and we make a joyful procession following the cross-bearer around the grounds and into the church.

In this case, the cross at the head of the procession is a wrought-iron one with the implements of the passion, decorated with palms and greens and streamers. It is bitter-sweet. It demonstrates the paradoxical tone of this feast. But for now we hold our palms and flags and decorations high, and with the passion of the children of Israel we sing out loud: "All glory laud and honor, to you Redeemer, King." "Hosanna, hosanna to the Son of David."

Remember, we are a marvelously human lot, and our feeling and passion was never meant to be checked at the church doors. If sports can bring thousands to shouting and waving flags and banners, what is it about our church-related rituals that make so many reticent and self-conscious? Liturgy is exactly concerned with what is most human about us. Theology and history do not tell us everything we need to know about religion. Beyond the rational, ritual and symbol allow us to risk powerful feeling expressions within the safety of a discipline or form. The powerful liturgy of these holy days must tap also our deepest and most human place, the feelings of the human heart.

Indeed, in many cases it takes some educating and coaxing of priests and leaders of public worship not to stand at such a distance from the passions of what make us human. That education and leadership, in turn, directed to the community assembled, can release a richness and a power, which can only be called a religious experience. Yes, we risk putting ourselves out. But to hold back or deny out of fear is to deny people a form to contain their human expression; it is to rob people of a religious life.

Once inside the church, we lay our palms aside and begin the prayers of the Mass and the reading of the passion of our Lord. The tone changes. We all participate in the readings and take the part of the crowd. We are aware of our human weakness that shouts praise and joy one moment and judgment and condemnation the next. After the eucharistic celebration is finished, the chicks become shared food.

The palms are brought home and the procession extended. We go from room to room, from garage to car to shed, and leave a blessed palm over the door or behind a cross or sacred image, over the hearth, over the bed. If you cannot bring your Palm Sunday chicks to church, then they are a part of the household procession and the buns become breakfast or afternoon tea.

Monday and Tuesday in Holy Week

These days are traditionally the days for "spring housecleaning." We put up freshly washed curtains, polish some silver in anticipation of the Easter festivities, wax the woodwork or turn the mattress: anything that shares in and points up our spiritual new life. We own little silver or copper, but in our house it has become something of a treat to haul out the silver teaspoons and the copper kettle that need a shine and put them into use again for the feast of Easter. Polishing away the tarnish is graphic and rewarding. These, too, are good days to bake and cook ahead for Easter.

It's a good idea to interview your relatives and see if you can collect some interesting recipes out of their past traditions that would be fun to experiment with and to incorporate into your own family traditions. Husband and wife can both dig into their ethnic heritage, either by remembering back to what was special in their own growing up, or by checking with mothers and grandmothers who would be willing to reminisce and share festive dishes. There is something very special about the yearly repetition of a smell or flavor. In a world that changes faster and faster, where little remains the same from year to year, it is satisfying and comforting to be able to rely on some things. The return of smells and flavors seems to validate the season at hand and remind us of past feasts.

There are some fine breads and cheese desserts out of eastern Europe which are traditional and not too difficult to make but would benefit from being made in advance of Easter and put aside.

We bake a cake rich with almond paste and cream that needs to rest in a cool place and "ripen" for several days before it is ready to be eaten on Easter. This torte has been part of a family tradition and comes from Germany.

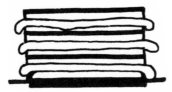

Paradise Torte

Grease well and flour four, round, 9″ cake pans. Heat oven to 350 degrees.

Cake layers:

1	**cup butter or margarine**
2	**cups sugar**
1	**whole egg**
4	**egg yolks (save the whites)**
1/2	**teaspoon salt**
1	**lemon rind, grated**
3	**cups flour**

Cream butter and sugar. Add eggs, salt and lemon rind. Work in flour. Dough will be stiff. Divide dough into 4 equal portions and pat into prepared pans making thin layers. Leave no edge or rim.

Topping:

4	**egg whites**
3/4	**cup sugar**
1/2	**pound almond paste, grated**
1	**teaspoon cinnamon**

Beat whites until soft peaks form. Fold into the egg whites, the grated almond paste, sugar and cinnamon. Divide mixture into four equal portions and spread on top of each layer. Bake the layers for 25 to 35 minutes or until the cakes are a rich golden brown. Cool slightly but remove from pans while still warm. (The layers come out of the pan as *crisp,* round disks.)

To assemble:

1 pint cream beaten until thick

Choose the layer with the most perfect bottom and invert it so that it is ready to become the top of the cake.

Divide the whipped cream into three equal portions and spread between each layer of the cake. Place the inverted layer on the top. Allow the whipped cream to ooze out between the layers somewhat by pressing on the top of the cake a little. Spread the excess cream around the sides of the cake and sprinkle almond slivers on the cream.

Keep the torte in a cool place (not refrigerator) to ripen. This will take several days, so allow time. Check the torte daily. Depending on the temperature and the weather, the torte will ripen in one to four days. When it is soft and settled, put it in the refrigerator.

Just before serving, decorate the top with a sprinkling of powdered sugar. A paper stencil or lace doily design can be created with the powdered sugar.

To serve, cut in a grid of small rectangular slices, because the torte is rich.

Easter Bread

We bake a sweet, eggy bread filled with chopped, dried apricots, dates and almonds and baked in a tall, well greased coffee tin. The tin should be half filled with the yeast dough before baking. In the oven it becomes a "resurrection bread," tall and impressive, as it rises over the top of the tin. We ice it with powdered sugar icing, flavored with almond extract or lemon juice. It is our variation of what the Russians make and call Kulich. Store it in the freezer for Easter breakfast.

Wednesday in Holy Week

This is a good day to plan on having a paschal meal. It can be on a very small and simple scale for your family if your children are still little and haven't a great attention span, or you can work out something larger with more details for a group of friends, each contributing one of the ritual dishes.

The celebration of the Christian paschal meal makes reference to the Jewish Passover celebration with some of the traditional foods and readings and the addition of readings from the New Testament. With the utmost sensitivity to what is a sacred and high feast for the Jews, it is important not to attempt an imitation of the Jewish festival, to tinker with what is not our own tradition. Rather, what we create should make a simple connection for us between the ancient Passover seder supper and our celebration of the Eucharist. It asks a new awareness of the Christian implication of our "deliverance from slavery." In the course of this sacred and sacrificial meal, the lamb of the chosen people becomes a powerful type of Christ, our paschal victim. The bread which the fathers had eaten in the desert now points toward the "true Bread of eternal life."

There are some very helpful booklets on how to serve such a paschal meal. They contain directions on how to prepare some traditional foods, what the tradition and meaning is behind the foods and gestures, and a selection of readings from the traditional Jewish celebration, exodus, and the New Testament.

You can make your paschal meal as extensive as you wish, or you can simply include some matzo (unleavened bread), wine or grape juice for the children and the story of exodus and the Last Supper.

If this ritual feels right for you and you feel comfortable with the symbolic implications, you can add to your ceremonies year by year as your children grow. If you have been telling them the stories of the exodus all along, the unleavened bread, the bitter herbs and salt water, the lamb and the "haroses" will come to mean something to them.

Another way to introduce small children to the story of the Jewish deliverance is to take one aspect of the exodus at a time during the weeks of Lent. Tell the story and prepare one of the seder foods that goes with the story, until, at the end of Lent, this ritual meal leads us into the Holy Thursday liturgies and the commemoration of Christ's last seder meal with his friends.

For the matzo/unleavened bread, tell the story of the manna in the desert and the bread made in a hurry during the exodus. (Ex 1:13–14) Relate it to the eucharistic bread.

For the wine or grape juice and roast lamb, tell the story of the slain lamb whose saving blood was sprinkled on the doorposts of the Israelites as they fled the Egyptians. (Ex 12)

For the moror (bitter herbs, parsley, radish, or green onion), tell of the bitter life of those who have no freedom and are enslaved.

Dip the herbs into a little dish of salt water and show them how the water tastes like tears.

For the haroses (a mixture of chopped apple, nuts, cinnamon and wine), show how it has become the color of bricks and tell how the children of Israel made bricks while in captivity.

Most important is to know that this is a feast of thanksgiving remembering that, once enslaved, we are freed, like the Israelites, by the blood of the lamb.

Taste and smell and touch and sound are powerful teachers that need few additional words, so one need not agonize over every analogy. We are thankful for Christ, our paschal victim, "who, dying, destroyed our death, and, rising, restored our life." This is a thanksgiving celebration for the eucharistic feast.

Holy Thursday

The best way to understand the liturgies for Holy Thursday is to look over the texts and rituals at home first. Children will want to know why the priest washes the feet of some of the community members. They will want to understand that Christ washed the feet of his apostles as a sign of his love for them and that he asks us to love one another in just that basic a way. The new commandment of the New Testament is: *Love one another as I have loved you.*

We all benefit from some thinking about how we can love each other as Christ asks us to. Such love is not always our first inclination. It is not always easy or romantic or rewarded. But it is always terribly basic and down to earth—like Christ washing the feet of his friends . . . and of his betrayer. Such love makes us all equals.

This day celebrates the Mass as a great feast of love. *The love of Christ has gathered us together. Let us rejoice in him and be glad, and let us love each other from the depths of our heart. Therefore when we are together, let us take heed not to be divided in mind. Let there be an end to bitterness and quarrels, an end to strife, and in our midst be Christ our God.*

From this feast we are instructed about the sacramental quality of the meal—every meal. Mealtime reminds us of The Meal. It begs us to work at a new atmosphere and understanding for our gatherings at the family table, for *where there is charity and loving friendship, there God ever dwells.*

Bells and Rattles

At church, in thanksgiving for the meal of the Eucharist, we hear the Gloria for the first time since Lent began. The Gloria, in fact, is sung, and if the church has big bells, they are rung throughout. If there are no big bells, little ones are rung.

Then, abruptly, the tone changes. The Gloria is finished. The bells are silenced. The organ, the guitars, the pianos are quieted. In the old days, the announcing bells were replaced with rasping wooden clackers. Not only did one miss the music of the bell, but one was doubly reminded of the loss by the shocking wooden noise. I could see church musicians create a variation on the wooden sound by turning their guitars around, strings inward, and thumping a hollow tympany on the back of the instrument as solemn "accompaniment" to the rest of the liturgy's music. Wooden sticks beaten together would also be appropriate.

I experienced Holy Week in a little village on the Main. People gathered there from all over Germany to celebrate the Holy Week and Easter liturgies. We assembled in a medieval castle which stood high on the cliffs overlooking the river, a string of villages and the rural countryside beyond. Throughout the week we learned to listen for the sounds of church bells, the bells in the village church directly at our backs, and the bells of half a dozen villages that spread out over the valley. After the bells of Holy Thursday's Gloria were silenced, all the church bells grew silent. With that the village boys appeared armed with their home-made wooden clackers and rattles. Throughout the valley you heard and saw them. With surprising seriousness they collected on the hour over the next three days. Then they walked through the village streets in a tight little crowd, first chanting something which sounded like a *Pater Noster,* and then in unison they let loose with a most ungodly racket and announced the hour.

The Bare Sanctuary

This kind of auditory contrasting is powerful and goes with what we also see. In church, after the Eucharist has been brought to a side altar with utmost reverence and ceremony, with flowers and candles, with incense and the chanting of the *Pange lingua,* we are struck by another contrast as priest and ministers return to the sanctuary and begin the stripping of the altar. The flowers, which we have not had all Lent but which were appropriate for this celebration of the Lord's Supper, are now carried away again. Cross and candlesticks and altar linens are removed. The sanctuary light is extinguished. The place is left hollow and empty.

We slip over to the altar of repose and spend some time before the Blessed Sacrament—Christ alone in the garden, Christ in his agony.

We join Peter, James and John. Untidy, unpredictable in our loyalties, we knew him for a moment, one glorious moment of ecstasy when we were with him on the mountain and his garments became like snow and he was transfigured before us. Like Peter—always hasty to take action—we would agree, when we wake up to the facts, that we should set up camp, here on the mountaintop, here amongst the peak experiences of our lives. This is a good show. This is worth keeping forever. But peak experiences are elusive and soon turn to another aspect of the truth: glory has its near desperate counterpart. And today in the garden, well, we cannot keep our eyes open. We fail Christ, and we fail our friends, not through malice or lack of charity, but because we cannot muster the understanding or the empathy in a moment of crisis. Such agony is too painful for us. We are tired when action is required. And we sleep.

We go home, and at home we carry on the keen auditory impression for the remainder of these three days.

Good Friday

On Good Friday, things are quiet. We hear no more bells, no music. No guitars are plucked; the piano is closed to idle plinking. No radio, TV or stereo breaks the quiet. In the car no radio or tapes are played. The simple meals are announced not with a bell, but with a wooden rattle or two sticks beaten together. The mood and atmosphere is entirely different. For years one of our children even woke us to his self-invented Good Friday rattle, as though the bells of the alarm clock might be too pleasing. I heard that in another family the children taped over the doorbell. Personally, I would like to muffle the phone.

It is a day to turn inward. It is the official Bad Day of the year. While the rest of the world calls us to its "spring break" entertainments, beach parties and kiddie matinees, we see how enticing it is to follow the crowds and we try purposefully to follow a different course. We go about the day's tasks but keep in mind the way of Christ's passion. Our projects and actions involve the youngsters as much as possible and include their creative participation.

Cleaning Out the Hearth

Somewhere I read about the sacred fire rites that Incas in the Andes performed and of similar rites performed by Mexicans, the Iroquois, the Eskimos, and the ancient Chinese. The similarity of these rites to each other and their likeness to our own Holy Week and Easter ceremonies would suggest that they have powerful roots in the unconscious.

On a given day at the onset of the festivals, the Inca villagers would fast for three days. After three days were over, they took the new fire directly from the sun in a ceremony where the sun's rays were caught on a curved polished plate and new fire was kindled on a little tinder of cotton. For the Incas this was the holy fire that would now roast the sheep and lambs offered to the sun and eaten at the festivals. Some of the new fire was also brought to the temple of the sun and kept burning the whole year. The Iroquois allowed their home fires to die out entirely. They cleaned out hearth and fireplace, strewed the ashes about and allowed everything to go cold. For three days they did without flame or fire, without warmth or cooked food. (The Chinese, in their festivals, called it the season of "eating cold food.") The Iroquois shaman supplied his people with the new, holy fire by going from hut to hut and relighting the home fires, allowing the people to be warmed and fed once again by the sacred flame.

Doing without Fire

On Good Friday, inspired by these ancient ceremonies and the additional meaning they lend our understanding of the new fire of the Easter night, we clean out our fireplaces and lay kindling to await the Easter fire which we will bring home after the vigil service. Some of our friends, equally intrigued by this ceremony and wanting to "do without" so as to better appreciate what we often take for granted, have taken the idea a step further. Each year for these three days they do without everything that requires a flame: the stove, the hot water heater. That means cold showers and food that requires no cooking. After the Easter ceremonies, the Easter fire, struck from flint and steel, blessed, praised, and shared, is carefully brought all the way home where pilot lights are renewed, candles and lamps are lit throughout the dark house and a new fire is lit in the fireplace.

The Cross at Home

Younger children can be set to making drawings for the Stations of the Cross, and if the weather allows, they post these through the woods or in the garden, and the family reads the passion and follows the pictures. The prayer corner, the little oratory, that we have made in a corner of the house has become a shrine for the veneration of the cross. The cross lies on a pillow, low, where all can kneel before it or sit and spend some quiet time. The children help cover it in greens or flowers from the garden. *Behold the wood of the cross on which hung the Savior of the world.* For children, the flowers, the cross, the silence, the wooden rattles, the simple meal, all set the tone and say more than words.

For the child in each of us this continues to be true. When in doubt about what to think on the theme of Christ's passion and death, the simple gestures and actions which we choose to make fill in and feed us back meaning. So much that has escaped us before about our own longing and yearning to be changed can be enacted in simple gestures. The cross becomes the outward sign of where the historical and the mystical intersect. Here, at the center, we find meaning for our daily lives.

Romano Guardini, the classical liturgist, in his superb and timeless little booklet *Sacred Signs,* gives us a meditation appropriate for our adoration of the cross by reintroducing us to the cross we have always available to us, the sacred sign we make over ourselves. It is not too difficult for the small ones among us to understand and even to act out as they listen to the words.

The Sign of the Cross

You can make the sign of the cross, and make it rightly. Nothing in the way of a hasty waving of the hand, from which no one could understand what you are doing—no, a real sign of the cross: slow, large, from forehead to breast, and from one shoulder to the other. Don't you feel that it takes in the whole of you? Gather up all thoughts and all feelings into this sign, as it goes from forehead to breast; pull yourself together, as it goes from shoulder to shoulder. It covers the whole of you, body and soul; it gathers you up, dedicates you, sanctifies you.

Why? Because it is the sign of the whole man and the sign of redemption. On the Cross our Lord redeemed all men. Through the Cross He sanctifies the whole man, to the very last fibre of his being.

That is why we cross ourselves before our prayers, so that the sign may pull us together and set us in order, may fix thoughts, heart and will in God. After prayers we cross ourselves, so that what God has given us may stay with us. In temptation, that it may strengthen us; in danger, that it may protect us;

when a blessing is given, that the fullness of life from God may be taken into our soul, and may consecrate all in it and make it fruitful.

Think of this when you make the sign of the cross. It is the holiest sign there is. Make it carefully, slowly; make a large one, with recollection. For then it embraces your whole being, body and soul, your thoughts and your will, imagination and feeling, doing and resting; and in it all will be strengthened, stamped, consecrated in the power of Christ, in the name of the Holy Trinity.

The Community Ceremonies

We go to church and gather with the greater family in the darkened and empty church for the Good Friday liturgy. The spirit, the gestures, the silence and the chants are stark and simple. The ministers, fully vested, prostrate themselves before the empty altar for a time of silence. We hear the passion of John read in parts and we take the part of the people. We think and pray, with the unique intercessions of this day, for the Church in this world, its leaders, its people, its unity with other believers, for those amongst us preparing for initiation into this Church. We pray for our Jewish brothers and sisters, for all who do not believe in Christ, and then for those who do not believe in God. We pray for those in public office. We pray for all people in special need. In a stylized ritual that is a dramatic unveiling and showing of the cross, we are invited to engage that sign and banner of our salvation. *Come, let us worship.* Between burning candles, the cross is brought to the people and the people come forward to venerate the cross. Either they kiss the cross, or in a variation of this recognition of our part in the sufferings of Jesus, another form is chosen. In our community, we come forward to a large wooden cross and each person pounds in a nail and returns quietly. The ancient chant of the Reproaches is sung to a hollow wooden tympany laid against the sound of our pounding nails. The Reproaches are chants of contrasts.

My people, what have I done to you?
How have I offended you: Answer me.

I led you out of Egypt, from slavery to freedom,
but you led your Savior to the cross.

Holy is God!
Holy and strong!
Holy immortal One, have mercy on us!

For forty years I led you safely through the desert!
I fed you with manna from heaven
and brought you to a land of plenty;
but you led your Savior to the cross.

I planted you as my fairest vine,
but you yielded only bitterness:
when I was thirsty you gave me vinegar to drink,
and you pierced your Savior with a lance.

I led you from slavery to freedom
and drowned your captors in the sea,
but you handed me over to your high priests.

I opened the sea before you,
but you opened my side with a spear.

I led you on your way in a pillar of cloud,
but you led me to Pilate's court.

I bore you up with manna in the desert,
but you struck me down and scourged me.

I gave you saving water from the rock,
but you gave me gall and vinegar to drink.

For you I struck down the kings of Canaan,
but you struck my head with a reed.

I gave you a royal scepter,
but you gave me a crown of thorns.

I raised you to the height of majesty,
but you have raised me high on a cross.

My people, what have I done to you?
How have I offended you?
Answer me.

Holy Saturday and the Vigil of Easter

The remaining daylight hours before the Vigil service are filled with the last preparations for Easter.

Easter Clothes and Easter Menu

Easter clothes are pressed or readied. Each family member needs something new or springlike to wear as a reminder of our baptismal garments and our new beginnings. One time, when I had a house with plenty of wall space, I hung each family member's baptismal robe on the wall to make a connection to our Easter dress. And I remember a time when Dorothy Day planned her Easter outfit. She only had a little change in her pocket, but it was sufficient. Delighted, she said it would buy her a pair of new shoelaces. The simplest sign is all we need.

The last errands are run and I hurry to get the groceries I still need. Lists are ticked off. Tomorrow's menu is gone over and completed as much as possible so that tomorrow will be free of work. In a quiet corner of the house where the children are excluded, one of the parents works on Easter baskets and some small gifts to be found in the garden (weather permitting) or in corners of the house tomorrow morning. In our house, the amusing rhyming clues to hidden treasure are the work of the papa rabbit. He seems to work best under pressure of a deadline, for there's no urging him to get at his clue writing until his Easter muses are ready. They have their own tradition and often don't begin to really inspire until the wee hours of Easter morning when everything is finally ready.

The Eggs

The egg is a symbol of new life and the breaking through from imprisonment to freedom. Egyptians buried an egg in the tomb with their dead. Ancient Germanic peoples did the same as a germ of hope for a new life hereafter. Greeks, even today, put painted eggs on the graves of their relatives.

Our painted eggs, if they have not been decorated bit by bit over the week and put aside, will need to be finished up now. In the early years when the children were small, we parents painted the eggs in the evenings after the children were in bed. They remained a surprise until Easter. Later, as the children joined in, we came to invite friends and neighbors to the house to prepare eggs with us in our kitchen.

Egg painting has always required a quiet sort of creative concentration, so as a group we seem a muttering, exclaiming lot as we go about our work. With enthusiasm we share a new technique or discovery here, and over there we check out what the other person is in such heavy concentration over. For some of the men it seems an especially rewarding experience. They don't allow themselves this kind of creative play very often. The process is by far more important than the product. By the end of the egg painting effort, it seems that we have made so many hard boiled and blown out eggs that we have to share creative ways to eat or save all this splendor.

There are those eggs that we paint with symbols of the resurrection and new life, the butterfly, the phoenix arising from fire and ash, flowers for a new springtime, chicks, and rabbits as signs of fertility and new life. Then there is the joyful word, ALLELUIA which is written on the "golden Alleluia egg," the best egg to find in the hunt on Easter morning.

Some eggs can be dyed in food colors and then, with the aid of a toothpick dipped in household bleach, decorated with white line drawings. The bleach on the pick takes away the color. Dab the extra bleach from the egg with a paper towel. Bleach, however, is not a safe medium for small children and caution must be used to protect table tops and clothing. A better variation for little ones is a set of wax crayons to draw on the egg with as a wax resist when dipped into dye.

When we had chickens, we loved the brown eggs just as they were with only the least amount of additional decoration, and once we had the exotic chickens that laid pale blue and green eggs. We blew those eggs out and still have them as a part of our Easter. They are a happy reminder of our agrarian ventures past.

Our very favorite way to color eggs is to wrap dampened skins of red and yellow onion around uncooked eggs and bundle them quite tightly into a small cloth or piece of hosiery. At the market our produce man has been alerted and he saves us a sack full of dry onion shells which he has rubbed off the onions. The more papery onion skins you have the better. Tie the ends of the bundle with rubber bands or wire twists. Then bring the eggs to a slow boil and hard cook them. Unwrap them and they reappear wonderfully marbled. Other eggs can boil alongside the wrapped eggs in the same water, and they take on an even, rich golden-red tone. Variations can be made by pressing herbs and leaves, flowers and fern against the wet eggs and then wrapping them in onion skins and cloth. These leave their imprint and sometimes their color against the egg. Rub a drop of vegetable oil all over the egg for shine. These eggs with their natural dye look organic and wonderful in a basket of real straw. The effect is a rich, subtle gold and bronze.

There are very good books available with instructions for Ukranian egg decorations. Some craft shops carry these along with the necessary tools, dyes and beeswax. This is a marvelous and satisfying folk art form, and, though it is time consuming, it is not as difficult as you may expect. Certainly it is an art form worth reviving. It seems to have the same centering and healing qualities that I think native American weavings and sandpainting must bring to the life of their creators. In our family, Sara has become the all-time expert in this batik egg-dying technique. Now that college spring break never seems to coincide with Easter, Sara takes "egg painting breaks" from her studies and over a week's time lays aside a cache of batik eggs to present to her friends on Easter morning as part of a dorm-style Easter brunch.

The Easter Egg Tree

We use blown out eggs to make an Easter egg tree. *Through the tree of knowledge, evil came into the world, but through the tree of the cross, we won life everlasting.* In the garden, we find a well-formed branch budding with new life, or if we are anywhere near a forsythia bush to force-sprout in time for Easter, we use its branches to make our Easter egg tree. We choose colored threads and string up the eggs. Over the years we have gathered a sizable hollow egg collection, so many that they won't all fit on one "tree." The extras we hang from the dining room chandelier and yet others we hang down like rain from a suspended wreath in the skylight.

With the eggs finished we set those we eat and share in baskets readied with straw. We prepare several baskets, and these we will take to church with us for the vigil. Besides the eggs, some contain breads, meats and cakes for a traditional Easter blessing. If you cannot inspire your parish community to join you in this ancient custom, at least arrange a family blessing of the Easter foods at home before brunch in the morning. Some of what we bring is shared food, a part of our community feast at the end of the vigil. We also bring a basket with a candle, a bottle for Easter water, and bells.

The Candle

We make or buy a fat candle to carry home the blessed fire and to use during festive mealtimes in the coming seasons. Recently one of the children asked that I burn it during the hours of an especially important and difficult exam. Experience has taught us to find a tall jar to set the candle in for carrying home this fire. The walls of the jar will help keep the flame from going out on the way.

The Water

We take down our special bottle in which we bring home the Easter water. This water gives us a year's supply of blessings. Elemental water, sometimes life-giving, sometimes terrifying in its destructive power, is something we too often take for granted. The Easter blessing of water urges us to reacquaint ourselves with its daily power. Lent has prepared us for the water of rebirth, for the reaffirmation of our baptism. Our bottle carries a small sample of our common experience home with us. We use it to bless everything and everyone that needs a blessing over the coming year. It reaffirms our commitment to the will of the Father. It makes ordinary things extraordinary—seeds in springtime, the harvest of summer, Advent wreath and Christmas tree. When a member of the family is very ill, or when someone must leave on a trip, we all sign him or her with this water. When the children were small, it gave them courage against the fears of night, and now, when they are grown, it blesses the newly licensed driver, the car or the long journeys back to the university.

Bells

Since our church does not have a bell, each member of our community is invited to bring a bell from home. One for each family member is tucked into a pocket or basket.

The Holy Night

Darkness falls. Everything is ready. We dress in our Easter clothes, all outward signs of the new, inner person. Our stomachs rumbling with this endless fast, we pick up our baskets of fragrant Easter foods, hidden under cloths. We take up our candle, bottle and muffled bells and we go off to church for the Easter Vigil service.

There we collect outside in the darkness with our friends around the carefully laid tinder, the construction of the scouts and campers amongst us. Priest and ministers join and greet us and then huddle, back against the wind, to strike a living spark from flint and steel. There is a silence; we are aware of every breeze. It is absolutely appropriate that this be a breathless moment. Every possibility of failure belongs to this moment as much as does success. The old rubrics that called for the use of flint asked essentially for the greatest and most skillful effort here, the fullest involvement in the archetype of this sacred moment. I remember as a child how my pastor licked that issue with a smug flick of his cigarette lighter (it had its flint) against a pile of coals doused in lighter fluid. We ached, in those days, for the tense mystery of that moment. There, there it comes. Blowing and fanning, the priest brings to birth the tiny spark, and it grows to a flame and then it climbs into a roaring fire. There is a stir of satisfaction in the crowd, and parents gently tug their curious children toward them as everyone steps back a pace. The fire is blessed and the huge Easter candle is lighted. *Christ yesterday and today, the beginning and the end, the Alpha and the Omega.* The candle, like the pillar of fire, is lifted high. *Christ our light,* the priest sings solemnly, and with gratitude we respond, *Thanks be to God.* We follow the light to the church door, and the priest intones the same message in an even higher pitch. Again we respond. The light from the one flame is passed now, from one to the next. We watch it spread a soft glow over the faces of the congregation. We continue the procession and bring our flames into the dark church. The priest, now arrived at the altar, holds high the great candle and in the highest pitch chants a third time, *Christ our light!* We answer in the same pitch, *Thanks be to God!*

Not enough can be said to recommend these ceremonies, crown and summit of the whole year's celebration. None is as ancient, none as human, none as profound. It is helpful to explain to small children all that will take place during this service. If they know what to look for and have a good place to see what is going on, they will pester you to take them back each year. The rites of the vigil service allow us to attend the holy transition between death and resurrection. The Exsultet proclaims the Easter mystery in word and chant.

> Rejoice, heavenly powers! Sing, choirs of angels! Exult, all creation around God's throne! Jesus Christ, our King, is risen! Sound the trumpet of salvation!

> Rejoice, O earth, in shining splendor, radiant in the brightness of your King! Christ has conquered! Glory fills you! Darkness vanishes for ever!

> Rejoice, O Mother Church! Exult in glory! The risen Savior shines upon you! Let this place resound with joy, echoing the mighty song of all God's people.

> It is truly right that with full hearts and minds and voices we should praise the unseen God, the all-powerful Father, and his only Son, our Lord Jesus Christ.

> For Christ has ransomed us with his blood, and paid for us the price of Adam's sin to our eternal Father!

This is our passover feast, when Christ, the true Lamb, is slain, whose blood consecrates the homes of all believers.

This is the night when first you saved our fathers, you freed the people of Israel from their slavery and led them dry-shod through the sea.

This is the night when Christians everywhere, washed clean of sin and freed from all defilement, are restored to grace and grow together in holiness.

This is the night when Jesus Christ broke the chains of death and rose triumphant from the grave.

Father, how wonderful your care for us! How boundless your merciful love! To ransom a slave you gave away your Son.

O happy fault, O necessary sin of Adam, which gained for us so great a Redeemer!

The power of this holy night dispels all evil, washes guilt away, restores lost innocence, brings mourners joy.

Of this night Scripture says: "The night will be as clear as day: it will become my light, my joy."

Night truly blessed when heaven is wedded to earth and man is reconciled with God!

Therefore, heavenly Father, in the joy of this night, receive our evening sacrifice of praise, your Church's solemn offering.

Accept this Easter candle, a flame divided but undimmed, a pillar of fire that glows to the honor of God.

Let it mingle with the lights of heaven and continue bravely burning to dispel the darkness of this night!

May the Morning Star which never sets find this flame still burning: Christ, that Morning Star, who came back from the dead, and shed his peaceful light on all mankind, your Son who lives and reigns for ever and ever.

It never fails: at the Exsultet eyes sting. Some of us juggle candle and books to fish for a hankerchief. At the very height of this proclamation, bondage and freedom are seen as belonging together, the passage from one to the other is possible only if one acknowledges the fact that both are one. *O truly necessary sin of Adam, O happy fault that merited us so great a Redeemer.* The season of atonement has been transformed to a great celebration of at-one-ment.

We put out our candles and settle in to hear the readings—primary and powerful stories that lie at the root of our belief. And we respond in songs. In one parish, the reader of the creation story was an old man with a fine, large beard. He looked like a patriarch. A father, his only son standing at his side, read the story of Abraham and his only son Isaac. A woman told, rather than read, the story of the march through the sea. She used simple words and powerful gestures. Each reader approached the sanctuary between candle-bearers and brought in a flowering plant to set at the base of the Easter candle or to place at the altar. Then they proceeded to the podium for the reading. Bit by bit, with each additional reading, lights were added and the sanctuary filled with flowers.

After the last reading from the Old Testament with its responsory and prayer, the altar candles are lighted, the priest intones the Gloria, and suddenly the church is flooded with light and music. I know a parish where a banner unfurls over the altar. It covers the crucifix and reveals a glorious cross made in bright colors and gold. Here, in this community, the moment has come for the people to pull out their bells from the muffle of pockets and baskets. Now we ring them enthusiastically throughout the Gloria. There are dinner bells and gongs, loud bells and tinkling ones, even a couple of clanking cow bells. When the church has no bell, we bring the bells to church and anything we have will do. We cannot help but grin and the children openly laugh with joy at the glorious cacophony. We hear Paul's letter to the Romans and the priest intones the Alleluia. We indulge in the sound and repeat over and over the expression we have denied ourselves for the weeks of Lent. The "death to self" of our Lenten sacrifices was worth it. Whatever we put into our mortifications we receive back again one hundredfold at this moment. The Gospel tells the story we have been waiting to hear: *He has risen from the dead and now he is going before you to Galilee.*

We proceed to the blessing of water. It stands before us in a huge earthen crock. It is our font. It is the womb of the Church. We sing the litany and then the priest breathes on the water and signs it with a cross. *At the dawn of creation your Spirit breathed on the waters, making them the wellspring of all holiness.* Then in a gesture filled with all the generative power of new beginnings, he plunges the Easter candle into the water three times. Here fire and water enhance, indeed wed each other, rather than quench each other. The opposites have come together. The fountain of baptism brings death to sin and at the same time is the source of new life, our own transformation in the risen Christ.

In this holy night two powerful elements have been blessed and spread through the community: first fire and now water. Here basic elements are contained, then blessed and then distributed in the most moving ceremony of our Church year. We rise out of our hopelessness and sin and darkness and finally are illumined by Christ our light. Share this light and it does not divide, it multiplies. *A flame divided but undimmed . . .* In the blessed water, we see *all who are buried with Christ in the death of baptism rise also with him to newness of life. Springs of water, bless the Lord.*

It is the business of the sacred, of religion, to actualize this paradox. When black becomes white, when night becomes day, when fire and water meet, when opposites unite, we can conclude that we are in the presence of a mystery. Sacred ceremonies are theatres in which consciousness is revived and actualized. The priest, putting awareness and action and feeling together through the medium of sign and sacrament, creates an act of unity basic to what is human and whole. Certainly this is the role of a priestly shaman.

Baptism is administered and we renew the promises of our own baptism. Then the priest sprinkles us all with a good shower of the new Easter water. We proceed to the eucharistic feast. *Christ has become our paschal sacrifice; let us feast with the unleavened bread of sincerity and truth, alleluia.*

At the greeting of the people, we may say to one another: "Christ is risen, Alleluia!" and respond: "He is risen indeed! Alleluia!" The priest concludes the eucharistic celebration with a greeting of peace surrounded in Alleluias and we respond in kind.

At the end of Mass, the family Easter foods which are placed on a table near the altar are blessed by the celebrants with the new Easter water and we get another shower ourselves. Some of the breads and cakes and eggs are shared directly after the services in joyful fellowship. Then we go home taking our fire from the Easter candle and our water from the great crock of blessed water with us.

Bringing Home the Fire

Bringing home the little flame, sometimes through drafts and rains, is an adventure in itself.

I can remember a blustery, rainy Easter night in the Pacific Northwest, where parishioners had witnessed the successful lighting of the Easter fire against all odds. Once inside the church, we felt blessed and victorious with our little flames.

After the services, and after the Easter feastings and greetings were over, we all trekked out to our cars in a blowing rain just trying to get our little flames as far as the car. Two young men approached us from the parking lot and told us they'd gotten all the way to their van, and in slamming the door their candle had gone out. They wanted a share in our flame and wanted to warn us that even closing the car door was a danger to getting our fire home successfully.

We shared our flame and crept into our car and, sure thing, when we closed the car door, even though we were ever so careful, our candle went out!

Well, the two young men had not driven off yet. They were sitting in their van watching to see how we would fare. Again, they shared their light with us and we had to laugh with joy and satisfaction at our fire-light fraternity. As they drove off the next family came knocking at our car window needing a light from our candle. We gave them a tip at how to close the car door and save the flame. Up and down the parking lot in the wind and the rain we heard the families laughing and calling out as flames went out and were rekindled. "Wow," said one of our kids. "This fire *is* magic! I know what you mean—you can give it away and you never lose; it only makes more."

At home we bring the fire—struck from a tiny spark, blessed, sung to, honored, shared and carefully tended on the journey home—to each dark room. Candles are lit, and pilot lights renewed. In the fireplace we light the kindling the children have provided over the last days and nurse it to a fine fire. Will there be embers left by morning? We wish each other another warm and happy Easter and turn in for what's left of the night.

In the morning we wake up to bright eggs and chocolates. One folk tradition says that the returning bells have spilled them into our homes and gardens. The bells had left for Rome, they said, on Holy Thursday after their last ringing. All the bells in the world had gone there for special blessings, and as they returned, ringing their way home during the Gloria, they have spilled Easter blessings and Easter eggs into our houses and gardens. That seems a warm and viable alternative to the Easter rabbit, if you are uncomfortable with him.

There is a great hunt and everyone is sent in search of eggs and treasure and tiny gifts. Some things are found by following rhyming clues and mysterious hints which some large papa rabbit, no doubt, spent the early morning hours conjuring up.

We play an Easter egg game. With a partner, we tap the ends of our Easter eggs together. The one whose egg cracks gives it to the winner and so on around the circle. The finder of the ALLELUIA egg is awarded a large chocolate rabbit or the like.

In households that would like to reduce the amount of sugar and chocolate eaten during this feast, there are creative and festive ways to celebrate with fruits. I know of a family that delights in a beautiful basket that is delivered to their front door each Easter by an anonymous rabbit. The basket is lined with a bed of crisp, fresh parsley, and nestled in that green bed are the largest strawberries you could wish for. This has become part of their family Easter breakfast.

The Easter breakfast table is a feast for the eyes. It is set with cakes and breads and meats and eggs. In some eastern European countries, this festive Easter table is left set and constantly replenished for all the guests who will visit over the next few days. If festive foods have not already been blessed the night before—or even if they have—we bless them now and bless each other with plenty of Easter water.

A Blessing for Easter Foods

A Blessing for Meat

O God, to deliver your people from Egypt, you instructed that a lamb should be slain and did ask that both sideposts of the door be sprinkled with its blood. So, too, was your own Son, our Lord Jesus Christ, slain for us as the true Lamb to deliver us from our sins. We ask you then to bless and make holy this creature of flesh, which we, your people, wish to eat in joy and celebration of the resurrection of the same Jesus Christ our Lord. Amen. Alleluia!

A Blessing for Bread and Cake

Lord Jesus Christ, living bread of eternal life, bless this bread, as you did bless the five loaves and in the desert, so that all of us who eat of it may receive health for our bodies and joy for our souls. Amen. Alleluia!

Or we read the Easter letter of Paul to the Corinthians:

Do you not know that a little yeast has its effect all through the dough. Get rid of the old yeast to make of yourselves fresh dough, unleavened loaves, as it were; Christ our Passover has been sacrificed. Let us celebrate the feast not with the old yeast, that of corruption and wickedness, but with the unleavened bread of sincerity and truth.

A Blessing for Easter Eggs

May you bless these eggs, O Lord, so that they will become healthful food for us, your people, who eat of them in thanksgiving for the resurrection of our Lord Jesus Christ, who lives with you forever and ever. Amen. Alleluia! Alleluia!

Blessings at Meals

During the meals of the day, as a part of the blessings, we try to include some of the readings that we will have missed if we did not attend church once again in the morning. That way we hear all the stories of the resurrection and hear the Easter Sequence too. We invite friends to the house, or we meet our friends from the community again at a nearby park where everyone brings one's Easter specialities and we share our meal as an Easter picnic.

Christ has become our paschal sacrifice; let us feast with joy in the Lord. Alleluia!

Easter Monday

Our Easter celebrations cannot end too abruptly. We've prepared too long for these mysteries to drop everything and go back to "business as usual."

For Christians, the whole of Eastertide, from Easter Sunday to Pentecost, is a concentrated continuation of the Passover feast.

Easter week itself had the tradition in the fourth and fifth centuries of being a week of intensified instructions for the newly baptized on the essence of a Christian life. The new Christians were celebrated by the whole community. They stood out from the crowd. They wore the white garments of their initiation for the whole week.

In the same spirit of enthusiasm for the resurrection of Christ, we nourish ourselves on the Gospels of Easter week. They are some of the best and happiest stories to tell children, the "new Christians" among us. They tell of the different appearances of the Lord amongst his friends but they also breathe of a new spirit and condition; they tell of a Christ who is risen and transformed. The risen Jesus could reach his friends as never before. His words burned in their hearts even before they knew the stranger who was speaking with them. But they recognized him in the breaking of the bread. Jesus, the risen Lord, revealed himself not as some ghost now totally separate from his earthly life, something to be feared. But new and transformed, he was yet human. He is one with us, and also one with the Father to whom he is connected in the mystery of the ascension. There is a full continuity between earth and spirit. And eating together is a most human way to reveal the eternal life we all share. The stories of Christ's appearances end either with such a meal or the conferring of a new sacramental power on the apostles. Christ's relationship to his friends is warm, but changed and charged. Each appearance begs us to strive for our own ultimate transformation.

It feels of particular significance that the risen Christ appeared to a woman friend first, Mary Magdalene. She was sent to the disciples to announce the Easter message. It is this transformed and risen Christ who charges the feminine with the new task, to stop feeling self-pitying or grieved, which only clouds reality, but to wipe tears away, to recognize the new truth, to run and spread the news of the resurrection, the truth of a new and wholly changed reality. This is an order and an ordination which cannot be overlooked any longer. Bernard of Clairvaux calls Mary and the other women at the tomb the "apostles to the apostles." Women who have heard this directive know to proclaim the Christian message with a new feminine wisdom and consciousness. Women have a great creative power and can join in making what is worn and old, boring and flat, into a new hope for a new world. "Behold, I make all things new."

Nor can we stop singing some of the old Easter hymns of comfort to Mary, mother of Jesus. *Be joyful, Mary, heavenly Queen, Gaude, Maria! Your Son who died was living seen, Alleluia! Laetare, O Maria.* And the other hymn of comfort to Mary, *O Queen of heaven, be joyful, alleluia! The Son whom you did bury in sorrow, alleluia! Rose in splendor as he promised, alleluia! Pray for your children, Mary, alleluia!*

The many repetitions of the Alleluia during this week are an open expression of Christian joy. Christian joy is the fruit of banished guilt and fear. It feels wonderful to sing out our joy. I lament the loss of a few of these very old Easter hymns and carols, the soaring Alleluias. Somewhere between the organ and the guitar some things of profound beauty fell through the slots and got lost. Did our rush to "be relevant" deny what is true for all times and all peoples? I taught them to our children along with the Sequence of Easter and hope that one day enlightened Church musicians will reinstate them, not as dusty museum pieces, but as treasures of our unique heritage and expressions of our ancient Catholic identity. During these days we listen to the Easter Oratorio of Schutz. Like familiar smells that announce the return of a traditional feast, the cyclic return of old and good paschal music makes the heart respond: Ah, it is Easter again!

While the season of Lent means to teach us to engage our guilt, our sins against ourselves and each other, and to accept our guilt as an incentive to suffer a change, Easter inspires us to get on with our work of becoming whole and offers us the reality of joy to reach for. Real joy is healthy. Health is the result of suffering and knowing our own woundedness. By knowing our fears and how they block us from growing we know our wounds. As the risen Christ shows us the wounds that brought him to death, we remember our own woundedness. Brought to consciousness by our own hard work during the Lenten seasons of our lives, our wounds are now transformed in the resurrection, and bring us to Christian joy.

So it is right and proper that we celebrate the days of Easter with joy. I will admit to having kept my children out of school on Easter Monday for years. The school holidays before Easter were steeped in preparations and anticipation. Now we needed time for rejoicing. I think the children liked that Monday holiday especially; it was so unlike us to take a "well day" off work and school.

On Easter Monday we have gone to an early Mass to hear the delightful Gospel and the Alleluias again. Then we have always found a body of water to visit and enjoy—a river, a lake, a stream, the marshes—fresh, life-giving waters like that which was blessed in the Vigil service, like the waters of our baptism which we remember at this time. The story of Emmaus seems to inspire a walk in nature. We see the evidence of transformation all around us in the new green of springtime.

When the children were small we would plan to meet another family or two, usually by the marsh waters near our home. That was the favorite Easter Monday picnic place. The marsh birds were actively expressing their rites of spring and with bird books and field glasses we would identify them and watch them nest. Sometimes there were baby ducks to feed.

Always we got wet. We learned about the traditions of getting wet on Easter Monday first from a favorite children's book which we have read and reread for years especially at Easter time. *The Good Master* by Kate Seredy tells of an Hungarian family, and the accounts of their Easter celebrations especially caught our interest. On Easter Monday, the young boys of the Hungarian villages went from house to house, and wherever young girls lived, they came up to the door, recited a blessing and then splashed the girls with water. The girls in turn invited them in and everyone feasted on Easter specialities, and the girls gave the boys some of their carefully painted eggs to take home. On Easter Tuesday they replayed the whole game in reverse.

Then a Polish friend of mine surprised me one Easter Monday morning with such a wet blessing, and "it took." Our children felt so inspired that it has become a part of our Easter Monday rites at the water's edge.

CHAPTER NINE

Pentecost

Come, Holy Spirit, fill the hearts of your faithful; and kindle in them the fire of your love. Alleluia.

The Ascension as Preparation for Pentecost

In the days after the resurrection, Jesus appears to his friends and prepares them for his leaving and for a new presence amongst them: "the gift which was promised by my Father"—the great outpouring of the Spirit, a baptism, this time not by water, but an infusion by fire and wind. After these final bodily appearances to the women and the apostles, Jesus is lifted up into a cloud and returns to the heavens. His place amongst us in time and in the flesh has come to an end.

In the mystery of Christmas, the divine unites with the human, and Jesus, the God-Man, spent time amongst us, in the body. This body suffered and died. And in the mystery of Easter, Christ arose in the body—not as a ghost, but bodily present for his last interactions. Now, in the mystery of the ascension, for the fruition of his redemptive action, the historical Jesus must disappear into the clouds of eternity so that his work can materialize in the hearts and actions of all of us, here and now.

The full revelation of Christ's mission does not seem to make sense to the apostles *until* he leaves them—bodily. Only then are they inspired with meaning, and they *receive the understanding,* the knowledge, that his mission is to be reembodied through their own ministry. In the mystery of the incarnation, Jesus, "by the power of the Holy Spirit, was born of the Virgin Mary, and became man"—Emmanuel, God-with-us. Now God comes again, not as man, but as Spirit *to become incarnate in us.* In our bodies and in one body to another, we carry on further, complete, the redemptive action of God. This time he does not reveal to us his truth from the outside but instills truth from the inside out. In the quickening, transforming action of the Spirit, we can carry and bring to birth the realization of redemption in the actions of our humanness, in the everyday interactions that the human experience presents.

In the nine days between Ascension and Pentecost (the original novena), we pray with Mary and the apostles, gathered together in community: Come, Holy Spirit! We ask to reverse the disruption, the enmity, the lack of communication in family and community that the story of Babel is sign and symbol of (First Reading, Pentecost Vigil). We know how often we have grown confused and have climbed too high in the stoic, uninspired towers we have built for ourselves as a way to holiness. We want literally to "build a stairway to paradise," to search for a God out there, and think that we can produce the architecture that gets us there. The letter of the law needs the inspiration of—the spirit of—the law, when we have lost meaning and forgotten purpose in the bustle of our actions. In the proud heights of our never-finished tower, in our isolation, we find we have lost our ability to communicate with each other and are bewildered in *the babble of tongues.*

In the mystery of Pentecost, we await *the gift of tongues*—the ability to hear and speak the word, each as we come to know it, understand it and proclaim it in the uniqueness of our personhood. The gift is to interpret the meaning of Christ's mission as it unfolds in our human experience, and through it we discover a common language. Meaning is what our waiting minds perceive and love, the word each heart understands. Come, Holy Spirit, sear and quicken us with a love that will imbue and recreate meaning in this worldly existence of ours.

When the Day of Pentecost Came

On Pentecost, fifty days after Easter and a feast already honored by the Jews as a harvest feast, we celebrate the roaring entry of the Spirit. We celebrate the fruits and effects of the driving wind and the scorching flame of the Spirit. The apostles are filled with a new wisdom and are prompted to express themselves, their timidity transformed by an infusion of divine enthusiasm. The harvest feast becomes the fruitful birthing of the Church, of people taking on themselves the work of redemption, of people who live by the Spirit.

Flesh and Spirit

Life "according to the flesh" is action based on what the world will think of us. (It is not our bodily existence, which together with the soul is made wonderful through the workings of the Spirit.) It is a life which is only skin-deep and functions from the outer layers of a shallow vision. It is prejudice, complacency, social preoccupations, pride of position, even heroic acts, done for the eyes of the world. Then we are "full of hot air." It is our ego which is inflated rather than our whole being, infused.

Life in the Spirit is different. The Spirit wells up from the center of our very being. It founds us and breathes into our actions the enthusiasm of love and a genuine creativity. Spirit means pneuma, breath, wind, air. Like the wind, we cannot see the Spirit, but we can see and feel its effect. We know when it is working. When the wind blows, it shakes the dead wood out of the trees. Leaves and twigs hurtle through the air. Or when there isn't even a breath of wind, we languish in the doldrums of its absence. We gasp and clamor for air when we are breathless. We breath deeply and sigh forth a great puff of relief when things turn out well. *Suddenly there came a sound from heaven as of a rushing wind.* The nature of an awakening, or of an inspiration is like that. Suddenly, it hits us. We say, "Aha!"

We Know the Spirit

The Spirit, elusive and "blowing where it will," is not as unknown to us as we sometimes think. That we cannot confine and define its nature does not mean we do not know it. Curiously, we know and recognize the Spirit manifest in the light and liveliness, the creativity or energy, the wisdom or the reverence in the life of the other. For it is through others that the Spirit ministers to us. And it is we who can draw out the Spirit in the other. We know it less well in ourselves and squirm self-consciously when others mention our own creative Spirit. But the Spirit dwells in our hearts so that it can minister beyond itself, so it can "matter" in the life of another.

Gifts of the Spirit and Fruits of These Gifts

The Spirit transforms what is just clever into wisdom. "Advice" is transformed through the Spirit's breath to counsel, comfort and healing. The Spirit illumines the truth so that it can be taken in, understood and integrated, not merely grasped by the mind but known in the heart. The Spirit imbues with meaning what has gone flat and tedious. Working from the inside out, it transforms a life lived "by the flesh"—a life which does not know its meaning. Motives are clarified and fortified and we stand in right relation to the wonder of the whole. The Spirit quickens what might otherwise remain unmoved. What is ordinary gains a fuller dimension. There is "nothing new under the sun" until, by the Spirit, we discover it, make it new and integrate it. Old truths are reinspired and lived. A boring relationship is transformed by the creative. Timidity is inspired to risk. It is dry formality made into a viable form. It is the every-day recreated in an extraordinary way. It is water made wine.

Sequence from Pentecost

Come, Holy Spirit, come!
and from your celestial home
shed a ray of light divine!

Come, Father of the poor!
Come, source of all our store!
Come, within our bosoms shine!

You, of comforters the best;
you, the soul's most welcome guest;
sweet refreshment here below.

In our labor, rest most sweet;
grateful coolness in the heat;
solace in the midst of woe.

O most blessed Light divine,
shine within these hearts of thine
and our inmost being fill!

Where you are not, man has naught,
nothing good in deed or thought,
nothing free from taint of ill.

Heal our wounds, our strength renew;
on our dryness pour your dew;
wash the stains of guilt away.

Bend the stubborn heart and will;
melt the frozen, warm the chill;
guide the steps that go astray.

On the faithful, who adore
and confess you, evermore
in your sevenfold gift descend.

Give them virtues's sure reward;
give them your salvation, Lord;
give them joys that never end.

Amen. Alleluia!

Paul's list of the fruits of a life lived in the Spirit are the perfect description of a healthy personality, fully human because it is truly Godlike. Love, joy, peace, patience, and the rest, each arising from the one before, are the wholly human response of a personality living fully their unique reality. Open to the Spirit of God's love, at peace with themselves, these are the people who heal those around them.

Family Practices

As one of the great feasts of the year, this birthday of the Church cannot slip past. Inspired by the roar of the Spirit's wind and fire, consider making a mobile. We hang ours in our "Holy Ghost hole," the skylight, or from the chandelier over the dining table. A red cardboard dove hovers on a thread with seven orange flames around it, marked with the seven gifts of the Spirit. It sways and dangles and moves in the drafts. Wear red clothes and eat red food—strawberries, perhaps, that look like tongues of flame. At each place at table make "name cards" with the gifts of the Spirit, and family members may choose where they sit today, selecting the gift they most love or most desire. At dinner, circle from one to the next and hear a word about each of the Spirit's gifts and the effect each brings. Then read "God's Grandeur" by Gerard Manley Hopkins. It is also a pleasant thing to gather with friends on an open field or in the park for an afternoon of kite-flying.

A Community Celebration

Our community arrives at church, everyone wearing reds. As we fill the church, the pinks and fuchsias, the oranges and reds make up a great, hot crowd. High in the sanctuary hangs a mobile of Spirit-doves with streamers and bells. The windows are opened and with the grace of God we get a real wind that puts the whole in motion.

At the reading from the Acts of the Apostles, the account of the Spirit's inspiration for all to speak their own languages, a group from the congregation steps forward. We line up before the community, and, after hearing the reading once in English, we begin, each of us in turn, to read it line by line in our own tongue. There are many in our community who speak a different mother tongue. Suddenly we are aware of the variety of our beginnings and the breadth of our experiences. We hear languages from all over: English, Spanish, French, Italian, Danish, German, Polish, Hindi, Chinese, even Farsi by one who has worked in the Peace Corps. In "utter amazement" we wonder: Are not all of these who are speaking from one neighborhood? For all our differences and for the variety of gifts of the Spirit that a community provides, we are suddenly struck and thankful that "to each person the manifestation of the Spirit is given for the common good. The body is one and has many members, but all the members, many though they are, are one body." (Second Reading of Paul to the Corinthians) This is indeed the wonder of Pentecost. Sometimes we fail to understand the Lord's teaching, but in the right spirit, we understand. We can speak up. We can come forward, each of us in our individuality, and feel assured and speak with authority and fire. For we can speak of the one truth, the fierce and tender love of the Spirit amongst us. So striking is the beauty of this variety in sound that sometimes we repeat the offering of this multilingual reading a second round. (Sometimes, when logistics allows, we share the experience with the Lutheran community members who worship directly after us in the same church, and we arrange to include their various nationalities in the reading. Another time, we had a Pentecost picnic with Lutherans, Episcopalians and Catholics, all gathered around a roaring campfire. We sang each other our Pentecost hymns.)

As prelude to the Gospel comes the ancient Sequence, *Come, Holy Spirit,* known since medieval times as the "Golden Sequence" because of its richness. Only a few feasts in the Church year have a Sequence, and because of their rarity and the no longer familiar quality of their ancient music, Church musicians are often unable to train a group to sing them. The hymn *Veni, Creator Spiritus* (Come, Holy Spirit) is a simpler substitute.

Because Pentecost falls at the end of the school year, we end our celebrations in church with a special recognition of those youngsters among us who are graduating and moving on to new situations. They are presented with a burning light, blessed and cheered on by the community; they are also charged with the mission to witness their faith in the new life ahead with the enthusiasm of a confirmed Christian. "Fear not to set fire to the world; discover and live the wonderful works of God."

Outside, we gather for cake and coffee. The cake is dusted with a sugar stencil of a dove and surrounded with red and orange and pink flowers, geraniums or hollyhocks. The table is orange and red with flowers. There is ferment, an energized rumble as people mix and mingle and catch up on each other's news and congratulate the graduates. Over us, wind socks and streamers in fiery colors catch the wind.

> ". . . Because the Holy Ghost over the bent
>   World broods with warm breast and with ah! bright wings."

(From "God's Grandeur" by Gerard Manley Hopkins)

CHAPTER TEN

The Feast of the Assumption

A great sign appeared in heaven: a woman clothed with the sun, the moon beneath her feet, and on her head a crown of twelve stars. Because she was with child, she wailed aloud in pain as she labored to give birth. Then another sign appeared in the sky: it was a huge dragon, flaming red, with seven heads and ten horns; on his head were seven diadems. His tail swept a third of the stars from the sky and hurled them down to the earth. Then the dragon stood before the woman about to give birth, ready to devour her child when it should be born. She gave birth to a son—a boy who is destined to shepherd all the nations with an iron rod. Her child was snatched up to God and to his throne. The woman herself fled into the desert, where a special place had been prepared for her by God. (Revelation 12:1–6)

Who is this mysterious woman, clothed with the sun, the moon under her feet? She is the woman of both heaven and earth. She is that primary force, the image and symbol of the feminine. She is that powerful, poetic, dream-woman who has evolved out of the elemental darkness of the night, out of the earth's fruitfulness, evolved from Great Mother, to Aphrodite, to Eve. She is the Church, she is Mary, she is Wisdom. At her feet, the devouring dragon threatens to swallow her child when it is born. But clothed with the sun, this woman has the aura of consciousness, the emergence out of the darkness and the destructive into Wisdom. This woman is type and symbol of all that is feminine in our experience. And as woman of the Apocalypse, John writes of her as an inseparable part of time's fullness, as she who becomes a part of the final events of history.

We hear this reading from Revelation, a powerful and poetic "dream" account of the archetypal feminine, on August 15, when the Church celebrates the mystery of the assumption of Mary into heaven. We hear about this mysterious woman giving birth to a child, the symbol of Christ, but also of the Church.

I see this feast as the ultimate celebration of the feminine—not just of Mary or of women, but of every aspect in nature and in our experience that carries the *Yin* element of our *Yin-Yang* totality. For this reason what follows is a rather extensive consideration of the mystery of the assumption and the meaning of that curious dogma. This chapter will not contain statements of fact so much as it will unfold as a process. It may be rather new territory for some and at times unfamiliar and strange, and that may be because the feminine aspects of our experience are still so much a part of our unconscious world.

The Poetic Church

It is the poetic Church that expresses the truths of the unconscious and speaks to us in myth and symbol. Then it provides an imagery or a clue to a profound wisdom, which touches our imagination, connects with our experiences and invites our creative interpretation. The ability to find meaning in the myths and symbols that the Church provides inspires an awakening to life and a personal transformation. Insight into religious meaning is already a religious experience. It uplifts and gives new courage and inspires lasting commitments from those who are willing to enter a mystery and apply imagination to what is elusive and subtle. The symbolic life, though it is elusive and subtle, is nonetheless able to disclose the real. It provides an inner truth which is certain and orienting, perhaps more so than those dogmatic rules or laws which we tend to identify with the Church. The poetic Church, as nourishment for and creative expression of the unconscious, is a Church which many are just beginning to appreciate.

The Intellectual Church

The Church, when it announces dogma and laws, too often forgets or dilutes its own rich, symbolic power by becoming overly rational or literal. Imposing intellectual understanding on truths that can only be understood symbolically or mythically confuses the levels on which we know things to be true.

Dogma comes from the Greek "to seem" or "to seem good." The ephemeral reality of what "seems good" cannot be restricted to what dogma has come to mean in the Church today: a rigid insistence that what is good on the level of intuition become right and proper and an unquestioned law, "essential to salvation," and to be believed literally. Our inclination to "nail down" a truth which is also a living religious process is to miss its power and the deepest meaning at its center. This truth lives and moves and breathes and cannot be contained and enforced as an ordinance. What is even more difficult about the literal understanding of such truth is that it blocks us from a much deeper understanding of a mystery—one that affects our whole life and our understanding of human existence. It blocks us from what is, indeed, essential to salvation!

The Dogma of the Assumption

The declaration of the assumption as a dogma is a good example of what we speak of here. For centuries, pious people understood something about the mystery of a human Mary and her incredible part in the incarnation.

Iconography depicted her "dormition" and assumption into heaven and tradition told a truth about the importance of her body—that she was taken to the same level of value as the divine. Devotion to Mary the Virgin Mother is seen in many countries where there are shrines and places of pilgrimage to a mysterious, dark Madonna who holds a certain power for the many devoted to her. In our own time, simple people and children in various parts of the world told of appearances of Mary in caves and grottoes and fields. A new surge of popular devotion to Mary arose simultaneously.

In response to the apparitions and this growing popular devotion to Mary, Pius XII in 1950 declared it a dogma that Mary, her soul and her incorruptible body, had been taken into heaven. (Insisting that this be believed literally is quite an assumption!)

At the time of its proclamation there was a great and varied reaction around the world. Some theologians responded with learned considerations, both dogmatic and historical. Some liberal theologians protested the dogma and felt seriously embarrassed. Outsiders felt this an example of the Church's medieval mentality. It caused tremendous concern in ecumenical circles. Some Catholics blushed and changed the subject. Other Catholics managed to avoid thinking about it at all. And some were content; they booked another trip to Lourdes. Hardly anyone understood the profound implications of this dogma as an expression out of the unconscious or dream language of the Church.

But Carl Jung, the Swiss Protestant psychiatrist, responded promptly, saying that the proclamation of Mary's bodily assumption into heaven was the most important religious event since the Reformation. Jung, with his deep respect for the symbolic life, with his skillful and creative imagination, could hear and see the symbol that the Pope was offering humankind. He indicated that this was the beginning of a new age—that now things would begin to happen.

For, while the Pope with this proclamation was responding to the growing popular devotion to Mary, he was also giving us, whether he was aware of it or not, a powerful, poetic image that emerged out of the Church's own soul or dream life. What had "seemed good" for centuries was emerging as an image that needed to be taken into the light of full consciousness. Mary, the archetypal feminine, once queen of all that was earthy, dark, unconscious, and frightfully fruitful, she who had been left to the darkness, where all that is feminine is feared or honored, served or oppressed—symbolically and literally—must now be raised into the light of our new understanding.

Out of the earth, in caves and dark grottoes, where the secrets of the inner world are revealed, the image of Mary appeared and prompted an expression of a powerful inner need. But the implications of either this movement or the proclamation of this dogma have still not reached our full understanding or realization. Few have opened themselves to the symbolic image which this dogma safeguards and encapsulates. Even the Church, rather than consider the message and meaning at the heart of such phenomena, has reduced its response to only a caution and wariness toward apparitions, apparitions which continue to be reported and continue to catch the attention of many. Perhaps there is embarrassment about the non-rational nature of these incidents, or perhaps the Church still thinks that it must "verify" or "authenticate" these dream-expressions, which in essence seems quite beside the point.

It is, in fact, wise to dilute the importance of place or persons when it comes to visions. That is because people want to rush to the sites of visions and localize them. Many come in search of, *again,* a literal Mary—to seek some outer, tangible proof, perhaps a miracle for themselves, or an immediate, private experience.

It is an old pattern with us—when we lose faith in the truth which is real but inner and elusive, we attempt to pursue it "out there" and make it tangible. Or the Church may make a rule or dogma around what it wisely intuits is right. It tries to firm up what is by definition undefinable with the demand for a literal or external understanding. Our belief in and understanding of the profound truth of myth is distracted by our insistence on outer proof. As parents we do something of the same thing when we set up "apparitions" of Santa Claus in department stores because our intuition still knows that somewhere there is a deep good at the heart of all this—whatever it was, we've forgotten—but we may as well nail all this down as a fact to children for as long as we can get by with it.

Visions as Voice of the Unconscious

Children are often the barometers of familial and collective states of consciousness, and their dreams, these visions, and the popular devotion that surrounds them are the expression of what Jung called "the collective unconscious" at work. Simple people and children will not always make the distinction between inner reality and outer reality. But their open nature and innocence makes them good candidates to receive and express messages out of the unconscious.

In no way are we to understand such a phenomenon as "only" a dream or as "merely" the expression of the unconscious. It is not important here that the Pope asserts as fact what seems physically impossible, for here religion deals with the reality of the inner world. Understanding and giving full value to the reality of the psyche gives us the dimension that we have been looking for. By this I do not mean psychologizing which often explains away and discredits religion. Psychologizing reduces the symbolic life to what is just indicative or evocative—pointing away from itself. Rather, the symbolic life is effective, a grace-filled sacramentality. Here the process is more important than the goal. The richness of dogma must be protected from reductionist thinking and from any kind of undervaluation of the psyche. That is to ignore and not believe in the continued workings of the Holy Spirit who operates out of the hidden places of the soul, who operates from the inside out.

Nor must we see dogmas as just absolutes that are handed us by the Church for us to bear—for us to be pinned down with in some confining way. Rather, here is a central truth which needs unlocking, which is part of a much larger picture, a divine mystery, a dynamic process which is inexhaustible. To this truth we must apply our creative imagination so that our faith is nourished. While we learn to interpret the symbolic language of this inner world, we will not come away with clear and formal statements. Instead we will feel and know: *Blessed is he who has not seen, but believes.*

The woman clothed with the sun and the Mary who appears in caves and grottoes is a vision of the archetypal feminine who needs to be incorporated into our consciousness, who must make the new difference in our understanding of the feminine and all that is feminine in our daily human experience.

The Holiness of Nature

Mary's message in the visions seems a basic Christian message: the need for our repentance and healing. There is plenty that we as a people must repent of and much that needs healing. Our large misunderstanding of the nature of feminine *materia,* indeed, of nature, has produced a materialism which has leached the earth of her riches and poisoned her life-giving soil. Ironically we destroy matter in sacrifice to materialism, the goddess we have created of holy matter. Matter is not God. It remains itself, but joined with God, in concert with God. When we do not believe in the holiness of matter, matter redeemed, or know it to be equal in value to the spirit, then we distort the truth and make of matter a divinity.

Our modern relationship to matter, deified in materialism, is analogous to ours to a woman, put on a pedestal. A woman knows great discomfort when, in a relationship, she is elevated to the position of an unattainable goddess. The pedestal is unrealistic. It leaves the human person isolated and alone and unknown. Furthermore, the pedestal is high and at any point she can topple from the height. And that fall is painful and brings her to an opposite place of misunderstanding. In the depths she carries the role of the witch or the concubine. Goddess is the flip side of witch or concubine. Materialism is just the flip side of the violent rape of all nature and her riches. The West seems particularly vulnerable to these dangerous inversions. We threaten to destroy all matter even as we try to accumulate it or dominate it. With this dangerously primitive mentality, we use sophisticated means to live out our heresy. Primitive cultures have goddesses because they have not yet evolved to the understanding that the earthly feminine is equal in value to the divine, because they do not know and take responsbility for the action which redeems and transcends. But, actually, I use the word "primitive" wrongly, for from what I know of our native Americans' reverence for and tender care of "our mother the earth"—what I know of "primitive" cultures' balanced interdependence with earth and matter—it is our own culture which seems clearly distorted and dangerously "primitive." It is we who refuse to be vulnerable to the nature of things and to take the steps in our own action which redeem and transform. The dogma of the assumption calls us to an essential understanding of, reverence for, and collaboration with the body, matter, the earth, and all that is feminine.

The Earth Is in Heaven

The doctrine of Mary's bodily assumption into heaven holds a lesson which we still must learn to understand and integrate into our way of being: Mother earth has been returned to the heavens. As in the incarnation, when the heavens were mated to the earth, now the earth is reunited to the heavens. The earth, in fact, is in heaven. Earth and heaven, matter and spirit, time and eternity, feminine and masculine can no longer be divided against each other.

Precisely as earthly, not as a goddess, but as a human, as a person, as woman, as material, as bodily (quite like ourselves!), as mortal but incorruptible, she completes and makes whole the Trinity by adding the fourth, forgotten element. She is queen of heaven, but not a goddess.

Jung said, "This results in a kind of quaternity which always signifies *totality*, while the triad is rather a process, but never the natural division of the *circle*, the natural symbol of wholeness. The quaternity as union of the Three seems to be aimed at by the *Assumption of Mary*. This dogma adds the feminine element to the masculine Trinity, the terrestrial element . . . to the spiritual, and thus sinful man to the Godhead."

Here opposing factors are once again reunited and made equal in value. Masculine and feminine, heaven and earth, body and soul, are not alike in nature but are equal in value. That dogma, though few were awake to its meaning, marked the beginning of a new age of understanding and integrity: for the validation of women in particular, for the feminine in the personality and development of men, for all aspects of the feminine factor in human life and experience wherever it is to be found. This dogma offers significant insight and implication for the unity of human experience.

The Power of Symbol Seeps into the Culture

But what "seems good" is not taken into our understanding and integrated with our experience by way of a bald statement of fact. To understand such elusive, non-rational symbols, we find our masculine, intellectual tools to be inadequate. It is like trying to eat broth with a fork. This is the domain of myth and not of science, so for many this is new territory. Here we are still clumsy, afraid, unbelieving and reactionary. We have been slow to rediscover our skills to interpret symbols. That is because we still are not convinced of the reality of the psyche—itself a feminine element. The poetic, the symbolic, the sacramental, the mythic is just as true and real as the rational and the historical. But the former is true on an inner level and the latter is true on an outer level.

The dogma of the assumption is a symbolic statement that says the feminine elements of reality are ready to be taken to a new level of consciousness. When such a powerful truth is ready to enter the collective awareness of an era, no one is exempt. Every aspect of life is touched, ready or not. For both historically and personally "things did begin to happen."

As scientists, we looked for a union with the great feminine—and used a fork for our broth. We sought the feminine amongst the moon and the stars, literally. With a powerful space program, we went to the moon, penetrated her mysteries, and found her barren. We turned around and there we found the elusive feminine, "glowing brightly as the dawn," fruitful, rich, but in grave danger. We regarded the vulnerable earth from this distance and surprised ourselves with a new tenderness and appreciation. So we began to gather up our litter—most faithfully while the "earth movement" lasted. White-skinned people began to see more clearly their injustices toward dark-skinned people. And these forgotten peoples gained a new sense of their worthiness and stepped into the light to assert their equality and demand their just due.

In the churches, pale, chalky statues of a sterilized Virgin were rolled quietly to the back and eventually into the janitor's closet where they gathered dust. And out of the closet came women themselves, blinking in the new light and too often brandishing their forks—their masculine tools. Men braced themselves. Some headed for cover; others struggled with dark, inner forces which often made them feel irritable, uncertain and touchy. But out loud, very loudly, we all proclaimed the equality of the sexes.

At first flush, it seemed that the forgotten feminine emerged "terrible as an army set in array." Whatever has been suppressed and denied, whatever we do not want to engage, whether painful or holy, whatever we stuff away under the manhole cover of our unconscious, begins to seep out slowly and disastrously or it simply explodes. On the surface we think that we have created a neat, rational way of life. But while order and reason, clarity and consciousness are vital to any kind of developed life, they are not the whole of life. For a while, such a rational, masculine system works well, and the sacrifices that we have made for this system have been necessary. But eventually, either by the grace of God or by some dreadful fate, the old pattern is shocked into change. The forgotten truth will always reemerge, roaring destruction like a dragon only because it must be recognized. This suppression of all that we deem inferior has already exploded during the most shameful periods of our own history— Auschwitz, Hiroshima. For these realities the Virgin of hidden places asks our repentance. Indeed we must repent or we cannot be healed. Belief in a new consciousness *is* "necessary for salvation." In some areas we have already begun the long road to reform and new feminine consciousness.

And Raised the Lowly to High Places

Old and long established structures have begun to topple. *He has confused the proud in their inmost thoughts. He has deposed the mighty from their thrones and raised the lowly to high places. The hungry he has given every good thing, while the rich he has sent empty away.* (Magnificat in the Gospel of the Assumption) After this long tradition of giving priority to masculine traits as the dynamic of our culture, we fast approach the overturning or self-destruction of this old order. Some people have caught the new insight and are at work. The old order of the Church simply is no longer what it was.

Everywhere there are little groups of people who support and minister to one another. They read the Gospel and integrate its message into the way they live their lives. Feminine and masculine roles have become more fluid. Ministerial roles in the churches are being served by women who are on their way to understanding and conceiving of a whole new idea of serving which is not servitude. *Behold the handmaid of the Lord. Be it done unto me according to your word.* As women understand their ordination to a new feminine wisdom and insight, they may compete for male roles both in the Church and in the world. But even this development continues to evolve and women may conceive that their service is not so much to fill the already existing male models, but to honor what is theirs by nature and to create and minister out of this feminine nature. Then the feminine will join and complement rather than overthrow and replace the masculine.

Rosemary Haughton (*The Passionate God,* Paulist Press, 1981), theologian and woman of exceptional insight, says that the revolution which we are at the edge of is not the usual revolutionary model, where the oppressed are now the oppressors. She says that with regard to the feminine in the Church, "It means that the vitality of the 'grass roots,' the place where things have always grown, is now recognized as having primary significance and is therefore to be served by those who formerly merely organized." (Madonna Kolbenschlag says that women no longer want to be the "cheerleaders" in the Church.) This place, this forgotten feminine, like the earth, must be loved and tilled and cultivated, so that the new possibilities can be brought to fruition. *For he has looked upon his servant in her lowliness; all ages to come shall call me blessed.*

Belief in the feminine as equal in value to the masculine can only come after we understand what the feminine values are and how they are *different* from the masculine. Feminine values, the *yin* quality in the nature of things, such as passivity, receptivity, acceptance, assimilation, incubation, the ability to wait, empathy, interdependence, care, cooperation, expression of feelings, an appreciation for being and the processes of becoming—all will develop as values that can become a part of the whole of human experience and not just properties of the feminine.

The feminine elements of nature and of human nature, given back their value, will first restore the value of the feminine to women and to womanhood. Most urgently the value of the feminine must be restored to womanhood. Women's freedom hinges on their own recognition, acceptance and integration of those values which are uniquely feminine—qualities particularly natural to women but enhanced and made useful through consciousness and understanding. A new psychology of women is already evolving, built on a different truth than the psychology of men. It honors and builds on the natural development of the feminine psyche which is founded on interpersonal attachment, relationship, interdependence, care, and cooperation.

Women, once they grow fully clear about their feminine nature, can make a powerful difference in our time. They can employ their masculine qualities without being merely reactionary, strident, imitative or aggressive. Fully founded in their feminine value, women can bring a new integrity to the problems of this world. They will work out of a confidence which is not just based on pleasing or on treating everyone the same, but on an ethic which augments equality and "justice for all" with a caring that crosses the breach of our human imperfections and imbalances. Here there can be no inequality, but, what is more, no person can be violated. Hoping for peace or being against war is not sufficient to the magnitude of our problems. Our energies need to be translated to a responsibility and a new, tender ministry for each other.

Independent action, a purely rational justice, competition, aggression, production, domination, intellectualization, all masculine qualities which we have valued over-long are rushing us into disaster. These qualities must be brought into balance or we will not survive. In this moment of crisis, we have to discover, name and integrate those *human qualities* of the feminine so that they will become more and more available to both sexes. With that men will become free to understand the feminine in themselves. Many men are on their way to calling into action their feminine side without weakness or embarrassment. As the feminine emerges into consciousness, the transformation of the old masculine order can be understood as an expression of humankind's inclination toward balance and unity.

As long as black remains the opposite of white, the left is the enemy of the right, down is the reverse goal of up, the earth is kept separate from the heavens, matter is considered lesser than the spirit—we continue to imply a value judgment which at some point will equalize itself by reversal or by transcendence. Transcendence is the only creative and healing solution.

As we struggle to bring together opposites and find the tension point at the center, we find that place to be both painful and joyous. It is a difficult place to meet, but the marriage of opposites brings to birth what is new and greater than the sum of its parts. Here, we touch the Sacred. The Sacred is touched and touches us at that painfully joyful moment when opposites unite, exchange the gift of their uniqueness, conceive and bring to birth the new, the Sacred, the salvific. *Holy is his name.* Between the dark and the light, between black and white, is not gray. Transcended, they create a rainbow.

A Family Celebration

It is the height of summer. The sun drenches the gardens which are abundant with flowers, fruits and vegetables. I'm struck with the riot of color. Our spring flowers were white and the pale, gentle shades of chalk. Our August garden has none of that delicacy. The leaves are dark green and shining with a hardy life. The flowers seem to reflect back to the sun its own strong yellows and bright reds and oranges. Some of the sunflowers have already grown heavy-headed with seeds. The seeds have formed a spinning pattern on each face. Where the seeds still bear a little star flower of their own, fat bees load up on pollen. It's curious how large and sturdy a plant can grow, far taller than

I am, from a single seed and in a single season—the melons too and the corn. The plants of August seem strong and hairy; they make my arms itch when I work amongst them. They must pull untold secrets out of the rich soil. The bees are busy on the zinnias and the lavender, too. Wherever the flowers have already completed their cycle, I collect the seeds into my shoebox and clip back the dry stocks. I carry an armload of zinnias to the house to arrange in a crock together with the snowy ball of blossom which some forgotten carrots have yielded. And I carry a bundle of fragrant lavender blossoms to dry in my kitchen.

My husband comes home at lunch hour from the office. He casts off suit and tie for garden clothes and is content to hoe and weed amongst his vegetables and flowers for an hour or so. The plants don't talk back. He clips and prunes and digs and trenches. He turns over and loosens and ties up and soaks. On Saturday, he tells me, we will take the time to give fish emulsion to the earth, or steer manure. It is the soil that we marvel at and celebrate, Mother Earth who incubates and feeds and sprouts what we have poked in her warm soil. And my husband, showered and tie still askew, hurries back to his office for the afternoon, glad to have nursed his garden that in turn has nourished him, glad to have sweated amongst his plants.

In August, we dry the herbs, invent new ways to accommodate the plethora of peppers. We rush the corn from stalk to pot, that ritual to save its sweetness. I see those corn stalks and think of the holy corn mother, Mary, I saw painted on the wall of the church in the Acoma pueblo; corn mother and dream sister to Demeter. We relish the ripe tomato slices, marinated in olive oil and lemon and herbed with sweet basil. We bring in apples and peaches as they ripen— the jays and mocking birds have had their share—and put up our surplus into jams and sauces. We share with friends and neighbors an abundance of zucchini that threaten to get up and walk if we don't harvest them at the right moment. It feels wonderful to exchange a sack of ripe tomatoes for a sack of plums. The college children plan on reaping this harvest once again—off shelves when they leave for school next month and go back to making their own meals.

Along roadsides and in the empty lots the earth continues to yield her gifts. There are stands of wild fennel with their golden umbrella flowers. They have seeds and flowers all at once. There are wild sunflowers and cat tails in the marsh. And all the grasses have developed heads of seed.

I remember as a child walking with my mother and sisters along the river banks, collecting every variety of grass seed that we could find. It was a part of our assumption rituals. The ears of grass were each different in color, from pinks to sage, and bore a variety of shapes. (It makes me think again of Demeter with the ear of corn walking over the fields with her daughter Persephone.) We brought these grasses home in great bouquets and prayed the blessing for herbs that the Roman Ritual offered for this day. It was our variation of a German custom that had the people collect wild herbs from the field which had healing powers and which were brought to the church on Assumption day for blessings. Later these were distributed and hung in barn and shed and house. In many countries, this is also the feast to bless fields and harvests and first fruits which are brought to the church.

Today we do something of the same. We gather a great basket of produce from the garden and make rich bouquets of flowers mixed with mint and basil and parsley. We plan our meal around whatever the earth has produced for us and bless both garden and its fruitfulness. We find some of the prayers or some readings from our native Americans about our mother the earth. Readings from anthropology have introduced us to peoples at one with nature and in love with the earth. We end up with some rounds to Mary and the *Salve, Regina.*

Once, when we lived in a place that had a thick wood and meadows, our family and some of our visiting relatives gathered wild flowers, ferns and herbs after Mass in the morning. After a festive breakfast we arranged these in crocks and hanging vases. During siesta time, while everyone else was quiet, my sister and I went into the woods and found a huge thick tree in a ferny clearing to make a kind of shrine there to the Virgin. We brought the pots of gathered flowers with us and a powerful, bright icon of Mary being lifted up to heaven by four angels. We hung the icon on the tree and surrounded her with the flowers and with some candle stubs set deep in jars. Then we went back to the house, and as late afternoon came, we gathered up the families and made a procession out to the woods. We sang songs to Mary. The children carried banners they had made and we wound our way into the darkening woods until we came upon the clearing. By some blessing, the last rays of light shot through a hole in the leafy ceiling and sent a beam directly illuminating the icon with a magic golden light. It lasted for the duration of our songs and readings. Then we lit the candles and sat in that place until it was time to return home.

Life in the City

I think that if I did not have a garden and were confined to a city apartment, I would devise some rituals that would bring me into nature or that would bring nature into my small living space. We need constant reminders that our mother the earth is the source of our nourishment and the foundation we walk on, no matter the layers of asphalt that separate us from her. I would take my family to the park or I would plan a camping trip that would reconnect us with the basic elements of earth and water, rain, wind, and weather. Or perhaps I would seek out those brave weeds and grasses that poke through cracks in the pavements and that thrive in empty lots that do not yet "wear man's smudge." I would build me a window box or fill me some pots of loamy soil on this day and start to grow something that I could tend. I would study the herbs and herbal medicines that women have always had a special talent with and would make up some ritual teas or flavor with them my green salad. I would make a vegetable dish or a fruit tart that would celebrate the greatest variety of this season's blessings.

If you cannot convince your worshiping community to have a special blessing on this day for herbs, fruit and flowers after the eucharistic service, have the blessing yourself at home. This blessing is a derivation of the old ones found in the Roman Ritual.

A Blessing for First-Fruits and Herbs

Psalm 65

Praise is rightfully yours,
God, in Zion.
Vows to you must be fulfilled,
for you answer prayer.

All flesh must come to you with all its sins;
though our faults overpower us,
you blot them out.

Happy the man you choose, whom you invite to live in your courts.
Fill us with the good things of your house,
of your holy Temple.

Your righteousness repays us with marvels,
God our saviour,
hope of all the ends of the earth
and the distant islands.

Your strength holds the mountains up,
such is the power that wraps you;
you calm the clamour of the ocean,
the clamour of its waves.

The nations are in uproar, in panic
those who live at the ends of the world,
as your miracles bring shouts of joy
to the portals of morning and evening.

You visit the earth and water it,
you load it with riches;
God's rivers brim with water
to provide their grain.

This is how you provide it:
by drenching its furrows, by levelling its ridges,
by softening it with showers, by blessing the first-fruits.

You crown the year with your bounty,
abundance flows wherever you pass;
the desert pastures overflow,
the hillsides are wrapped in you,
the meadows are dressed in flocks,
the valleys are clothed in wheat,
what shouts of joy, what singing!

Leader: The Lord is gracious to us.

Response: The earth brings forth her fruit.

Leader: He waters the mountains from the clouds.

Response: The earth is refreshed by his rains.

Leader: He makes green the grass lands for cattle.

Response: And the plants that feed us, his people.

Leader: He blesses the wheat that springs from the earth.

Response: And the wine that brings joy to the heart.

Leader: Oil that makes the face lustrous and shining.

Response: And bread to give strength to the heart.

Leader: At the Lord's command, he heals our suffering.

Response: And frees us from want.

Leader: Lord, put bread on the table of those who are hungry.

Response: And to those who have bread, make them hungry for justice.

Prayer

Lord, at your command you created for us this heaven and this earth, seas, lakes and rivers; all that we see and cannot see. You adorned the earth with plants and trees for our use and to feed every one of your creatures. You arranged that each kind bring forth fruit in its kind, to be the nourishment of all creatures and a healing medicine to our bodies when we are sick. Bless † this variety of herbs and fruits, flowers and grasses which we bring before you today and also bless those which we have left behind in the fields to live out the full cycle of their service. Bless this holy earth on which we stand. Bless the farmers of this soil, the tenders and harvesters of your bounty. Without them and their diligence we would not know this richness. Bless us, Lord, and transform all the natural powers which we gather together in our offerings here and in our hearts and with your grace transform all life with your blessing. May we be nourished by the fruits of this earth, share them with all humankind, and use them in peace. Amen.

Holy Mary, Virgin Mother, whose assumption we celebrate today, your crowning in heaven, with Father, Son and Spirit, crowns all nature with a blessedness that makes heaven and earth one. Your own human nature which was the font itself of God's own Son, Jesus, fruit of your womb, is proof that what surrounds us is holy and worthy carrier of the redemptive. Let us never misuse this sacred earth, her fruits, her soil, her adornment, life or riches. Let us always return to her soil worthy nourishment to replenish and not poison her. Let us never misuse those who tend the earth. Their work is holy and noble. May we take from earth's offerings without greed or waste. Let us share with earth's people, her gifts in full justice and love. Amen.

A Celebration for Community

In our community, the assumption as celebration of the feminine is a day that we extend to the nearest Sunday so that the greatest number of people can participate. This time it is the women who plan the ceremonies. The church is decorated with wild flowers and blooms that hold seeds—cat tails and giant sunflowers and huge stalks of fennel that smell of licorice and are bright yellow and pale green with their umbrellas. At the entry procession, the community sings an *Ave Maria* in rounds. We have put the Responsorial Psalm to a special chant and at the Gospel, when the reading brings us to Mary's quotation of the Magnificat, the women of the community chant it.

The homily is prepared and delivered by one of the women in the community. Either the dogma of the assumption or the life of Mary as we know it from the Gospels provides us the themes. The references to Mary throughout the Scriptures point up feminine qualities of great power—each fully necessary to the incarnation and redemption—receptivity, waiting, incubation, allowing, being. Each year the homilist passes her task along to another woman in the community who will prepare herself for next year's presentation. At the offertory, women and men chant back and forth to each other a song which demonstrates the complementary roles of Mary and Christ, of feminine and masculine:

Mary the Dawn

> Mary the dawn, Christ the perfect day,
> Mary the gate, Christ the heavenly way.
>
> Mary the root, Christ the mystic vine,
> Mary the grape, Christ the sacred wine.
>
> Mary the wheat sheaf, Christ the living bread,
> Mary the rose-tree, Christ the rose blood red.
>
> Mary the font, Christ the cleansing flood,
> Mary the chalice, Christ the saving blood.
>
> Mary the Temple, Christ the Temple's Lord,
> Mary the shrine, Christ the God adored.
>
> Mary the beacon, Christ the haven's rest,
> Mary the mirror, Christ the vision blest.
>
> Mary the Mother, Christ the Mother's Son.
> Both ever blest, while endless ages run.
> (From *Our Parish Prays and Sings,* Liturgical Press, 1959)

We have revived the Ave Maria in Gregorian Chant and sing it in Latin for Communion. After Communion, we have a blessing for the fruits and flowers of this earth. Communities can use the blessings cited above in the family celebrations or write something of their own.

Ours is written as poetry by one of the women, Odette Filloux, and read before we adjourn. It is a blessing made especially for our corner of nature and how we experience it.

A Prayer for the Blessing of Herbs, Plants, and Flowers, on the Assumption of the Blessed Virgin Mary

Sancta Mater
Domina Rerum
Mistress of things created of matter
Holy Mother
On this your August fest
We bring for you to bless and nurture in nature,
not the priced garden-rose by vase enclosed
or the pallid orchid corsaged and pinned
nor the ribboned bouquet tied-up in paper robe
or the herbal bundles crushed in scented sachets
. . . (though, we confess, for their grace
there is a time and place . . .
but don't we see them here, already, more than abundantly blessed?) . . .

instead, into your care we dare entrust today
—to help us preserve and thus deserve—
the flower of the field, the lily of the valley
yet neither torn nor shorn
improved or worn
but left, well in place in their wilderness.

Of the summer hills all of the frill-corolled dills;
in April, the pastel hues of verbenas overtaking the mesas
with the mustards that spring up
yellow
from among the tender green shoots of the plateaux;
by the rustling stream, the rushes, and the fresh blue cress where it hushes
next to all of the mints' lushes;
on the canyons' slopes the ancestral California oaks,

of sage and bushes
    the berry, the bay and the rosemary,
with further the juniper
    thyme and silver lavender,
while, mountain-high the pinyon pine.

All those mille-fleured and spice bearing
creatures
as odoured, adorned and ordered by the Creator.
We ask you anew, Virgin Mother of God,
    Lady arrayed in gold,
    but most of all bold maiden-servant of old,
to endow them with your protection
so we may forever rejoice in the creation,
singing in a single voice
the very praise you yourself raised:

    "Tell out, my soul, the greatness of the Lord
    Rejoice, rejoice, my spirit, in God my Saviour.

    . . . the arrogant of heart and mind he has put to rout
    he has brought down the monarchs from their thrones
    but the humble have been lifted high.
    The hungry he has satisfied with good things
    the rich sent empty away." . . .

And may the blessing of almighty God, Father and Son and Holy Spirit, come upon those creatures and remain for all time. Amen.

We end with a rousing folk rendition of The Seven Joys of Mary, and recess.

Outside, we gather around our table which is decorated for the occasion with garden flowers and offerings of fruits and vegetables from community members. The fruit and vegetables and flowers are sometimes shared and traded among us. Large round wheels of bread are passed from member to member and guest to guest—a small corner of it is torn off by each to be shared and eaten. It is a whole wheat bread full of honey and baked in a pizza tin—circles of tiny buns all baked into one large wheel. For the occasion, it has baked in it all manner of seeds for the fruitfulness of this season. It will have sunflower seeds, wheat berries soaked and plumped, great lots of poppy seed, some anise or fennel here and there for a surprise, and cardamon. We have herb teas and coffee. After the celebration, we take our share of fruits and flowers and go home. For the rest of the morning, tucked in the hiding places of the mouth, an occasional poppy seed turns up—tiny, tasty reminder of earth's endless bounties.

CHAPTER ELEVEN

Vision of the Whole

Autumn

It is autumn. We are in a village, strange to us. I open the window, then the shutters of our guest room to look out over the town. A burst of biting air suggests there was a killing frost in the night. Over there, over the slate rooftops, I see a church steeple. It is Sunday, so we wrap up against the sharp morning air and venture into the narrow streets. We peer into back gardens that have been well prepared against this frost. Apple trees have been picked clean; some plants have been hooded and blanketed against the cold. But even the tough mums have been killed during the night. It is cold and it is utterly quiet. Not a wind stirs and no one in the village seems to be awake. We round a corner and come upon a park, a long terraced stretch which overlooks the rooftops and has a view into the river valley. It is a park with only a row of benches interspersed with a long line of chestnut trees. They are a blazing yellow—each leaf like a giant, drooping glove. The yellow is so shocking that we halt in our steps to stare. In the utter stillness we hear only the noise of the leaves falling. Plop, plop, plop-plop. Up and down the row, every tree is losing its leaves—right now in front of our eyes. The trees are raining down their leaves with steady determination. Was it the frost that caused this event—or the first rays of sun? We stand in silence and watch. Within half an hour, we see a whole row of golden trees turn utterly bare before our eyes. Gaunt and black, the empty branches reach at the sky. At the foot of each tree is a perfect pile, yellow as sunlight, a gift from the tree to its own roots. By the time the villagers wake, autumn is over.

Autumn looks like nature's end, and if we did not know nature's cyclic pattern we would not believe this was a dormancy and that a transformation would occur with springtime. It is an end that we have come to know as necessary to a new beginning. Summer's abundance and sun drenched extroversion is finally over. The harvest has been gathered indoors. The garden's excess has been turned under the earth one last time. While we return to the earth the riches that she shared with us and allow the rotting melons or the bright leaves to be turned back into the soil, I think of that interdependence and of something Lewis Thomas said: "We have always had a strong hunch about our origin, which does us credit; from the oldest language we know, the Indo-European tongue, we took the word for earth—*Dhghem*—and turned it into 'humus' and 'human'; 'humble' too, which does us more credit." So it is that with the death of summer, the dormancy of nature, it is ultimately our own dormancy in the grand scheme of things that we celebrate. In anticipation, a woodpile has been stacked against the winter upon us. We ourselves are pleased to return indoors to build home fires, to turn inward, to love the settling in of lying fallow with the rest of nature.

A Year Ends

The Church's message coincides with this mystery of apparent death and finalities. We consider in these days the saints who have gone before us. We consider the souls of our forebears, known and unknown, who have died. Just as the harvest has been gathered into barns, as the children have been collected into schools, the saints and souls have been gathered as a heavenly harvest or brought before our consideration, because it is the nature of things. The Sunday readings, as we inch again toward Advent's new beginnings, have been picking up the themes of endings, a looking for Christ's presence with us, now in glory, in the fullness of time.

Halloween and All Saints Day

All Saints Day is the celebration of those who have contributed successfully to the creation of the kingdom. The saints were not perfect, but they were whole, holy, and they were certainly human. They lived their unique fate with creativity and participated in the evolution of human consciousness. Such a great feast, as every great feast, is preceded by an "eve" or vigil. At sunset, we turn toward the coming celebration of the next day. We launch our celebration of all that is holy with a consideration of all that is "unholy".

All Hallows eve, or Halloween, carries these overtones. A Christian veil has been thrown over the ancient, pre-Christian festivals for the dead which celebrated both good souls and evil. The feasts of All Saints and All Souls were placed on top of ancient feasts. So some of the old traditions entered and mixed with the new practices. The ancient British Celtic traditions of fire festivals on this last night of October, of fear of witches and invitations to ghosts, have prevailed to this day in parts of Great Britain. Witches, animals, but most especially cats, into which witches were said to have transformed themselves, may have been burned in this, one of the major Celtic seasonal fires of the year. Together with the unseen witches, the souls of the dead hovered unseen in the sky. Witches and demons went wild and played tricks on their night and needed to be placated with food and sweets. What is unseen and unknown is so often treated as evil or dangerous. But with a contrasting intuitive gesture, the ancients also felt that, on this night when autumn made its transition to winter, the dead departed, returned to their old homes to be invited to the fireside, to be warmed and fed, by the living. These people were herdsmen more than farmers, and since they brought their cattle in from the frozen fields and housed them in shed and stall and fed them, they would do as much for the ghosts of their dead. Invitation into the light of consciousness does make unknown dangers safe, indeed full of energy and blessing.

These ancient practices still color the way people enter into Halloween festivities today. Going from door to door dressed as a witch or a ghost to beg for food or coins on this night is certainly connected with these ancient rites. In other countries food is placed on graves, or special cakes called soul cakes are handed out to children who sing at the door, or these are given to poor beggars. Dunking for apples may have been connected to the celebration of the goddess Pomona to whom orchards were dedicated and whose feast was held on November 1. Pumpkin faces, or turnips hollowed out into jack-o-lanterns, can be found in many parts of Europe. Their candle fire may be connected with the ancient Halloween fire.

Halloween, it seems, has many of the same overtones of Carnival with its costumed disguises, its permission for mischief, its engagement of darkness, danger, and the depths of the yet unconscious mysteries. (See Chapter on Carnival and Lent.) At Halloween, everything spooky, unseen, mysterious, or otherworldly connects to the souls of the dead which the Church celebrates in its feasts at this time of the year. Perhaps it is a time to channel some very basic human fears and fascinations. I find that where I live, the power of dressing up for Halloween holds a growing appeal, even with adults. They are not exempt from the need to engage and discharge all the feelings that this season calls up. One Halloween I went to a party where everyone was invited to arrive in a disguise and bring along a "witches' brew" to share. Another Halloween, I did my banking with the Medici family and had my blood drawn by a vampire.

Family Celebrations

Since many families fear that the mischief is turning quite dangerous, and the candy collecting has gotten out of hand, they arrange celebrations with more planning and a greater channeling of feelings for the children. In some households the treats that are passed out are healthy and nutritious. So as not to be "toothless as a jack-o-lantern," the children are given pumpkin seeds, which have been roasted and salted as part of the pumpkin carving ritual. Small cans of fruit and vegetable juices to be taken in school lunches make good giving. Apples, raisins and nuts are healthy. Some people, using a European custom, might make gifts of a little bundle of kindling for hearth fires or a few lumps of coal, called black diamonds, to add to the warming of winter evenings.

Some families make parties of carving the pumpkins and carve other squash and turnips as well for a variety of creative expression. Mask-making is a delightful undertaking for both children and adults. A simple mask to make uses a standard, 8½ by 11″ sheet of paper, white or colored. Fold the paper in half lengthwise. Measure up 2 inches from the bottom to allow for a chin. Now cut into the fold a half of a mouth, frowning or smiling. Up an inch from the mouth, cut an inverted "7" for a nose into the fold. Then poke the scissors through both layers of paper at once to cut an eye. Slash the top of the paper to make hair. Open the paper and you have the basis of your mask. Round the chin if you wish, add teeth, lashes, mustaches, ears, horns, whatever you fancy. Paint, color, or decorate the mask with colored papers. Now fold the mask in its original halves again and make a two inch slash into the cheeks from the open ends and a one inch slash in the center of the chin. Open the mask and pull the slash of each cheek over itself to make a little formed cheek. Staple in place. Do the same with the slash in the chin to form a point on the chin. Staple. Now the mask has taken on dimensionality. With that you have the basic idea; now the variations and possibilities are as broad as your imagination. A group making masks together can offer each other humor and inspiration and trade colored paper scraps with each other for the ornamentations. Thin paper plates can be folded in the same manner and made into masks. They are sturdier for wearing. Paper masks make fine wall decorations as well.

Community Celebrations

In our community we anticipated All Saints Day with a party on Halloween. We began with a skit which the children put on about one of their own name-sakes. Daniel was chosen. They read about him in the Old Testament and interpreted the lions that surrounded him as the temptations and invitations to pride that are a part of their own lives. The lions, all dressed in brown bag frills and sporting rope tails, assailed poor Daniel with their own views of life, and Daniel, wise in interpreting visions and dreams, could also interpret the motive of these lions and was not to be devoured. He tamed them, one by one, with his insight and vision. Finally the king himself came into the pit, bearing in a false god. "Just fall down and worship this god and you will be saved"—and he held a gleaming football trophy aloft. But brave Daniel didn't fall for that one either and the king and all his people believed in the one true God of Daniel.

The next part of the party dealt with more patron saints among us. All present had prior instructions to research their name, patron saint or namesake, a person they looked up to, living or dead, saint or hero, and learn some major things about this person. Confirmation names, either those which we had already chosen for ourselves or those which the young people were considering, were especially popular. We created a long time-line on shelf paper, roughly separated into Old Testament Time and New Testament Time. At the start of the line we drew Adam and Eve under the tree of knowledge. At the center, we drew a cross rooted in a manger bed. At the end, we drew a symbol of Christ in glory, a cross with rays like a sun. We marked off the eras roughly into centuries, B.C. and A.D. People came before the group and we played twenty questions with them until we caught the saint or important personality they wished to depict. After we guessed the name, we learned some more about this person. Then a sign or symbol was drawn on the time-line in the century this patron saint or namesake lived.

We saw how each saint prepared the way or participated in the mystery of the incarnation or contributed to the fulfillment of time. We saw that we were to become the saints of the twentieth century and that we were called to make our personal and unique contributions to the history of consciousness. As a medieval theologian put it, we are dwarfs who stand on the shoulders of the giants who went before us, and we are grateful for the height they lend to our vision. While sainthood is in the service of the whole, our final contributions to the healing of humankind are also distinctly individual. Elie Wiesel put it this way: "There are one thousand and one gates leading into the orchard of the mystical truth. Every human being has his own gate. We must never make the mistake of wanting to enter the orchard by any gate but our own."

A Church for All Saints

I love this story which comes to us out of the medieval legends of Jacobus de Voragine. According to his accounts called *The Golden Legend,* the feast of All Saints was first celebrated in about the year 605. It was instituted so that no saints would be forgotten or offended. It was also instituted in order to rededicate to all these saints a temple which had been previously a Roman temple, the Pantheon, dedicated to all the gods. The Romans said they had built this temple at the command of Cybele, the mother of all the gods. It was bigger and higher than any of their other temples. The base of this temple was designed to be circular to signify the eternity of the gods. The story of how it became so grandly vaulted and how it came by having its famous hole left in the roof is related here by this archbishop, de Voragine. Since it seemed that the vault of the building would be too wide to be supported, as soon as they built up the walls to a given height, they filled the whole interior with earth and buried coins in the earth. Over the mounded earth they completed the large roof. They let it be known that anyone who wished to help dig out the temple could carry away the earth and keep any coins that they found in the process. Apparently this caused the temple to be cleaned out very quickly. On the top of the roof the Romans constructed a gilded bronze battlement, on which stood statues of each of the gods representing each of the Roman provinces. Eventually this battlement collapsed and thus left a hole open to wind and weather, an opening in the roof which is there to this day.

When the Pope took over this temple from the Romans, he dedicated it to Mary and to all of the martyrs. Just as the Romans had come in great crowds to honor the gods, now the Christians came to celebrate on the feast of Mary and the martyrs, May 12. But the crowds that came to Rome for the feast were so large that the food supplies were quickly exhausted. For that reason the feast was later moved to November 1. The new harvest and the completed vintage allowed a greater food supply. The feast then became solemnly observed throughout the world, this time to honor all the saints. So the temple that was first constructed for all the Roman gods is now a church dedicated to all the saints—with a hole in the ceiling where heaven and earth unite.

Community Ceremonies for the Feast of All Souls

After All Saints Day, we have All Souls Day, so that we can remember all the dead, known and unknown, who have gone before us—the "communion of saints." In many places the graves in the cemeteries are specially blessed and a special service is held in the churches to remember the dead. One of the five sequences of the year is sung or recited at church on this day, the *Dies Irae*.

On the Sunday after All Souls Day, our community celebrates a special service for the dead. The *Dies Irae* is sung and we are invited to go up to the altar in solemn procession and write on a large card the names of our friends and relatives who have died. This large sheet remains on the altar for the rest of the month.

For many, these days are helpful and lend a healthy opportunity to grieve and engage that pain of loss which we suffer for the special people in our lives who have died. It is a comfort to have each other, both when we lose someone in death, but even as we continue to grieve. I have a friend who falls into a sadness at this time of year. It happens that her father died in November and that event, which she has not yet fully come to terms with, together with the very nature of the season, adds to her great discomfort. She feels so despondent that she dreads the anniversary, would like to avoid thinking about it, and feels frozen in place, as though she were unable to accomplish much during these days. One day some of us talked. My friend opened up about her unfinished relationship with her father. She engaged her great sadness.

"Maybe *do* something now?" I suggested after the feelings were set free. "Make some simple gesture for your father—a little ritual."

On November 2, in the evening, she phoned. "I want to tell you, I went to church this morning and then my daughter and I went to my father's grave," she said. "I've always gone to my father's grave, but to bring my mother and then I'd wait for her. But today I went for my own reasons. I brought a plant, and while my daughter busied herself about the names on the markers, I sat at the edge of his headstone and I talked with him. It felt almost like the days when I was a child and sat on his stomach and we tussled and played. I saw that some grass seeds and leaves had fallen on his stone. I brushed these away. Suddenly it felt like I had *done* something for him; it was terribly simple, but it felt so right. I feel different now."

Another friend told me of the death of his mother. He was especially grateful that the hospice where his mother spent the last days of her brief illness allowed his little nieces and nephews to visit her frequently. Dying was not reduced to a medical problem, it was a part of the human condition. The presence of the children was a warm and human part of this reality. "The day before she died," he told me, "they were sitting on her bed and she was reading *Heidi* to them. They'll never forget that."

Family Ceremonies

This is a good day, a good season, to recall family friends, neighbors or relatives who have died. It is a time to make a trip to the graveyard, to tend to the family graves, to bring flowers and to tell the stories we remember about these people. I know a woman who sets out a picture of her friends and relations who have died. She lights a little candle next to each picture and thinks about them. It might be a good idea to take out some few heirlooms or the family photo album and go through the pictures of those who have died and have a story telling session that keeps alive the legends that surround these persons. It is perfectly appropriate to remember both the good things and the bad things. We realize that one day people may look at a picture of us. What will they remember our great deeds, or very simply how we got along with our families, our motives, our attachments, our human struggles? What goals do we have now that we hope to accomplish before we die? Families could share these ideas.

A form of therapy, built on the principles of a Japanese philosophy, suggests an exercise which "helps us accept our feelings, know our purpose and do what needs doing." The exercise is to write your own obituary, your epitaph and a eulogy for your own funeral. It is designed to stimulate the awareness that we are all going to die and to engage the feelings that come when we consider what we have done with our lives. What still needs doing will certainly emerge in the process of this brave exercise. This may be something you can do with one trusted friend or alone as an entry in your journal.

On a simpler level we can talk about our own death and our fear of the unknown with our family. We can talk about the way in which we would like our funeral conducted and how and where we would like to be buried. It is right to use the word "death" and not disguise it in expressions like, "passing away," or "falling asleep." Death is what it is. Children may have had their first experience with the death of a pet. It is a perfectly real experience which may need to be included and which helps them with death's mysteries. They may mourn the loss of a beloved grandmother or grandfather. Talking about the feelings of loss, remembering the days when they were important to our lives, is a healing exercise.

Children will want to know about life after death. They will want to know what heaven and what being with God is like. Wouldn't we all like to know more about heaven! But heaven is both unknown to us and yet, perhaps, familiar! For it is rooted in our real lives and loves. We have tastes of heaven and we know what it is to "dance with God" in those religious experiences which mark our days and are at the center of those rituals and relationships that suddenly touch and transform us. We can review those views and tastes of heaven that we have all experienced.

"Do you remember how happy it makes you to splash in the lake? To jump on the old couch? Remember how you feel when you dance, when you see the first snow? That's a small taste of heaven, just a lick of it. Do you remember how glad you were to see Daddy after his long trip? That's just a sniff of heaven. What else makes you terribly happy that might be a little foretaste of heaven?"

We say that the old Chinese practiced "ancestor worship." When they moved, they took the remains of their forebears with them. They made death a part of their everyday lives—as a part of the earth from which they lived. We live in a time that so glorifies youth and everything new that we have lost respect for the old, for our roots, for our heritage of traditions. I think that "ancestor worship" is really an engaging of our own place in history and in the grand scheme of things. We recognize who has contributed to who we are and that we contribute to those who come after us.

This is a good month to work on the family tree, to update the family will and to put everything in order as, together, we engage our own deaths. Speaking with one another about these issues prepares us, bit by bit, for our own inevitable death. Our own contributions on the continuum of time are small blips, but they have lasting and living effects. We are learning to live out, passionately, our unique role in our bodies—as our bodies become spiritual, as spirit is one with the body. Death may be the great leveling experience but finally in death our soul lives on to join the "communion of saints." And the body delivers its last service to the earth, humble, human, humus.

The Kingdom

On the feast of Christ the King, we consider the kingdom which is sign and symbol of a unitive wholeness. The kingdom of heaven is near at hand, we hear—so near in fact that the kingdom of God is within you. God's kingdom is not *of* this world, but it is fully brought into being *in* this world, here and now.

Voting with the right wing or cheering for the left wing is our attempt to create a kingdom outside of ourselves, but the kingdom we ultimately discover is "not of this world." It is not a perfect government, nor is the kingdom of God only a pie in the sky which we get in a better day than this one. It is a process in which each of us participates. It lies in our individual, inward relatedness to God. The kingdom God has prepared for us becomes ours as we participate personally, with growing consciousness, in its ultimate unfolding and fulfillment. In knowing ourselves, in living out creatively our unique way, and in loving relationship with our fellows, the process takes place and we inherit the kingdom. The transcendent God is also a personal reality. Transcendent and personal, our relationship with God is enacted in the present, but it is also forward-looking as we evolve as a people, aware and participating in God's plan for us, as we help bring about the equalization of every inequity and imbalance.

> Come. You have my Father's blessing! Inherit the kingdom prepared for you from the creation of the world. For I was hungry and you gave me food, I was thirsty and you gave me drink. I was a stranger and you welcomed me, naked and you clothed me. I was ill and you comforted me, in prison and you came to visit me. . . . I assure you, as often as you did it for one of my least brothers, you did it for me. (Mt 25:34–40)

Thanksgiving

We do not have an official Thanksgiving Day in the Church, and yet we would have to agree that this American harvest feast is a religious feast. Perhaps it is one which needs to be brought to the churches and kept safe there. Our impressive energies that commercialize every religious expression might need the energies of the churches to hold this one in check and to help us develop the feast fully. A beautiful liturgy has been designed for this day, with some rich readings from Scripture that describe our thanksgiving, our reverence for the earth, and our responsibility to share the earth's goods.

Harvest festivals and thanksgiving rituals go back as far as our knowledge of ancient culture and religion goes. The "grain mother" was honored by ancient Greeks and the Indo-Europeans. In the Christian world, she is Mary at the height of August. In many parts of the world, the grain harvests are celebrated in wreaths or dolls made of wheat sheaves, ears of grain, straw, husks or flax. Our autumn arrangements of dry weeds, grains and flowers celebrate the fields' harvest too.

The Pilgrim origins of the first Thanksgiving feast carry strong Christian overtones that recall the feast day of St. Martin on November 11. St. Martin's Day (Martinmas) was actually the Thanksgiving Day of medieval days that celebrated stocked barns and cellars. On this day, people went to church and then had games and dances and processions. They feasted at a huge midday meal of roast goose and new wine from the grape harvests. This feast was kept throughout central Europe, and the goose was retained by the Dutch even after the Reformation.

It was from them that the Pilgrims who came to the New World in 1620 learned of the ancient harvest festival. In the autumn of 1621, they decided to celebrate a thanksgiving and went to hunt the traditional goose. Apparently Governor Bradford sent four men "on fowling" to prepare for such a feast that would celebrate the fruit of their labors. They found some wild geese and also a number of wild ducks and turkeys. With those turkeys, they began one of the truly American traditions that we have. Native Americans, noted for their great hunting skills and the sort of boundless generosity that kept many old world people alive when they first came, contributed lobsters and oysters and fish. I am sure they also introduced the wild cranberries, sweet roots and pumpkins that are a beloved tradition of the American Thanksgiving dinner to this day.

A Family and Community Celebration

This is a feast that is truly meant to gather the whole family together—the personal and extended family—and when that is not possible, or over and above that, friends, neighbors, foreign students, single men and women, and those in need of our love and bounty. If you are looking for persons in need of your plenty, ask at your church. The pastor may have a name or two for you. (In fact, it has been known that the pastor will add his own name to that list.) I know a family that has made it their custom to help cook and serve the Thanksgiving dinner that is offered by the local Catholic Worker. They are so satisfied by the experience that they tell me they could never go back to celebrating with just their own, small family.

The day begins well with a family and community celebration at church. The liturgy can be introduced with a procession led by a cross designed of wheat sheaves and bound with ribbons and flowers. Or the community processional cross can be decorated with sprays of wheat, flowers and streamers and carried in. An offertory procession can bring forward gifts from the community of canned goods and dried grains and beans to be distributed later where there is need. This day's reading from Luke 12:15–21 reminds us of a right attitude toward our bounty.

> Jesus said to the crowd, "Avoid greed in all its forms. A man may be wealthy, but his possessions do not guarantee him life." He told them a parable in these words: "There was a rich man who had a good harvest. 'What shall I do?' he asked himself. 'I have no place to store my harvest. I know!' he said. 'I will pull down my grain bins and build larger ones. All my grain and my goods will go there. Then I will say to myself: You have blessings in reserve for years to come. Relax! Eat heartily, drink well. Enjoy yourself.' But God said to him, 'You fool! This very night your life shall be required of you. To whom will all this piled-up wealth of yours go?' That is the way it works with the man who grows rich for himself instead of growing rich in the sight of God."

At home, before the Thanksgiving dinner is served, a search for an appropriate meal prayer might take you to the accounts we have of native American prayers and songs which praise "our mother the earth." Or the Responsorial

Psalm from today's Eucharist is one of several readings which would make an appropriate Thanksgiving meal prayer (Ps 67:2–3, 5, 7–8):

The earth has yielded its fruits;
God, our God, has blessed us.

May God have pity on us and bless us;
    may he let his face shine upon us.
So may your way be known upon the earth;
    among all nations, your salvation.

The earth has yielded its fruits;
God, our God, has blessed us.

May the nations be glad and exult
    because you rule the peoples in equity;
    the nations on the earth you guide.

The earth has yielded its fruits;
God, our God, has blessed us.

The earth has yielded its fruits;
    God, our God, has blessed us.
May God bless us,
    and may all the ends of the earth fear him!

The earth has yielded its fruits;
God, our God has blessed us.

Vision of the Whole

The Lord says: My plans for you are peace and not disaster; when you call to me, I will listen to you, and I will bring you back to the place from which I exiled you. (Jer 29:12–14)

In these last days of the Church year, the readings are not often as encouraging and peaceful as those just quoted. We hear more about the destruction of Jerusalem and Christ uses the apocalyptic language that Old Testament writers used in times of crisis, a literary voice that tells of cosmic disasters announcing the final "day of the Lord." It is sobering language, and it causes us to think on Christ's coming at the time of death and both our collective and individual calling forth to be gathered into heavenly barns.

The sunset of all humankind, however near or far away, is in process of evolution. Any contribution that we make to the fullness of time—to the creation of history—is finally a personal matter and draws on our efforts to fully become ourselves, each one of us in her or his unique life. Our personal self-realization also contributes to the universal community. Each of us, as we succeed or fail to call up into human consciousness the revelations that lie waiting for our transformation, contributes to or fails in the process that becomes the only way to change the course of human events and bring its healing. The kingdom of God, the beatific vision, the vision of the whole becomes real, in the flesh of our daily living. The unitive vision is revealed in our very humanness, in the interplay between our bodies and the creative spirit, between one person and another. Each of us carries the grace which can express and illuminate what is our common foundation, our creative and life-giving Center.

The course of time is changeable through individuals as we accept the grace to cooperate with the healing energies of the inner world, where the source of awareness is found and hence where the healing of history can take place. This is an especially vexing concept for us because individual work is slow work and we are a people who like to make sweeping changes, fast. We dread, if we do not outright reject, the effort that individual change requires. We think meaningless the effort of a single individual and say, "What's the use!" With that we want to dismiss whole areas of concern from our minds, because we feel too small and helpless.

The work of a Dorothy Day or a Mother Teresa was never a work that began with goals to launch a sweeping world movement. Both have, nonetheless, contributed irrevocably to the slow growth of human awareness. Each of these women has found comfort and validation in the "useless" efforts of Jesus, efforts which first become real and effective as they are lived in our own lives. Love, the ultimate ingredient for wholeness and healing, can only be transmitted person to person. The work of love is small and slow-going. But like the effect of water on rock, it makes real change.

A mother prepared her little daughter for her enrollment at a new school.

The first day of school had already gone well. It had been exciting and successful. But on the second day of school, the child was grumpy and slow to get prepared for school. The mother's first reaction was the temptation to cajole and coax the child with cheerful suggestions and reminders of everything that had gone well and was sure to be marvelous today. Yesterday was great, wasn't it? It was an automatic attempt to offer a cheery balance to the child's dark mood. But the mother chose to forego the automatic inclination. Her attempts would only deprive the child of creating her own, deeper balance. Rather, the mother wisely understood her daughter's mood. She took a moment to put herself in the girl's shoes and felt what it was the child might be struggling with. She gave her daughter the words that failed her, words that engaged her fears.

"Perhaps today won't be as fine as yesterday. You are new in the classroom. You haven't made any friends yet so you will feel lonely. Maybe the teacher won't turn out to be as charming as you thought she was. She'll probably make you work hard today and the work will be new and strange . . ." Bravely engaging the unknown and the dark possibilities, the girl eventually began to cheer up visibly. She ate her breakfast, gathered up her school books and chattered happily as they went to the car.

This kind of patient growing and being is never meant to be dramatic or noticed. But it is a "feminine" attribute which we have not yet learned to value. I heard another story, of a woman who learned that the firm she had been working in for some years made one little part of a nuclear warhead. She allowed herself to think about this without being defensive. One day, it occurred to her that she might look for other work because she felt that in conscience she couldn't contribute to this enterprise. She mentioned her concern to a friend who was a lawyer.

"Look," he said, "do what you want. But remember, they'll just hire someone else to take your old job. Your gesture isn't going to make a bit of difference." Out of a practical frame of mind, he dismissed as useless what seemed an impractical gesture. The "masculine" mentality, that also happens to make weapons that make a BIG difference, canceled out the "feminine" consciousness as though it had no place in this universe.

If we continue to think of God on the periphery of the world, as far removed from our humanness, as external to history, we sin against the Spirit, who lives and works from the inside of our humanity outward into the making of our days. If we think of God as distant and other, we give away our part in the whole revelation of God-with-us. The final harmony and wholeness of our own beings and hence of history will be settled before its time and we will bring about, in fact, a termination of time and history and not its completion.

While the history of consciousness, while theology, while the creation of society as we know it thus far may have had to emphasize the masculine elements of order, intellect and the rest, the time is quickly approaching where the incarnation of God in our very matter and humanness, the realities of evil and the healing quality of the feminine must be brought to consciousness. Otherwise we will have tipped the scales away from wholeness and we will create our own "final day." By distancing ourselves from the reality of God incarnate in our humanness, by putting God far out into space and making the divine unreachable, we will have played out, in fact, the very role we think is God's and we will have split all times and peoples asunder.

We consider this an age of secularization—of non-belief. Indeed we no longer hold bloody crusades in the name of God, but the religious energies of the soul continue to live on and do their work. Our religious fervor will not be stilled, because religious instincts belong to us as the spiritual element of our basic human make-up. So we continue to project our deep religious nature, dangerously, onto exteriorized beliefs of a political, conquesting, competitive, divisive and warring nature. When the religious energies within the human psyche go into action—untransformed into a faith experience—they carry on as a blind faith. They are projected to create destruction and to wage the battles through time that are conducted by masses of people who leave their personal decisions to whoever it is that currently leads the herd and professes the creed that has caught the collective fancy. But transformed, through the painful work of each individual as she or he unfolds a life of growing consciousness, the God within confers grace. No matter how small the step taken, that grace is for the good of all time and all people.

Looking at the Message on a Medieval Church Portal

Over many Romanesque and Gothic church entries, the final judgment day of the Lord is depicted, carved in stone relief, in a form called the tympanum. (The Cathedrals of Moissac, Vezelay, Autun, and Conques—all in France—are good examples of what I describe here.) Seated at the top of a huge and elaborate scene is a Christ who looks down on the last days of human life. The tympanum is like the high point in a drama of apocalyptic magnitude. The actors everywhere scramble in response to a director, but this scene has never before been rehearsed, the players not having known "the day or the hour." The trumpets of the avenging angels blow, and each terrorized creature, coming forth from a grave, responds according to his or her own fate. The stone figures seem to vibrate with tension. Souls are weighed on the Godly scales of justice. A demon pulls down his side of the scale, hoping to win this soul for his own fiery kingdom. To the left hand of the Christ in majesty, the damned—knights and bishops amongst them, the lustful and the proud—are stuffed, like vegetables into a processor: a gaping, toothy maw of hell, to be spat out onto a lower level of endless agony, to suffer in isolation forever. To the right, the blessed saved, reaching and crawling, shoving and pulling are lifted into the doors of heaven to rest, finally, on Abraham's bosom and to meet with Mary and other saints and even our first father, Adam. Left and right, good and bad, sheep and goats, the great division is played out on the tympanum and the tension is electric. I think that for years—I don't know how long—we may have been reading the tympanum in reverse order, that is, from the top down where we attribute to Christ the qualities of Judge and Great Divider. We read, in that order, that it is a Christ—"true on the outside"—who is the one to cause our great split and division. What is more, his judgment leaves us split for ever and ever.

I have seen outside of at least one cathedral door, much further down, between the great portals themselves and at eye level, the tree of knowledge of good and evil with Adam and Eve on either side. (It may have been in Bourges?) It would seem appropriate to begin our reading of this message in stone down here with the tree in Eden. In any case, we might begin our reading from the bottom up; then the whole issue begins at the beginning and can be taken personally, "on the inside." Our taste for this fruit was the beginning of our splitting off from God. Good and evil, right and left, masculine and feminine and all the divisions of divisions are the choices that mark the process of our human growth in consciousness. Personally and collectively, this is the arena where we create our own heaven and make our own hell. It is the dangerous and painful process that we must make back again to our ultimate unity and harmony with the Christ of Majesty. *O happy fault, that merited so great a Redeemer.*

Crowning the whole story, at the very center and over and above the turbulent drama, we see the Christ of majesty, an image of peace and equity. *My plans for you are peace and not disaster.* He sits in the center of an almond shape, called the *mandorla,* the areole that contains the image of the holy. It is the ellipse shape, the third form that occurs when two circles overlap. He is seated where left and right have merged and reveal a new truth, greater than the sum of oppositions. Often he holds a book inscribed with an Alpha and an Omega—the beginning and the end. He is neither the first nor the last; he is over and above both. Outside of time, he is the fullness of time, he is eternal. Sometimes, especially in ancient illuminations where color was used, he is seated on a rainbow within the *mandorla.* The rainbow is the place where black and white meet and are not gray, but every color in the spectrum.

This is the image of wholeness, where outside is turned inside, where paradox comes to rest and can contain and transform opposites. This image in the *mandorla* contains the same psychic, symbolic power of the Eastern *mandala* which is a circle. Jung understood the mandala as essentially a symbolic, religious image which belongs to all people in all times. It indicates the creative presence of God at the center of the person, a creative center in the soul basic to every human and the expression of wholeness. In Christianity we see the mandala image in the concept of the mystical rose, in the rose window of many cathedrals, in the four equal arms of the cross, in the image of the four evangelists surrounding Christ, in Mary, the matrix of the world—all of them en-circling a Center point of great creative energy.

These symbols underscore the two-sided nature of reality. They describe reality as made up of dualities and they indicate that exclusive commitment to one or the other side is indeed lopsided, not whole, and in grave need of heal-ing. Such healing can only be found in including the forgotten opposite and finally in transcending the contradictions, reaching a center of awareness, a new faith, numinous and charged with meaning, broader, deeper, more ex-pansive, than anything that came before.

This new, expansive faith is emerging. It is a faith that will come to allow the truth of contradictions and even know them as painful, but necessary to the process of the divine and human amending each other. The human psyche is singularly intent on healing the rupture between the human and the divine. That is why the language of the soul keeps producing the symbols, the dreams, the images that insist on the final union between God and humanity.

The Second Advent

Individually and personally, the crisis in the second half of life is analogous to the historical crisis we are currently standing at the brink of. The second half of life introduces us to the "second Advent." Christ is revealed to us so often in every slipped stitch that we let fall or that fate encouraged us to drop in our first years and which now must be picked up and considered again. This time we consider the slipped stitch, or the "road not taken," from the outside in. We do not act out, do not relive literally, what we have missed, but take our reality into our full consciousness and make it our own. The incarnation that this sec-ond Advent heralds will not produce a flesh and blood baby boy. It will be the redemptive act which takes flesh in the heart and in the realization of God-with-us, God centered in our every human relationship.

A husband does not drop his wife who bores him and go back to marry his high school sweetheart and honestly solve the problems of his soul. He has merely projected, again, his dilemma as being outside of himself and not cen-tered within him. His honest untangling of his drives and impulses, his longings and feelings as an inward call for his inner healing and wholeness is a deeply religious process. He learns to take back the projections of God to the outside and learn the symbolic language that life is serving him up. Jung felt that psychic illness in the second half of life could not be cured without a rediscovery of a religious attitude and an experience of the transcendent. The transcendent may come, "like a thief in the night," and "we will not know the day or the hour."

By the same token, a nation which claims to have the "one true system" and which will destroy any other system that lies in its path has exteriorized its collective religious problem. Ideology has become the externalized God. Co-operation, empathy, creative solutions, forbearance are the stitches we have let drop. Who knows how long and how far we have to push the exteriorizations, how close to disaster we must press before we learn that divine intervention will not come from outer space but lies in each person's call to bring redemption to birth in greater harmony, in fullness of being, in an ever deeper awareness.

God invites humankind to join him as co-creator in the ongoing process of creation. But the making of this world is finally a personal matter which can come to something only by the tolerance and indulgence, indeed an empathy, we have for each other's differences. Any truth that we espouse now still awaits its transcendence in an awareness of God-with-us which is deeper and broader and richer than any we know now. All that we have divided must be brought together into a wholeness. A new Advent is already begun.

> What we call the beginning is often the end
> And to make an end is to make a beginning.
> The end is where we start from . . .
>
> We shall not cease from exploration
> And the end of all our exploring
> Will be to arrive where we started
> And know the place for the first time.
>
> (From *Four Quartets* by T. S. Eliot)

References and Related Readings

Benziger, Bernard, ed. *The New American Sunday Missal*. Collins World, Cleveland-New York 1975.

The New English Bible, Oxford University Press, Cambridge University Press, 1970.

The Jerusalem Bible, Darton, Longman and Todd, London 1966.

Campbell, Joseph. *The Masks of God: Primitive Mythology*. Viking, New York 1959.

————, *The Mythic Image*. Princeton University Press, Princeton, N.J. 1974.

Dourley, John P. *The Illness That We Are: A Jungian Critique of Christianity*. Inner City Books, Toronto 1984.

Eliade, Mircea. *Cosmos and History: The Myth of the Eternal Return*. Harper and Row, New York 1959.

————, *The Sacred and The Profane: The Nature of Religion*. Harcourt, Brace and World, New York 1959.

Eliot, T.S. *The Complete Poems and Plays,* Harcourt, Brace and Company, New York 1958.

Frazer, Sir James George. *The Golden Bough*. Macmillan, New York 1958.

Gilligan, Carol. *In a Different Voice*. Harvard University Press, Cambridge, Massachusetts 1982.

The Golden Legend of Jacobus de Voragine. Trans. by Granger Ryan and Helmut Ripperger, Arno Press, New York 1969.

Grivot, Denis, and George Zarnecki. *Gislebertus Sculpteur D'Autun.* Trianon Press, France 1960.

Guardini, Romano. *Sacred Signs.* Sheed and Ward, London 1930.

———, *The Church and the Catholic and The Spirit of the Liturgy.* Sheed and Ward, 1935.

Haughton, Rosemary. *Beginning Life in Christ.* Newman Press, Westminster, Maryland 1966.

———, *The Gospel Where It Hits Us.* Ave Maria Press, Notre Dame, Indiana 1968.

———, *The Passionate God.* Paulist Press, New York/Ramsey, N.J. 1981.

Hopkins, Gerard Manley. *Poems and Prose of Gerard Manley Hopkins,* ed. W.H. Gardner. Penguin Books, Harmondsworth, Middlesex, England 1953.

Huisinga, Johan. *Homo Ludens, a Study of the Play Element in Culture.* Beacon Press, Boston 1950.

Huxley, Francis. *The Way of the Sacred.* Doubleday, Garden City, New York 1974.

Jung, C.G. *Mysterium Conjunctionis.* Collected Works, Vol. 14. Pantheon Books, New York 1958.

———, *Psychology and Alchemy.* Collected Works, Vol. 12. Pantheon Books, New York 1958.

———, *Psychology and Religion: West and East.* Vol. 11. Pantheon Books, New York 1958.

———, *The Symbolic Life.* Vol. 18. Pantheon Books, New York 1958.

Kavanagh, Aidan. *On Liturgical Theology.* Pueblo Publishing, New York 1981.

Kennedy, Eugene. *A Sense of Life, A Sense of Sin.* Doubleday, Garden City, New York 1975.

McGlashan, Alan. *The Savage and Beautiful Country.* Houghton Mifflin, Boston 1967.

McKnight, George H. *St. Nicholas His Legend and His Role in the Christmas Celebration and Other Popular Customs.* Corner House Publishers, Williamstown, Massachusetts 1974.

Mueller, Therese. *Our Children's Year of Grace.* Pio Decimo Press, St. Louis, Missouri 1943.

———, *Family Life in Christ.* Liturgical Press, Collegeville, Minnesota 1959.

———, *Ideas for the Christian Homemaker.* Abbey Press, St. Meinrad, Indiana 1965.

Opie, Iona and Peter. *The Lore and Language of Schoolchildren.* Oxford University Press, London 1959.

Pieper, Josef. *Leisure the Basis of Culture.* Pantheon Books, New York 1952.

The Roman Ritual, The Blessings, Trans. and ed. by Philip T. Weller. Bruce Publishing Co., Milwaukee 1946.

Turnbull, Colin M. *The Human Cycle.* Simon and Schuster, New York 1983.

————, *The Mountain People.* Simon and Schuster, New York 1972.

Vann, Gerald, O.P. *The Son's Course.* Collins, London 1959.

Weiser, Francis X. *Handbook of Christian Feasts and Customs.* Paulist Press, New York 1958.

————, *The Holyday Book.* Harcourt, Brace, New York 1956.